Entity Framework Tutorial

Second Edition

A comprehensive guide to Entity Framework with insights into its latest features and optimizations for responsive data access in your projects

Joydip Kanjilal

BIRMINGHAM - MUMBAI

Entity Framework Tutorial

Second Edition

First published: October 2008

Second edition: August 2015

Production reference: 1190815

Published by Packt Publishing Ltd.
Livery Place
35 Livery Street
Birmingham B3 2PB, UK.

ISBN 978-1-78355-001-2

www.packtpub.com

Credits

Author
Joydip Kanjilal

Reviewers
Konstantinos Athanasoglou
Abhishek Luv
Jason De Oliveira
Nicholas Suter

Commissioning Editor
Kevin Colaco

Acquisition Editors
Kevin Colaco
Douglas Paterson

Content Development Editor
Riddhi Tuljapurkar

Technical Editor
Prajakta Mhatre

Copy Editors
Charlotte Carneiro
Ameesha Smith-Green

Project Coordinator
Sanchita Mandal

Proofreader
Safis Editing

Indexer
Tejal Soni

Graphics
Disha Haria
Jason Monteiro
Abhinash Sahu

Production Coordinator
Manu Joseph

Cover Work
Manu Joseph

About the Author

Joydip Kanjilal has won a Microsoft Most Valuable Professional (MVP) award in ASP.NET. He is a speaker and author of several books and articles. He has over 18 years of industry experience in IT, with more than 12 years in Microsoft .NET and its related technologies. Joydip is currently working as a Principal Architect at SenecaGlobal IT Services Private Limited, Hyderabad. He has been selected as an MSDN Featured Developer of the Fortnight (MSDN) a number of times and has also been a Community Credit Winner at `www.community-credit.com` several times. He has authored the following books:

- *ASP.NET Web API: Build RESTful Web Applications and Services on the .NET Framework* by Packt Publishing
- *Visual Studio 2010 and .NET 4 Six-in-One* by Wrox Publishers
- *ASP.NET 4.0 Programming* by Mc-Graw Hill Publishing
- *Entity Framework Tutorial* by Packt Publishing
- *Pro Sync Framework* by APRESS
- *Sams Teach Yourself ASP.NET Ajax in 24 Hours* by Sams Publishing
- *ASP.NET Data Presentation Controls Essentials* by Packt Publishing

He has authored more than 250 articles for some of the most reputable sites, such as `www.msdn.microsoft.com`, `www.code-magazine.com`, `www.asptoday.com`, `www.devx.com`, `www.ddj.com`, `www.aspalliance.com`, `www.aspnetpro.com`, `www.sql-server-performance.com`, `www.sswug.com`, and so on. A lot of these articles have been selected at `www.asp.net`, Microsoft's official site on ASP.NET.

He has years of experience in designing and architecting solutions for various domains. His technical strengths include C, C++, VC++, Java, C#, Microsoft .NET, AJAX, WCF, web-based APIs, REST, SOA, design patterns, SQL Server, operating systems, and computer architecture.

He can be contacted at:

- `http://aspadvice.com/blogs/joydip`
- `http://www.infoworld.com/blog/microsoft-coder`
- Website: `www.joydipkanjilal.com`
- Twitter: `https://twitter.com/joydipkanjilal`
- Facebook: `https://www.facebook.com/joydipkanjilal`
- LinkedIn: `http://in.linkedin.com/in/joydipkanjilal`

Writing a book has always been a rewarding experience for me. My special thanks to the entire Packt team for providing me with the opportunity to author this book—and turn this idea into reality. I am also thankful to the entire management team at SenecaGlobal for their continued support. I was delighted by the warm welcome I received when I joined the company and also for the inspiration I received from the management team here. I am very happy to be a part of this wonderful team.

My deepest respect and gratitude to my parents for their love, blessings, and encouragement. My special thanks to my wife for her continued inspiration and support. I am also thankful to my sister, and little Jini in particular, for their support.

Thank you all so much!

About the Reviewers

Konstantinos Athanasoglou holds a diploma and an MSc in electronics and computer engineering from the Technical University of Crete, Greece. He has been involved in speech and web application development on the .NET stack for more than 5 years.

He participated in the architecture and development of an automated framework that enabled the rapid prototyping of speech applications.

He is now part of the core development team at AirFastTickets, a rapidly growing online travel agency with offices in New York, Piraeus, London, Frankfurt, and Istanbul. It is now a major OTA in Greece.

Abhishek Luv received his BCA degree and completed a course on Startup Engineering taught at Stanford University via Coursera.

He has been developing and designing websites and web applications for the last 3 years. During these years, Abhishek has been involved in Microsoft technologies such as C#, ASP.NET, ASP.NET MVC, SQL Server, Entity Framework, Orchard CMS, and many more.

He is currently working as a freelance .NET web developer and an instructor at Develop2Deploy (`http://develop2deploy.com/`).

He is also the founder of the Orchard CMS Indian Community website (`http://orchardproject.net.in/`) and a contributor to the official Orchard CMS documentation website (`http://docs.orchardproject.net/Contributors`). He has created numerous online courses on Orchard CMS (`https://www.udemy.com/courses/search/?q=orchard`).

He loves sharing his knowledge and experiences via his online podcast at http://www.softwaredevelopmentpodcast.in/, teaching courses on web development at www.udemy.com, and coaching and mentoring college students and newbie developers.

Outside of his normal day-to-day activities as a freelance .NET web developer and instructor, he is also a cofounder of a video training start-up called *The Video Trainer* (https://www.thevideotrainer.in/) where he trains and coaches individuals, professionals, and teaches them how to create their own stunning videos for the Web. You can reach him at abhishek@abhishekluv.in.

Jason De Oliveira works as a CTO for Cellenza (http://www.cellenza.com), an IT consulting company specialized in Microsoft technologies and the Agile methodology in Paris, France. He is an experienced manager and senior solutions architect, with a lot of skills in software architecture and enterprise architecture.

Jason works for big companies and helps them realize complex and challenging software projects. He frequently collaborates with Microsoft, and you can find him quite often at the Microsoft Technology Center (MTC) in Paris.

He loves sharing his knowledge and experience via his blog by speaking at conferences, writing technical books and articles in the technical press, giving software courses (MCT), and coaching coworkers at his company.

Since 2011, Microsoft has awarded him with the Microsoft Most Valuable Professional (MVP C#) award for his numerous contributions to the Microsoft community. Microsoft seeks to recognize the best and brightest from technology communities around the world with the MVP award. These exceptional and highly respected individuals come from more than 90 countries, serving their local online and offline communities and having an impact worldwide. Jason is very proud to be one of them.

Feel free to contact him via his blog if you need any technical assistance or want to exchange knowledge on technical subjects (http://www.jasondeoliveira.com).

Jason has worked on the following books:

- *.NET Framework 4.5 Expert Programming Cookbook* (English) by Packt Publishing
- *WCF 4.5 Multi-Layer Services Development with Entity Framework* (English) by Packt Publishing
- *.NET 4.5 Parallel Extensions Cookbook* (English) by Packt Publishing
- *Visual Studio 2013: Concevoir, développer et gérer des projets Web, les gérer avec TFS 2013* (French)

I would like to thank my lovely wife, Orianne, and my beautiful daughters, Julia and Léonie, for supporting me in my work and for accepting the long days and short nights during the week, sometimes even during the weekend. My life would not be the same without them!

Nicholas Suter has been a full-stack Agile software developer and architect, specialized in Microsoft technologies since 2003. He has also been a .NET and C# MVP since 2014, and works as much in a web environment as in Windows client applications for Cellenza, a consulting firm in Paris, France.

He focuses on software patterns and practices in Agile, clean code, and craftsmanship environments. He wrote a book on web development called *Visual Studio 2013: Concevoir, développer et gérer des projets Web, les gérer avec TFS 2013* (French). He also writes for his personal blog (`http://www.nicholassuter.com`) and Cellenza's blog (`http://blog.cellenza.com`).

www.PacktPub.com

Support files, eBooks, discount offers, and more

For support files and downloads related to your book, please visit www.PacktPub.com.

Did you know that Packt offers eBook versions of every book published, with PDF and ePub files available? You can upgrade to the eBook version at www.PacktPub.com and as a print book customer, you are entitled to a discount on the eBook copy. Get in touch with us at service@packtpub.com for more details.

At www.PacktPub.com, you can also read a collection of free technical articles, sign up for a range of free newsletters and receive exclusive discounts and offers on Packt books and eBooks.

https://www2.packtpub.com/books/subscription/packtlib

Do you need instant solutions to your IT questions? PacktLib is Packt's online digital book library. Here, you can search, access, and read Packt's entire library of books.

Why subscribe?

- Fully searchable across every book published by Packt
- Copy and paste, print, and bookmark content
- On demand and accessible via a web browser

Free access for Packt account holders

If you have an account with Packt at www.PacktPub.com, you can use this to access PacktLib today and view 9 entirely free books. Simply use your login credentials for immediate access.

Table of Contents

Preface vii

Chapter 1: Introducing the ADO.NET Entity Framework 1

- **What you should know** 3
- **Looking back** 3
- **What is the ADO.NET Entity Framework?** 5
  - Is Entity Framework just another ORM? 6
- **A comparative analysis of Entity Framework and other ORM tools** 7
  - LINQ to SQL and .dbml files 11
- **Entity Framework architectural components** 11
  - The Entity Data Model 12
  - How is the EDM represented? 15
  - The Object Model (O-Space) 16
  - LINQ to Entities 17
  - Entity Client 17
  - Entity SQL 18
    - Avoiding complex joins 19
  - The Object Services Layer 20
  - Features and benefits at a glance 21
- **System requirements** 22
  - Support for persistence ignorance 22
  - Support for T4 code generation 23
  - Support for lazy loading 23
  - Support for POCO change tracking 23
  - Better n-tier support with self-tracking entities 24
  - Support for code-first, model-first, and database-first approaches 24
  - Support for built-in functions and UDF support 25
  - Support for model-defined functions 25
  - Enum support 26

Spatial data types support 27
Other enhancements 27
Performance improvements in Entity Framework 6 28
New features in Entity Framework 7 30
Summary 30
Chapter 2: Getting Started 31
Designing the UserAuthentication database 33
Creating the EDM 34
Creating the Entity Data Model using the ADO.NET Entity Data Model Designer 35
Creating Entity Data Model using the EdmGen tool 41
The DataSource controls 44
The ObjectDataSource control 44
The SqlDataSource control 45
The SiteMapDataSource control 45
The XMLDataSource control 45
The LinqDataSource control 46
The EntityDataSource control 46
Implementing our first application using the Entity Framework 46
Summary 54
Chapter 3: Entities, Relationships, and the Entity Data Model 55
Entities, entity types, and relationships in the EDM 56
What is an entity? 56
Defining entity sets in the EDM 57
Extending the existing entity types to create derived entity types 61
Association sets, associations, containment, and multiplicity 63
What are entity containers? 65
Exploring the Security EDM 67
The Mapping Details window 68
The Entity Model browser 70
The EDM layers 72
The CSDL schema 72
The SSDL schema 79
The MSL schema 81
Entity classes 85
Summary 88
Chapter 4: Working with Stored Procedures in the Entity Data Model 89
Creating a database using model-first development 90
Creating stored procedures 105

Mapping stored procedures to functions in the EDM **108**
Mapping the create, update, and delete functions to entities in the EDM 111
Mapping stored procedures with no entity set 113
Executing stored procedures using the EDM **113**
Mapping stored procedures that return custom entity types **114**
Summary **116**
Chapter 5: Working with Entity Client and Entity SQL **117**
An overview of the E-SQL language **118**
From T-SQL to E-SQL **118**
Why E-SQL when I already have LINQ to Entities? **119**
Features of E-SQL 120
Operators in E-SQL 121
Arithmetic operators 121
Comparison operators 122
Logical operators 122
Reference operators 122
Type operators 123
Set operators 123
Operator precedence 124
Expressions in E-SQL 124
Query expressions in E-SQL 124
Identifiers, variables, parameters, and types in E-SQL 125
Row 126
Collections 126
Reference 127
Canonical functions in E-SQL 128
Mathematical functions 128
Aggregate functions 128
String functions 129
Bitwise functions 129
Date and time functions 130
Data paging using E-SQL **130**
Working with the ADO.NET Entity Client **131**
Let's get into action 133
Building the connection string 133
Creating an entity connection 134
Opening the connection 134
Executing queries using the entity command 135
Closing the connection 136
Other operations with E-SQL **138**
Inserting a record using E-SQL 138
Inserting a record with a foreign key constraint 139
Retrieving native SQL from EntityCommand 139
Transaction management in E-SQL 140

Deferred, eager, and lazy loading 142
Summary 143
Chapter 6: Working with LINQ to Entities 145
Introducing LINQ 146
Why LINQ? 146
Understanding the LINQ architecture 147
LINQ to XML 148
LINQ to SQL 148
LINQ to Objects 149
LINQ to Entities 150
Querying data using LINQ to Entities 151
LINQ to Entities and Entity Framework 151
Differences between LINQ to Entities and LINQ to SQL 152
Parallel LINQ 153
Operators in LINQ 153
Aggregation 154
Projections 155
Ordering 155
Quantifiers 156
Restriction 156
Conversion 157
Element 157
Set 158
Querying data using LINQ 158
Expressions in LINQ to Entities 161
Constant expressions 162
Comparison expressions 162
Initialization expressions 164
Null comparisons 165
Navigation properties 165
Immediate and deferred query execution 166
Retrieving entity data from the Security database 168
Summary 170
Chapter 7: Working with the Object Services Layer 171
What are Object Services? 172
Features at a glance 174
The SecurityDbEntity's DbContext class 174
Querying data as in-memory objects 176
Using Entity Framework 7 176
Performing CRUD operations on objects 177
Attaching and detaching objects to and from ObjectContext 178
Serializing and deserializing entity instances 180

Change tracking and identity resolution using ObjectContext 182
Understanding the code-first, model-first, and database-first approaches to domain design 183
Using the code-first approach 184
Using the model-first approach 185
Using the database-first approach 188
Inheritance in Entity Framework 188
Table-per-Hierarchy 189
Table-per-Type 190
Table-per-Concrete Type 190
Implementing complex types in the EDM 192
State management, identity management, and relationship management 193
Reading objects from the Security database 196
Inserting objects from the Security database 197
Editing objects from the Security database 198
Deleting objects from the Security database 198
Summary 199
Chapter 8: Working with WCF Data Services 201
Introducing WCF Data Services 202
How do WCF Data Services and Web Services differ? 202
What is Representational State Transfer (REST)? 202
Why use WCF Data Services? 204
The features at a glance 204
Exposing data as a service using WCF Data Services 205
Why do we need REST? 205
Resources in REST-based architecture 207
The REST architectural constraints 208
The client-server model 208
Stateless 208
Cacheable 209
Code on demand 209
The uniform interface 209
Resource management 209
REST attributes 209
WebServiceHost 210
WebHttpBinding 210
WebHttpBehavior 210
WebOperationContext 210
WebMessageFormat 211
The WebGet attribute 211
The WebInvoke attribute 212
UriTemplate 212

REST-based Web Services 213
What is the OData Protocol? 214
Working with WCF Data Services and Entity Framework 217
Working with OData Services using WCF and ASP.NET MVC Framework 222
Working with Protobuf WCF Services 225
Protocol Buffers 225
Creating Protobuf-net objects 226
Integrating Protobuf.NET with Visual Studio 227
Implementing the WCF Service 227
Specifying binding information 228
Summary 229
Appendix: Advanced Concepts 231
REST and REST-based service frameworks 231
Ruby on Rails 232
Restlet 232
Django REST 233
The Flickr REST API 233
The Google API 233
Yahoo Social REST APIs 234
Exploring OData 234
HTTP methods, request, and response codes 236
Abbreviations 238
New features in Entity Framework 7 238
Suggested reading 239
Index 241

Preface

The ADO.NET Entity Framework, the next generation of Microsoft's data access technology, is an extended Object Relational Mapping (ORM) technology that makes it easy to tie together the data in your database with the objects in your applications. This is done by abstracting the object model of an application from its relational or logical model. It is an extended ORM in the sense that it provides many additional features that a traditional ORM does not.

This book is a clear and concise guide to the ADO.NET Entity Framework. Packed with plentiful code examples, this book helps you learn the ADO.NET Entity Framework and ADO.NET Data Services and build a better data access layer for your application.

The intent of writing this book is updating you to the latest trends and developments as far as Entity Framework is concerned.

What this book covers

Chapter 1, Introducing the ADO.NET Entity Framework, is an introduction to the basics of the ADO.NET Entity Framework (EF), its usefulness, features, and benefits.

Chapter 2, Getting Started, discusses how you can get started with EF, create an Entity Data Model (EDM), and write a program to query data.

Chapter 3, Entities, Relationships, and the Entity Data Model, gives a detailed explanation of entities, relationships, and each of the sections of the EDM.

Chapter 4, Working with Stored Procedures in the Entity Data Model, provides a sample application that illustrates how to perform CRUD operations against the EDM.

Chapter 5, Working with Entity Client and Entity SQL, discusses the Entity SQL query language and how to work with the Entity Client provider.

Chapter 6, Working with LINQ to Entities, includes a detailed discussion on LINQ to Entities with many code examples.

Chapter 7, Working with the Object Services Layer, provides a detailed discussion on the Object Services Layer and its helpful and useful features.

Chapter 8, Working with WCF Data Services, provides an introduction to WCF Data Services, the REST architectural paradigm, and how these can be used with the EDM to perform CRUD operations.

Appendix, Advanced Concepts, covers a few advanced concepts. These include: REST and REST-based service frameworks and OData. We would also explore the HTTP methods and the request and response codes. Lastly, we would take a look at the new features in Entity Framework 7.

What you need for this book

To learn the concepts covered in this book, the reader should have a proper understanding and working knowledge of the following:

- ADO.NET
- ASP.NET
- C#

To execute the code samples in this book, the following technologies should be installed on your system:

- Visual Studio 2013 or later
- SQL Server 2012 or later
- Windows 7/Windows 8 or higher

Who this book is for

This book is for C# developers who want an easier way to create their data access layer. You will need to be comfortable with ADO.NET, but you do not need to know anything about the Entity Framework. Along the way, we will create some ASP.NET applications, so familiarity with this will be helpful. The book is a clear and concise guide to the ADO.NET Entity Framework 6 with plenty of real-life code examples.

Conventions

In this book, you will find a number of text styles that distinguish between different kinds of information. Here are some examples of these styles and an explanation of their meaning.

Code words in text, database table names, folder names, filenames, file extensions, pathnames, dummy URLs, user input, and Twitter handles are shown as follows: "Entity Framework 6 now provides support for spatial data types using `DbGeography` and `DbGeometry` types."

A block of code is set as follows:

```
public class User
    {
        public virtual Int32 UserID { get; set; }
        public virtual String UserName { get; set; }
        public virtual String CreatedBy { get; set; }
        public virtual DateTime CreatedDate { get; set; }
        public virtual String ModifiedBy { get; set; }
        public virtual DateTime ModifiedDate { get; set; }
    }
```

When we wish to draw your attention to a particular part of a code block, the relevant lines or items are set in bold:

```
static void Main(string[] args)
        {
            DataContextDataContextvar context = new
            DataContext(GetConnectionString());
            context.CreateDatabase();
        }
```

Any command-line input or output is written as follows:

```
edmgen /mode:fullgeneration /c:"Data Source=.;Initial
Catalog=SecurityDB;User ID=sa;Password=sa1@3;" /p:SecurityDB
```

New terms and **important words** are shown in bold. Words that you see on the screen, for example, in menus or dialog boxes, appear in the text like this: "You can see that the **Convert to Enum** option is enabled."

Warnings or important notes appear in a box like this.

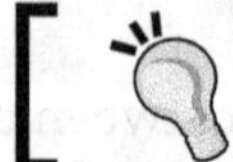

Tips and tricks appear like this.

Reader feedback

Feedback from our readers is always welcome. Let us know what you think about this book—what you liked or disliked. Reader feedback is important for us as it helps us develop titles that you will really get the most out of.

To send us general feedback, simply e-mail `feedback@packtpub.com`, and mention the book's title in the subject of your message.

If there is a topic that you have expertise in and you are interested in either writing or contributing to a book, see our author guide at `www.packtpub.com/authors`.

Customer support

Now that you are the proud owner of a Packt book, we have a number of things to help you to get the most from your purchase.

Downloading the example code

You can download the example code files from your account at `http://www.packtpub.com` for all the Packt Publishing books you have purchased. If you purchased this book elsewhere, you can visit `http://www.packtpub.com/support` and register to have the files e-mailed directly to you.

Errata

Although we have taken every care to ensure the accuracy of our content, mistakes do happen. If you find a mistake in one of our books—maybe a mistake in the text or the code—we would be grateful if you could report this to us. By doing so, you can save other readers from frustration and help us improve subsequent versions of this book. If you find any errata, please report them by visiting `http://www.packtpub.com/submit-errata`, selecting your book, clicking on the **Errata Submission Form** link, and entering the details of your errata. Once your errata are verified, your submission will be accepted and the errata will be uploaded to our website or added to any list of existing errata under the Errata section of that title.

To view the previously submitted errata, go to `https://www.packtpub.com/books/content/support` and enter the name of the book in the search field. The required information will appear under the **Errata** section.

Piracy

Piracy of copyrighted material on the Internet is an ongoing problem across all media. At Packt, we take the protection of our copyright and licenses very seriously. If you come across any illegal copies of our works in any form on the Internet, please provide us with the location address or website name immediately so that we can pursue a remedy.

Please contact us at `copyright@packtpub.com` with a link to the suspected pirated material.

We appreciate your help in protecting our authors and our ability to bring you valuable content.

Questions

If you have a problem with any aspect of this book, you can contact us at `questions@packtpub.com`, and we will do our best to address the problem.

1
Introducing the ADO.NET Entity Framework

Welcome to our journey into mastering the popular data access technology from Microsoft named **Entity Framework**. At the time of writing, Entity Framework 7 hasn't been released—so we will use Entity Framework 6.x throughout this book but at the same time discuss what's new in Entity Framework 7.

Object Relational Mapping (ORM) technology has been widely in use for over a decade. ORMs are used to convert data between incompatible type systems. These are tools that encapsulate calls to the underlying database and enable you to query and manipulate data using an object-oriented paradigm.

The figure that follows illustrates the persistence layer that is responsible for reading and manipulating data to and from the database. Now, this persistence layer can be your ADO.NET library, a wrapper around the ADO.NET library, or an ORM:

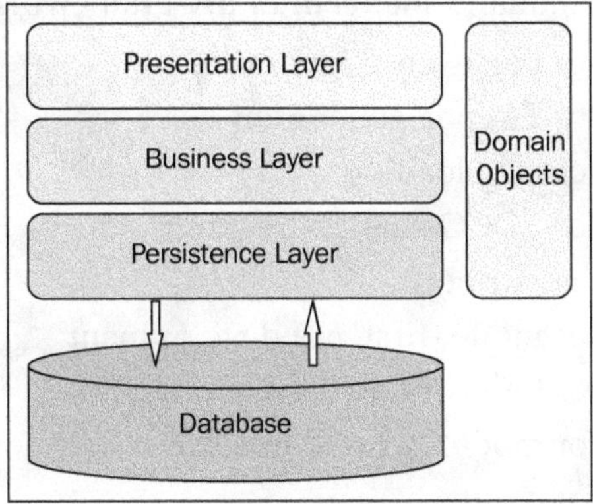

We will explore more on ORMs later in this chapter. The **ADO.NET Entity Framework (EF)** is an extended and open source ORM technology from Microsoft that abstracts the object model of an application from its relational or logical model. That is, it isolates the object model from the way the data is actually represented in the relational store. This framework makes the conceptual model real by using an extended entity relationship model called the **ADO.NET Entity Data Model**. In this book, we will examine Entity Framework 6 in order to leverage its existing and enhanced features to design and implement applications that are robust, high-performing, persistence, ignorant, and scalable. We will explore each of these features as we read through the chapters of this book.

This chapter will give you an introduction to Entity Framework and also provide you with a brief understanding of the related terminologies. We will revisit each of the Entity Framework architectural components as we progress through this book. Our journey through Entity Framework 6 has just begun!

In this chapter, we will cover the following points:

- An overview of Entity Framework
- Entity Framework architectural components:
    - The Entity Data Model
    - LINQ to Entities
    - Entity Client
    - Entity SQL
    - The Object Services Layer
- A comparative analysis of EF and other ORMs
- New features and enhancements in Entity Framework 6:
    - Support for persistence ignorance
    - Support for T4 code generation
    - Support for lazy loading
    - Support for POCO change-tracking
    - Better n-tier support
    - Support for model-first and development
    - Support for built-in functions and UDF
    - Support for model-defined functions
    - Support for enums
    - Support for spatial data types

But, before we delve deep into this amazing technology from Microsoft, let's take a quick look at the prerequisites to learning the concepts covered in this book.

What you should know

As Entity Framework 7 has not been released and isn't mature yet, we will use Entity Framework 6.x in this book while discussing the features of Entity Framework 7 as we move ahead.

To learn the concepts covered in this book, you should have a basic understanding of the following:

- Programming using ADO.NET
- C# 5.0
- Using the Visual Studio 2013 IDE
- Working with the .NET console and web applications
- SQL Server 2012 or later

Looking back

Data-centric applications have two perspective layers. They are the **data model** and the **object model**. While the data model defines the way data is defined and stored, the object model defines how the same data will be represented to the user in the presentation layer or how it is exposed to the other layers of the application. The data model of the application usually deals with the storage and retrieval of the application's data to and from the relational store.

The relational store is used for data persistence, consistency, concurrency, and security. It contains the application's data and typically comprises a set of tables, views, functions, procedures, and relationships. You typically use T-SQL to query against the relational store, which returns result sets that contain columns and rows of data.

However, the data returned doesn't necessarily match the application's object-oriented programming model. Usually, we don't use the data returned in the same form in which it is returned from the relational store. We write the necessary code to transform the data returned from the relational store into business objects in the data access layer of the application. Similarly, you need to write code to transform your application's business objects into a form that can be persisted into your relational store. But, what if the schema of the underlying relational store changes?

Here's exactly where an ORM fits in. The figure given next shows how objects in an application can be mapped to the relational store by using a mapping layer. This mapping layer is provided by the ORM. An ORM is a method of representing the relational tables as entities in the object world. ORMs came onto the market to provide you with a framework using which you can connect your applications to the underlying database without having to write much code. Most importantly, you can use ORMs to connect to any database, increase development productivity, ensure database independence, and database portability.

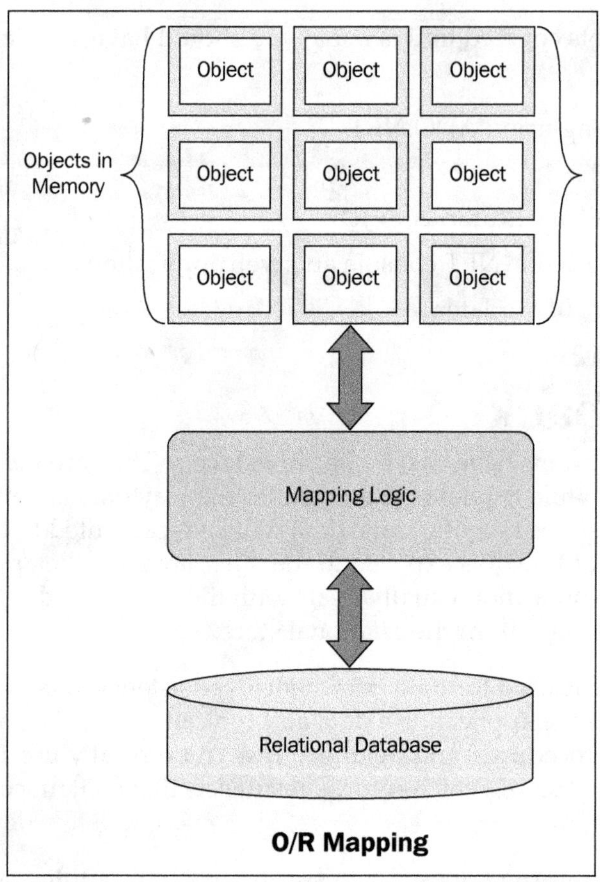

O/R Mapping

To bridge this apparent mismatch between the data and the object models, ORM tools have evolved. They are used to reduce the code required to transform your application's business objects into a form that can be persisted into the relational store and vice-versa.

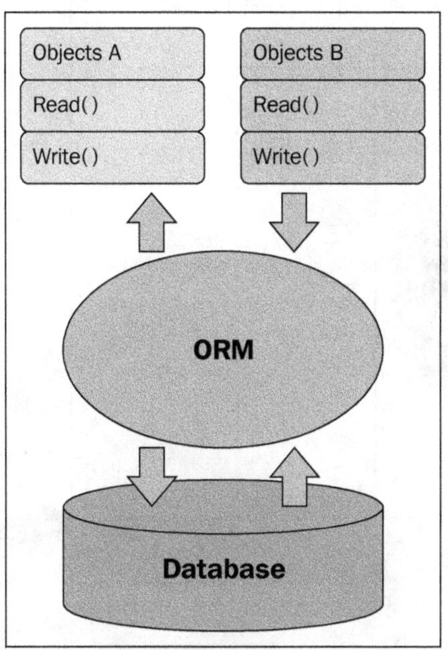

Microsoft first released its ORM by the name of LINQ to SQL, which shipped with .NET Framework 3.5 and Visual Studio 2008. However, LINQ to SQL was restricted to working with SQL Server databases only. Entity Framework is an attempt by Microsoft to provide you with an extended ORM built on top of the ADO.NET provider model and enable you to connect to and work with any database.

What is the ADO.NET Entity Framework?

Entity Framework is a type of ORM. It is a development platform that provides a layer of abstraction on top of the relational or logical model. In doing so, it isolates the object model of the application from the way the data is actually stored in the relational store. Developers can use the ADO.NET Entity Framework to program against an object model rather than the logical or relationship model.

This is illustrated using the self-explanatory diagram that follows:

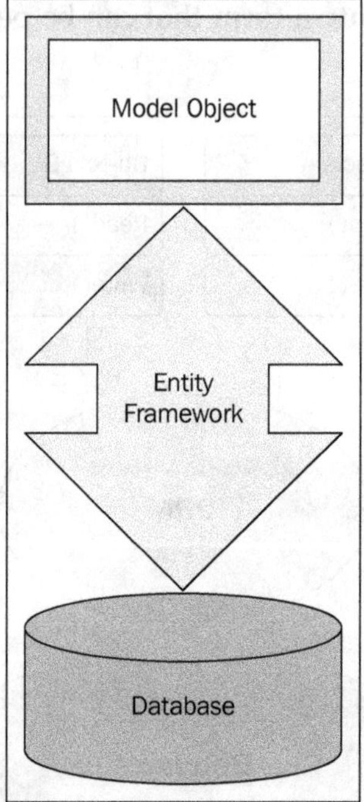

This level of abstraction is achieved using the **Entity Data Model (EDM)**—an extended entity relationship model. The EDM reduces the dependency of your domain object model on the database schema of the data store in use. We will discuss more on this topic later in this chapter.

Developers can use the ADO.NET Entity Framework to work with domain-specific properties such as employee name, employee address, contact details, and so on, without having to be concerned with how the actual data is stored and represented in the underlying data store. The framework can take care of the necessary translations to either retrieve data from your data store or perform inserts, updates, and deletes. Also, Entity Framework provides support to cache data automatically by default.

Is Entity Framework just another ORM?

The ADO.NET Entity Framework is an extended ORM technology from Microsoft. We say it is an extended ORM because it has many additional features compared to a typical ORM. ORMs often use metadata and factory classes to retrieve data or collections of data.

Factory classes are based on the factory design pattern and are used to create instances of classes without exposing the instantiation logic to the client.

On the contrary, using Entity Framework, you can easily map your data to be accessible in a relational representation in the database to objects, no matter how the mapping is implemented. You can expose different data views to your application without having to change your relational schema. In essence, this allows the applications to have their own view of the data. The applications can even reuse the same views of data among themselves.

The major difference between Entity Framework and ORM tools is the EDM and the former's ability to query data using strongly typed LINQ. You can even use Entity SQL, a T-SQL-like query language to query the EDM, to execute dynamic queries. In addition to what a typical ORM framework provides, the Entity Framework provides and supports entity inheritance, entity composition, and a flexible, loosely-coupled, three-tiered model consisting of the conceptual model, the mapping layer, and the storage model. Please refer to the *Appendix* section for links to resources on this topic.

Entity Framework even enables you to extend the existing schema. In other words, you can extend the generated entity classes to create your own custom entity classes. You can define relationships of any kind such as one-to-one, one-to-many, and even many-to-many.

A comparative analysis of Entity Framework and other ORM tools

Data access strategies have changed over the years. From **Remote Data Objects (RDO)**, **Data Access Objects (DAO)**, to ADO.NET, the industry has seen a marked improvement in the way data is accessed these days.

ORM tools enable you to access data from persistent storage devices without having to bother about how the underlying data is actually stored. NHibernate is a lightweight ORM tool for .NET. It has a statically compiled counterpart called Fluent NHibernate. Fluent NHibernate provides you with an XML-less, compile safe, automated NHibernate mapper with LINQ support. Domain modeling is an area where Entity Framework scores over NHibernate.

Consider the following entity class:

```
public class User
    {
        public virtual Int32 UserID { get; set; }
        public virtual String UserName { get; set; }
        public virtual String CreatedBy { get; set; }
        public virtual DateTime CreatedDate { get; set; }
        public virtual String ModifiedBy { get; set; }
        public virtual DateTime ModifiedDate { get; set; }
    }
```

Downloading the example code

You can download the example code files from your account at `http://www.packtpub.com` for all the Packt Publishing books you have purchased. If you purchased this book elsewhere, you can visit `http://www.packtpub.com/support` and register to have the files e-mailed directly to you.

The following class illustrates how you can create a mapping for the preceding class by extending the generic `ClassMap<T>` class:

```
public class UserMap : ClassMap<User>
    {
        public UserMap()
        {
            Table("Users");
            Id(x => x.UserID).GeneratedBy.Identity();
            Map(x => x.UserName);
            Map(x => x.CreatedBy);
            Map(x => x.CreatedDate);
            Map(x => x.ModifiedBy);
            Map(x => x.ModifiedDate);
        }
    }
```

The following code example illustrates how you can create a data gateway for the `User` entity class:

```
using FluentNHibernate;
using NHibernate;
using FluentNHibernate.Cfg.Db;
using FluentNHibernate.Automapping;
using NHibernate.Cfg;
```

```
using NHibernate;
using FluentNHibernate.Cfg.Db;
using FluentNHibernate.Automapping;
using NHibernate.Cfg;
using NHibernate.Tool.hbm2ddl;
using System.Reflection;
namespace Packt
{
    public static class DataManager
    {
        private static ISessionFactory sessionFactory = null;
        private static readonly string businessObjectsNamespace =
        "Packt.Entity.Mappings";
        private static readonly string connectionString = @"Data
        Source=JOYDIP-PC\SQLServer2014;
        Initial Catalog=Security;Integrated Security=True";
        private static ISessionFactory SessionFactory
        {
            get
            {
                if (_sessionFactory == null)
                {
      //Code to create a new session factory instance and load the
      business entities
                }
             return sessionFactory;
            }
        }

        public static ISession OpenSession()
        {
            return SessionFactory.OpenSession();
        }
    }
}
```

Note that you can make a call to `DataManager.OpenSession()` to open the database connectivity session.

Entity Framework 6 is a mature ORM and comes up with many powerful features. When you use Entity Framework, you can concentrate more on writing application logic rather than writing the database connectivity code. This reduces development time and effort greatly.

Language Integrated Query (**LINQ**) is a query translation pipeline that you can use to integrate your queries into the object model. LINQ provides you with a framework that you can use to access relational data in a strongly typed way. LINQ provides a great way to query in-memory objects.

Here are the various forms that LINQ comes up with:

- **LINQ to objects**: This is used to query in-memory objects or a collection of in-memory objects
- **LINQ to XML**: This is used to query data retrieved from XML data sources
- **LINQ to SQL**: This is used to query data retrieved from SQL Server database
- **LINQ to DataSet**: This is used to query data from a DataSet or a DataTable
- **LINQ to Entities**: This is used to query data exposed by the EDM

The LINQ library contains two primary interfaces that all generic collection classes implement. These are the `IEnumerable<T>` interface and the `IQueryable<T>` interface. While the former exposes an enumerator to iterate over a collection of a given type `T`, the latter provides a functionality to query a data source that will implement this interface. Also, `IQueryable` allows you to filter data on the server side.

The following diagram illustrates how these interfaces are related:

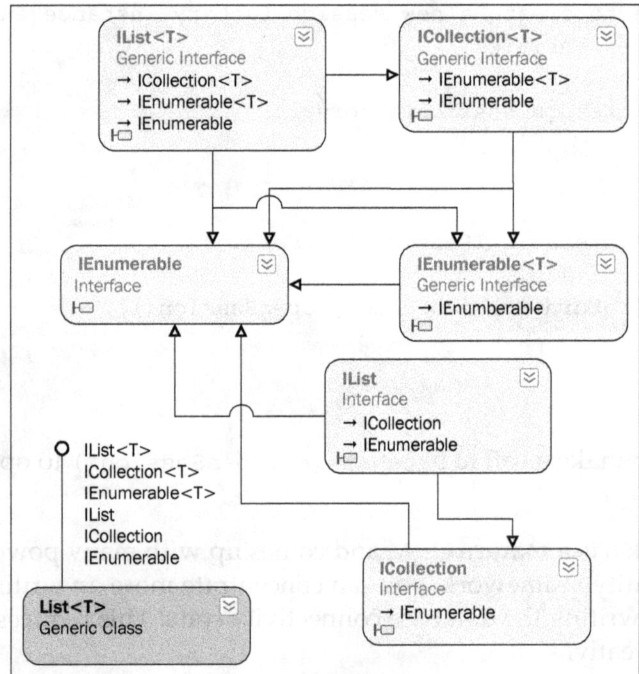

Important interfaces of the LINQ library

LINQ to SQL and .dbml files

LINQ to SQL allows you create an object model that maps to the tables in the relational database. The object relational mapping implementation of LINQ to SQL handles the execution strategy of the SQL queries. A database markup language file, also known as `.dbml` file, is generated by the Visual Studio IDE when you drag and drop database tables from the solution explorer onto the LINQ to SQL design surface. When each table is dragged on the design surface, a class is created for each table. These classes are known as **entity classes** and they are partial classes.

Both LINQ to SQL and ORM share certain common behaviors in terms of designing, mapping entities with relational database, and querying entities.

Developing non-LINQ to SQL data-centric applications may consume a lot time and effort in trying to build custom components that will interact with the data source. LINQ to SQL maps tables to classes, which helps architects to design a better n-tier architecture, thus improving productivity.

The properties in the entity classes are mapped to the columns in the table with an appropriate data type mapping scheme. Hence, a compile time check is performed that reduces runtime errors.

Entity Framework architectural components

Entity Framework comprises the following components:

- The Entity Data Model
- LINQ to Entities
- Entity Client
- Entity SQL
- The Object Services Layer

Note that the **Conceptual Model Layer**, **Mapping Layer**, and **Logical Model Layer** are all parts of the EDM. The following image illustrates the layers of the ADO.NET Entity Framework and how they are related to each other:

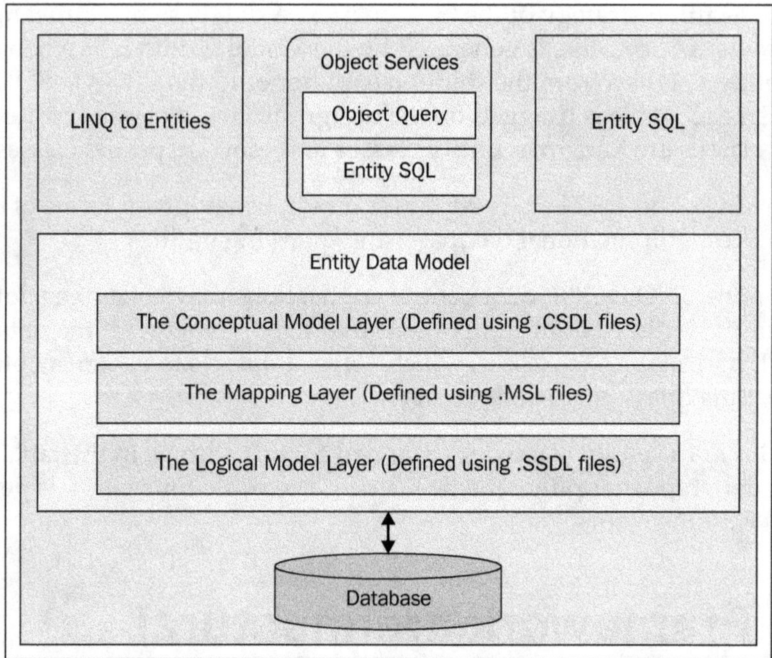

ADO.NET Entity Framework: the architectural components

We will now discuss each of the components of the Entity Framework technology stack in the following sections.

The Entity Data Model

The **Entity Data Model (EDM)**, an extended entity relationship model, is the core of Entity Framework. You can generate an EDM using the `EDMGen.exe` command-line tool or using the ADO.NET EDM Designer—a new Visual Studio template. We will discuss how an EDM can be generated from a relational schema in the next chapter.

For additional information, please refer to `http://msdn.microsoft.com/en-us/library/bb896270(v=vs.110).aspx`.

The following image illustrates where exactly the EDM fits in:

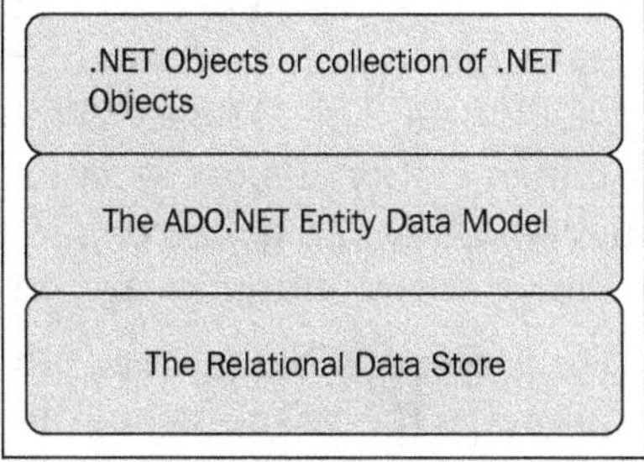

The Entity Data Model

The EDM abstracts the logical or the relational schema and exposes the conceptual schema of the data using a three-layered approach. It comprises the following layers:

- The Conceptual Model Layer or the Conceptual Data Definition Language Layer (C-Space)
- The Mapping Layer or the Mapping Schema Definition Language layer (C-S Space)
- The Storage Layer or the Logical Layer or the Store Space Definition Language Layer (S-Space)

The following image illustrates the layers of the EDM:

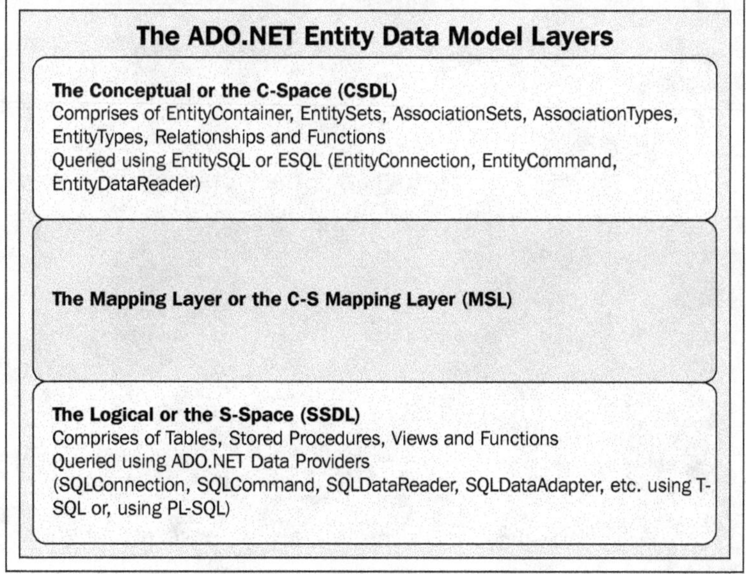

The Entity Data Model layers

Let's explain each of these layers in detail:

- The Conceptual Layer or the C-Space Layer is responsible for defining the entities and their relationships. It defines your business objects and their relationships in XML files. The C-Space is modeled using CSDL and comprises EntityContainer, EntitySets, AssociationSets, AssociationTypes, EntityTypes, and functions. You can query this layer using Entity SQL or ESQL (EntityConnection, EntityCommand, and EntityDataReader).
- The C-S Mapping Layer is responsible for mapping the conceptual and the logical layers. That is, it maps the business objects and the relationships defined in the conceptual layer with the tables and relationships defined in the Logical layer. It is a mapping system created in XML, which links or maps the conceptual and the Logical layers. The C-S Mapping Layer is modeled using Mapping Storage Layer or the MSL.
- The Logical or the Storage Layer (also called the S-Space) represents the schema of the underlying database. This comprises tables, stored procedures, views, and functions. It is modeled using SSDL and queried using the database providers. A database provider is an API to connect to and perform CRUD operations against a database. As an example, if the database in use is SQL Server, the ADO.NET data provider for SQL Server will be used. Hence, we use SQLConnection, SQLCommand, SQLDataReader, and SQLDataAdapter using T-SQL or PL-SQL if our data store is a SQL database.

Here is what a typical EDM looks like:

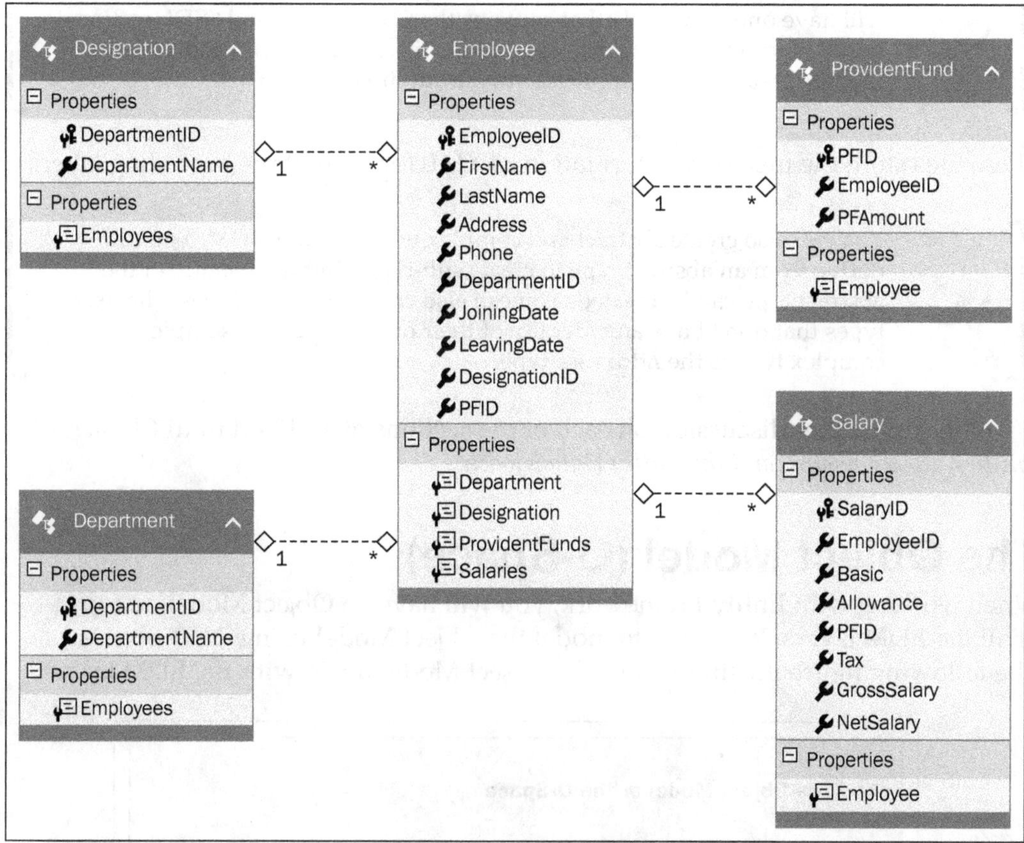

An ADO.NET Entity Data Model at a glance

How is the EDM represented?

The EDM uses the following three types of XML files to represent the C-Space, C-S Space, and the S-Space respectively:

- **Conceptual Schema Definition Language (.CSDL)**: This represents the C-S Space and is used to map the entity types used in the conceptual model
- **Mapping Schema Language (.MSL)**: This represents the C-S Space and is used to map the logical model to the conceptual model
- **Store Schema Definition Language (.SSDL)**: This represents the S-Space and is used to map the schema information of the Logical layer

If you use the ADO.NET EDM Designer tool to generate your EDM, you will have one `.edmx` file that contains the CSDL, MSL, and SSDL sections bundled into one single file. At runtime, the `.csdl`, `.msl`, and `.ssdl` files are created in the application's output directory.

These files store the metadata information as XML for each of the preceding layers.

You can also create abstract and complex types in your EDM. You can derive from an abstract type to create sub-types, but no instance of the abstract type can be created. You can also create complex types. That is, types that don't have any identity of their own. A typical example of a complex type is the `Address` type.

We will skip further discussion on each of the sections of an EDM until *Chapter 3, Entities, Relationships, and the Entity Data Model*.

The Object Model (O-Space)

When working with Entity Framework, you will have an Object Model on top of all the EDM layers. You need to model the Object Model using .NET objects. The following figure illustrates how the Object Model fits in with the EDM layers:

The Object Model or the O-Space
The O-C Mapping Layer
The Conceptual Model or the C-Space (Modeled using CSDL)
The Mapping Layer or the C-S Space (Modeled using MSL)
The Logical Model or the S-Space (Modeled using SSDL)

The Object Model and its relationship with other layers

The Object Model layer contains .NET objects and a collection of .NET objects, types, properties, and methods. You can use the Object Model or the O-Space Model to query your business objects, or the collections of your business objects, using LINQ to Entities or Entity SQL. The C-Space and O-Space models are actually mapped by the O-C Mapping Layer using code attributes applied to the O-Space Model.

LINQ to Entities

LINQ is a query translation pipeline that has been introduced as part of the C# 3.0 library. It comprises a set of query operators for different data sources (LDAP, objects, CSV, XML, entities, SQL, and so on). It is an extension of the C# language (it's actually a series of extension methods) and provides a simplified framework to access relational data in a strongly typed, object-oriented manner.

LINQ to Entities is a Microsoft technology that enables you to query your business objects from within the language in a strongly typed manner. You can use LINQ to Entities, a superset of LINQ to SQL, to query data against a conceptual data model, namely, the Entity Data Model. You will learn more about LINQ and LINQ to Entities in *Chapter 6, Working with LINQ to Entities*.

Here is an example of a typical LINQ to Entities query:

```
AdventureWorksEntities ctx = new AdventureWorksEntities();
            var query = from e in ctx.Employees
               select e;
            foreach (var employee in query)
                Console.WriteLine (employee.EmployeeID);
```

> LINQ to Entities rests on top of Entity Framework's Object Services Layer and the LINQ to Entities queries are internally translated to canonical query trees. This, in turn, gets converted internally to corresponding SQL queries in a form expected by your underlying database.

Entity Client

The Entity Framework allows you to write programs against the EDM and also add a level of abstraction on top of the relational model. This isolation of the logical view of data from the Object Model is accomplished by expressing queries in terms of abstractions using an enhanced query language called Entity SQL.

EntityClient, the gateway to entity-level queries, is the Entity Framework's counterpart of ADO.NET's SQL client or Oracle client that uses Entity SQL or E-SQL to query the conceptual model. You create a connection using the entity connection, execute commands through entity commands, and retrieve the result sets as entity data readers. The MSDN states:

> "*The EntityClient provider is a data provider used by Entity Framework applications to access data described in a conceptual model.*"

Entity SQL

Entity SQL is a data store independent derivative of T-SQL that supports entity inheritance and relationships. You can use it to query data using the conceptual schema. You can even build your own dynamic queries. These E-SQL queries are internally translated to data store dependent SQL queries. This translation of the E-SQL queries to their data store-specific query language like T-SQL, (it doesn't need to be only T-SQL, however, it is the supported one), is handled by the Entity Framework. Entity SQL or E-SQL may not be as strongly typed as LINQ is, but you have the flexibility of executing dynamic queries using it, much like T-SQL.

Strongly typed data access is one of the most striking features of LINQ. LINQ queries are checked at compile time. This is unlike SQL queries, which are only detected at runtime.

But, why do you need Entity SQL when you have LINQ to Entities to query data through your EDM? You can, using Entity SQL, compose queries that are difficult to determine until the time the query is executed. On a different note, Entity SQL is a full text-based query language that you can use in much the same way as you use the ADO.NET data providers.

Here is an example that shows how you can use Entity SQL to insert data into your applications:

```
using (EntityConnection conn = new
EntityConnection("Name=PayrollEntities"))
           {
               try
               {
                   conn.Open();
                   EntityCommand cmd = conn.CreateCommand();
                   cmd.CommandText =
                   "PayrollEntities.AddNewEmployee";
                   cmd.CommandType = CommandType.StoredProcedure;
```

```
            cmd.Parameters.AddWithValue("FirstName",
            "Joydip");
            cmd.Parameters.AddWithValue("LastName",
            "Kanjilal");
            cmd.Parameters.AddWithValue("Address",
            "Hyderabad");
            cmd.Parameters.AddWithValue("DepartmentID",
            4);
            cmd.ExecuteNonQuery();
        }
        catch (Exception ex)
        {
            Console.WriteLine(ex.ToString());
        }
    }
```

To query data from the EDM, you have three choices—Entity SQL, LINQ to Entities, and Object Services.

Avoiding complex joins

You can use Entity SQL to avoid complex joins as you will typically be querying against a conceptual model of the data. As an example, if we want to display employee names and the department names in which they work, we would have to join the information of the `Employee` and the `Department` tables and then filter the unwanted columns to retrieve only the information that is required. Such traversals become a nightmare as you add additional tables and therefore require more complex joins.

When you implement your Object Model using object-oriented programming languages, you expose the object's relationships to other objects of its kind using properties. This is in contrast to the approach we just discussed. Hence, designing an Object Model using this approach is cumbersome. This is exactly where Entity Framework fits in; it represents the conceptual and logical model of data while using grammar that is common to both.

Here is a code snippet that explains how you can use Entity SQL to avoid complex joins in your application's code. The following T-SQL query can be used to retrieve employee data split across three tables, namely, `Employee`, `Department`, and `Salary`:

```
Select Employee.FirstName, Employee.LastName,
Department.DepartmentName, Salary.Basic
```

```
from Employee
INNER JOIN
Department on Department.DepartmentID = Employee.DepartmentID
INNER JOIN
Salary on Salary.EmployeeID = Employee.EmployeeID
```

This is how you would use Entity SQL to achieve the same result:

```
Select FirstName, LastName, DepartmentName, Basic from Employee
```

In the previous example, `EmployeeData` is an entity that has been derived from the `Employee`, `Department`, and `Salary` entities.

The Object Services Layer

As well as querying the conceptual model, you might, at some point, have to work with entities such as in-memory objects or a collection of in-memory objects. To do this, you need Object Services. You can use it to query data from almost any data store, and with less code.

> You can query data from the EDM by either using Object Services or EntityClient. However, if you require change tracking, be aware that only Object Services provides this feature. Note that in either case, the ADO.NET data providers are responsible for talking to the underlying database.

Note that the Object Services Layer internally uses an `ObjectQuery` object for query processing. To use object services, you should include the `System.Data.Objects` and `System.Data.Objects.DataClasses` namespaces.

Here is an example that shows how you can use Object Services to retrieve data:

```
using (ObjectContext ctx = new ObjectContext("Name=
PayrollEntities"))
            {
                ObjectQuery<Employee> data =
                ctx.CreateQuery<Employee>("PayrollEntities.
Employees");

                foreach (Employee emp in data)
                {
                    Console.WriteLine(emp.EmployeeID);
                }
            }
```

In addition to enabling you to perform **create**, **read**, **update**, and **delete** (**CRUD**) operations, the Object Services Layer provides the following additional services:

- Change tracking
- Lazy loading
- Inheritance
- Optimistic concurrency
- Merging data
- Identity resolution
- Support for querying data using Entity SQL and LINQ to Entities

You will learn more about Object Services later in the book. The Object Services Layer leverages an **Object Query** object internally to process the data. Note that the Object Services Layer supports querying data using both Entity SQL and LINQ to Entities.

Features and benefits at a glance

Here is a quick look at some of the features and benefits of Entity Framework:

- It provides support for an increased level of abstraction on top of the underlying data store
- It provides support for extensibility and seamless querying of data using Entity SQL and LINQ
- It is a flexible schema that can be used to store the mapping information
- There is a reduction in the amount of **Kilo Lines of Code** (**KLOC**) needed to write data access code in your applications
- It contains a powerful Object Services Layer
- It provides support for a full text-based query language
- It provides support for persistence ignorance
- IT provides support for lazy loading

KLOC refers to Kilo Lines of Code, a unit of measuring the amount of source code in your programs.

System requirements

To run the programs given in this book, you should have the following elements installed on your system:

- Visual Studio.NET 2012 or higher
- SQL Server 2014 or higher

Entity Framework 6.0 can be downloaded from NuGet at `https://entityframework.codeplex.com/releases/view/87028`.

Note that Entity Framework 6.0 already ships with Visual Studio 2013, so there is no need to download it if you use this version of Visual Studio.

Now let's take a quick look at each of these new features. We will explore each of these features in detail as we move through the chapters.

Support for persistence ignorance

Support for persistence ignorance was introduced in Entity Framework 4.0. Persistence ignorance, as the literal meaning implies, is a concept that enables you to build your applications in a way that can just ignore the underlying data store in use. In essence, you can build applications that can have different persistent technology in future.

You can now create your own **Plain Old CLR Objects** (commonly known as **POCO**) that are decoupled from any specific persistence technology. To provide support for POCO, all you need to do is just turn off code generation in the model in your Visual Studio 2013 IDE.

You can simply clear the values of the **Custom Tool** property of your EDM and save it again. Once you have done this, you have to create your own custom object context by deriving your custom object context class from the `ObjectContext` class. Then you can define the data members and properties in your custom object context class as per your needs.

Support for T4 code generation

T4 is a code generation technology that was introduced in Visual Studio 2008. T4 templates not only give you advantage to customize the generated code, they also generate less code, concealing a lot of redundant functions that were present in the old generated code. Entity Framework 6 provides support for T4 code-generation templates. You can also customize these templates as needed.

Support for lazy loading

Lazy loading is a concept that enables an entity to be loaded late– it's loaded on demand actually. Entity Framework 6 provides better support for lazy loading. To enable deferred loading (it is turned off by default), you should make use of the **DeferredLoadingEnabled** property. Please check out this URL for more information on lazy loading `http://msdn.microsoft.com/en-us/library/vstudio/dd456846(v=vs.100).aspx`.

Deferred loading works with both code-generated entities as well as your Plain Old CLR Objects – commonly known as POCO entities.

Support for POCO change tracking

Entity Framework 6 enables you to easily track changes to POCOs. Note that Entity Framework 6.0 provides support for the deferred or lazy loading of entities with POCO classes through the usage of proxy types. Here is an example:

```
var result = (from emp in PayrollDataContext.Employee
.Include("Department") where emp.DepartmentID == 12 select
emp).Single();
```

Please check out this URL to find out more about lazy loading:

`http://msdn.microsoft.com/en-us/library/vstudio/dd456846(v=vs.100).aspx`

We will explore more about POCO classes and lazy loading later in this book.

Better n-tier support with self-tracking entities

Entity Framework 6 provides better n-tier support and support for self-tracking entities. Self-tracking entities are those that enable each entity to track any changes to themselves so that you can pass it across process boundaries and persist the entire object graph. Entity Framework 6 includes T4 templates to generate entities that have the ability to track their own changes on the client side.

Support for code-first, model-first, and database-first approaches

Entity Framework 6 now enables you to generate your Data Model from the conceptual model. You can now create your entities and then use Visual Studio 2013 to generate the database based on a predefined conceptual model.

In the code-first approach, the domain model is first defined using POCO classes and then the database is created from these classes. This approach is popular and provides much more control over your code—you just need to define the database mappings and leave the creation of the database entirely to Entity Framework. Note that as your code drives the database, manual changes to the database are not recommended in this approach.

The figure given next illustrates the three approaches and why and when each should be used:

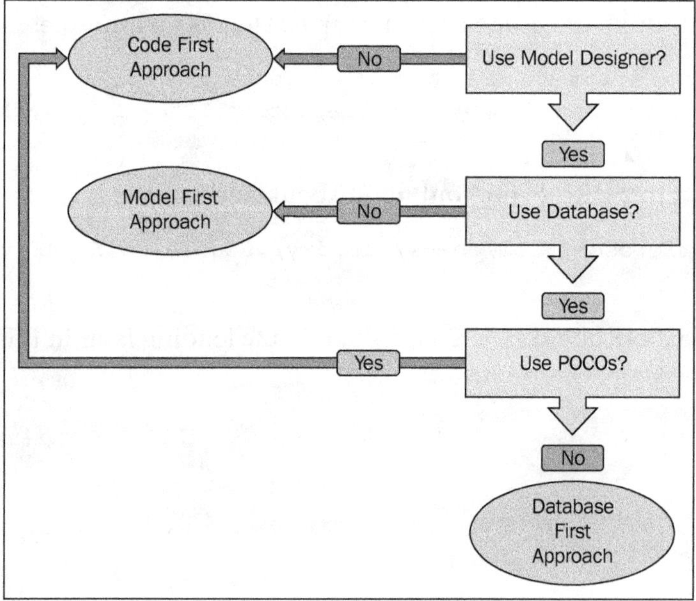

In the model-first approach, you create your entities, relationships, and the inheritance hierarchies directly on the design surface of the EDM Designer in Visual Studio and then generate the database from the model designed. If you need additional features, you can use partial classes. In essence, in this approach, the model drives and defines the database. This is also known as the **model-driven approach**. This approach is good for small projects, but with complex databases and large projects this is not a preferred approach as you don't have much control over the database. Also, making manual changes to the database schema is also not recommended.

In the database-first approach, you would create your database first and then generate your model using the ADO.NET EDM Designer from this database.

Support for built-in functions and UDF support

Entity Framework 6 provides support for you to use SQL Server functions directly in your queries. Here is an example:

```
from emp in PayrollDataContext.Employee
where new[] {"january","february","march"}.Contains(SqlFunctions.
DateName("mon
th", emp.JoiningDate))
orderby emp.EmployeeID
select new
{
 emp.EmployeeID,emp.JoiningDate
};
```

Support for model-defined functions

Entity Framework 6 now provides support for model-defined functions that can be defined in the CSDL using eSQL. Note that model-defined functions support LINQ to Entities and can also be called Object methods. Here is an example:

```
<Function Name="GetEmployeeAge" ReturnType="Edm.Int32">
    <Parameter Name="Employee" Type="Self.Employee" />
      <DefiningExpression>
        Edm.DiffYears(Employee.BirthDate, Edm.CurrentDateTime())
      </DefiningExpression>
</Function>.
```

In this section, we just gave you an introduction to the new features in Entity Framework 6—we will cover details of each of these features in the forthcoming chapters of this book.

Enum support

Enum support is a much-awaited feature that enables you to have enum properties in your domain classes. In Entity Framework 6, you have enum support both in the EF Designer as well as using a code-first approach. To create an enum in Entity Framework 6, all you need is to create a scalar property of type `Int32` in the EDM, select it, right-click on it, and then select **Convert to Enum**. The following image illustrates this:

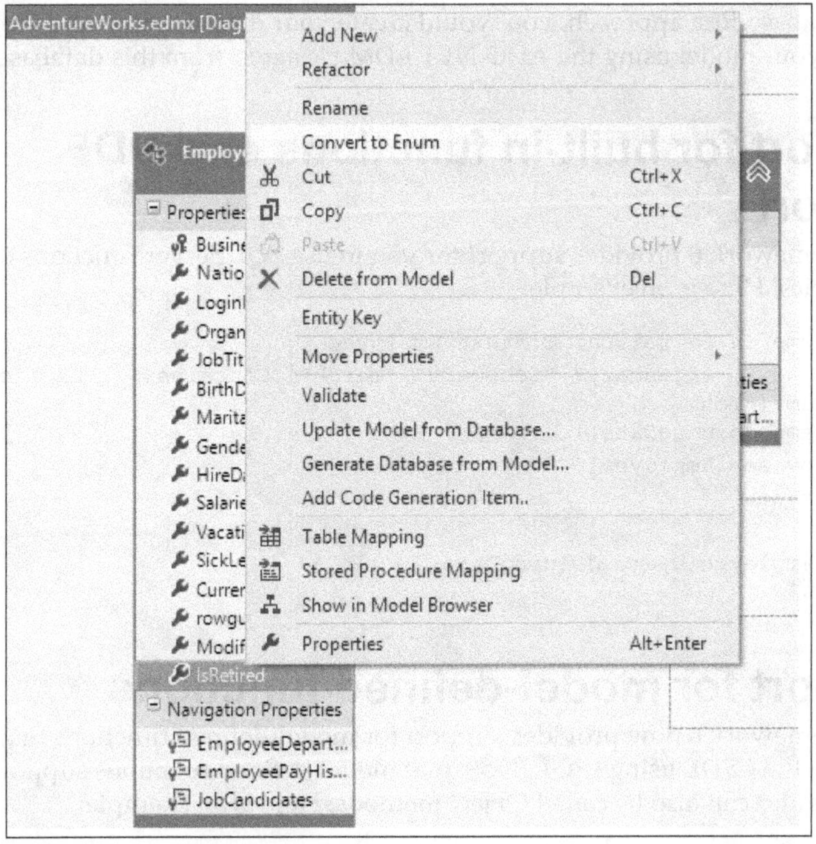

In the preceding image, **IsRetired** has been introduced as a scalar property of type `Int32`. You can see that the **Convert to Enum** option is enabled.

Spatial data types support

Spatial data types are actually geography and geometry-related classes that allow us to work directly with such data inside the SQL Server. Spatial data can be of two types – the **geometry data type** that provides support for planar or Euclidean (flat-earth) data, and **geography data type** that can store ellipsoidal (round-earth) data such as GPS latitude and longitude coordinates. Entity Framework 6 now provides support for spatial data types using the `DbGeography` and `DbGeometry` types. You can include spatial data in your models both using the EF Designer, as well as using code-first. You can find out more about spatial data types from this link: `http://technet.microsoft.com/en-us/library/bb964711.aspx`.

> Some of the new features in Entity Framework 6 such as enum support and spatial data types will work with .NET Framework 4.5 and above.

Other enhancements

In Entity Framework 6, `DbContext` is the default generated context. It is not new though. It is a wrapper around `ObjectContext` generated using T4 templates. Here is an example:

```
public AdventureWorksEntities()
        : base("name=AdventureWorksEntities")
    {
    }

    protected override void OnModelCreating(DbModelBuilder
    modelBuilder)
    {
        throw new UnintentionalCodeFirstException();
    }

    public virtual DbSet<Department> Departments { get; set; }
    public virtual DbSet<Employee> Employees { get; set; }
    public virtual DbSet<EmployeeDepartmentHistory>
    EmployeeDepartmentHistories { get; set; }
    public virtual DbSet<EmployeePayHistory>
    EmployeePayHistories { get; set; }
    public virtual DbSet<JobCandidate> JobCandidates { get;
    set; }
    public virtual DbSet<Shift> Shifts { get; set; }
}
```

The other enhancements in Entity Framework are shown as follows:

- **Task-based asynchronous operation**: This allows Entity Framework to take advantage of .NET 4.5 asynchronous support with asynchronous queries, updates, and so on. Entity Framework 6 now provides support for a simplified approach to asynchronous programming. Entity Framework 6 can now be used to run async queries and also save data asynchronously.
- **Enhanced support for stored procedures and functions in code first**: This feature allows you to map stored procedures and database functions by using the code-first APIs.
- **Support for custom code first conventions**: This is a feature that allows you to write and register custom code conventions with code first.

Note that the third-party providers for Entity Framework 5 are not compatible with Entity Framework 6. This implies that if you are using the SQL Server or SQL Server Compact editions, you should update the database providers.

Performance improvements in Entity Framework 6

In Entity Framework 6, query performance has been improved a lot. One important performance improvement is in precompiled queries. A compiled query is one that is stored as a parsed tree in memory so that it needn't be regenerated with every subsequent call. You can create compiled queries in two ways: creating an `ObjectQuery` class with `EntitySQL` and also using the `CompiledQuery.Compile` function. Compiling expression trees into SQL every time is an overhead particularly for queries that are complex. This is exactly why compiled queries were introduced.

The earlier versions of Entity Framework contained the `CompiledQuery` class that you could use to precompile the query and then execute the query as and when needed. So, in essence, when using precompiled queries, the SQL to be executed is figured out only once (during precompilation) and this is then reused each time the compiled query is executed.

Note that if you are using `CompiledQuery`, you should make sure that you are using the query more than once. This is because it is more costly than querying data the first time.

Now, what were the downsides? You cannot use `CompiledQuery` using the `DbContext` API as it only works with `ObjectContext`. Note that the support for compiled query was revoked from the `DbContext` API due to some technical limitations. If you use a code-first strategy, you will most likely be opting for the `DbContext` API. Thankfully, Entity Framework 6 solved this problem, so you no longer need to make this choice.

With Entity Framework 6, you have a feature called **auto-compiled queries** — this works very different from the way `CompiledQuery` works. You no longer need to write code to compile each query and then invoke as needed. How does it work then? Entity Framework stores the generated SQL in the cache using a background thread and then as and when needed (based on the calls made), it searches the compiled queries in the cache. This is illustrated in the following image:

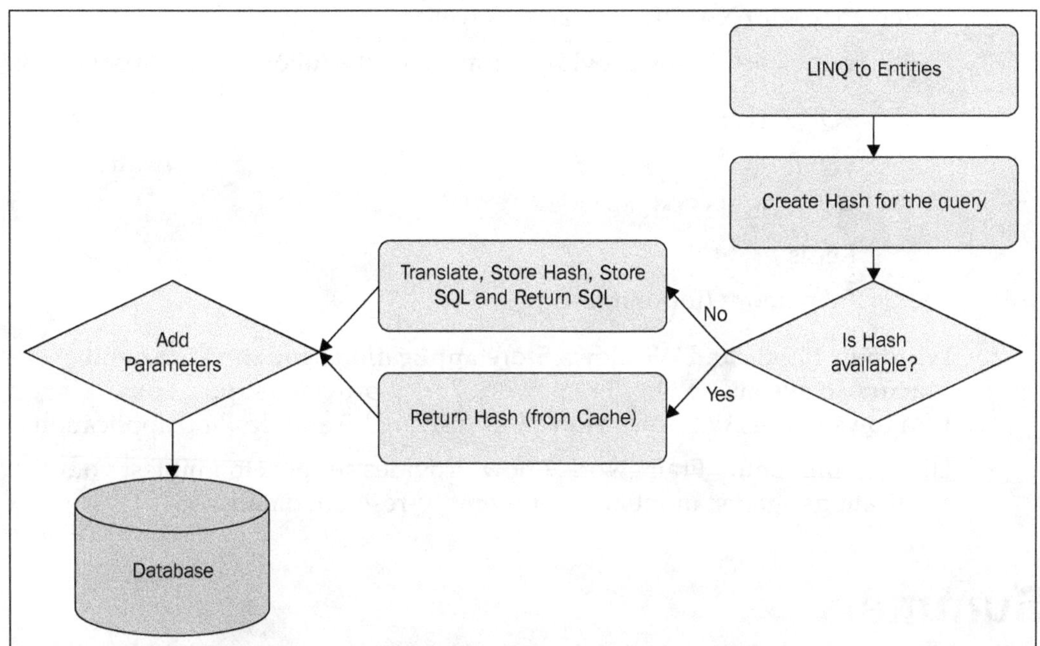

Auto-compiled query in Entity Framework

You can also turn off query caching if you need to. The new `ObjectContext.ContextOptions` property allows you to control the default behavior of the query compilation. This property is set to `true` by default, but you can set it to `false` to turn off the auto-compilation of your queries. Here is an example:

```
dataContext.ContextOptions.DefaultQueryPlanCachingSetting = false;
```

If you are using `DbContext`, you should cast to `IObjectContextAdapter`, as shown in the following code:

```
((IObjectContextAdapter)dataContext).ObjectContext.ContextOptions.
DefaultQueryPlanCachingSetting = false;
```

New features in Entity Framework 7

Entity Framework 7, a major redesign of the ORM, is the latest version of Entity Framework with the vision of "New Platforms, New Data Stores."

Some of the striking features of this release include support for the following:

- **Non-relational data stores and in-memory data**: You can now use Entity Framework with NoSQL databases as well.

  Entity Framework 7 now provides support for the following data providers:

  - SQL Server
  - SQLite
  - Azure Table Storage
  - Redis
  - In memory (for unit testing)
- **Windows Phone and Windows Store applications and the Linux and Macintosh systems**: Entity Framework 7 now provides support for Windows Phone, Windows Store, and ASP.NET 5 and desktop applications.
- **Unit testing**: Entity Framework 7 now provides support to unit test your applications against in-memory or memory-resident databases.

Summary

Entity Framework mainly addressees how easily you can persist and query your data with many added services. You can use Entity Framework to focus on the object model rather than the logical model. In other words, you can add a level of abstraction on top of your relational store.

In this chapter, we explored Entity Framework and the architectural components of Entity Framework, and provided a comparative analysis between Entity Framework and other ORM tools. In the next chapter, you will learn how to get started with Entity Framework.

2
Getting Started

In the previous chapter, we took a look at Entity Framework, including its architecture and its features. We also had a look at the new and enhanced features in Entity Framework 7. Note that Entity Framework 6.0 ships with Visual Studio 2013, but you can also install it via NuGet if needed. Also, Entity Framework 7 is yet to be released.

In this chapter, we will design our `Security` database, create an Entity Data Model (EDM) on top of it, and then use the EntityDataSource control to bind data exposed by the EDM to a GridView control.

The DataSource controls are those that are used to connect to a data source and then retrieve data from those data sources. If you use DataSource controls, the need of writing tedious code to perform **Create, Read, Update, Delete** (**CRUD**) operations on data-based controls is eliminated. The EntityDataSource control is a DataSource control that can connect to the data exposed by the EDM to perform CRUD operations.

In this chapter, we will cover the following points:

- Designing the `UserAuthentication` database
- Creating an EDM for the `UserAuthentication` database
- Introducing the EntityDataSource control
- Implementing our first application using Entity Framework 6

The latest version of Entity Framework is Entity Framework 7. As of this writing, Entity Framework 7 hasn't been released. It will be released as a "pre-release" at the same time ASP.NET 5 is released. You will be able to install the pre-release version of EF 7 using NuGet.

There are many changes coming up in Entity Framework 7—it is being rewritten from the ground up. The major goals of Entity Framework 7 include its support for new platforms and new data stores. So, support for additional providers will also be included in Entity Framework 7:

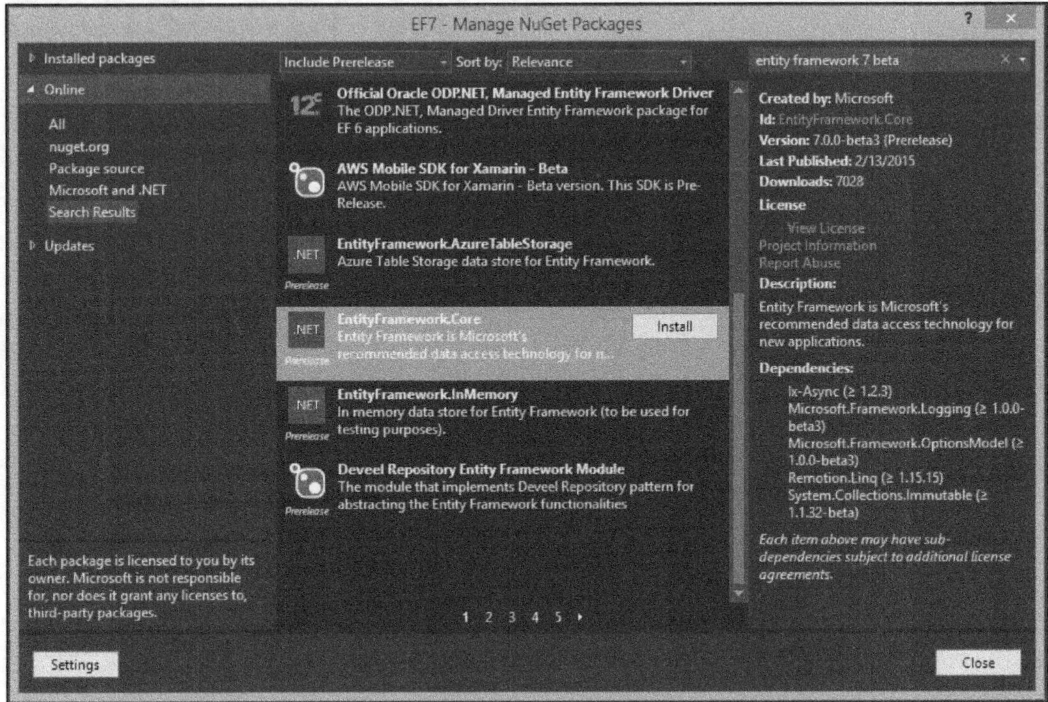

We will start this chapter with a discussion on our `UserAuthentication` database that we will be using throughout this book, followed by a discussion on how we can create an EDM using the `Security` database.

Designing the UserAuthentication database

Before we begin implementing a simple application that shows how data retrieved from the EDM can be consumed, let's take a quick look at the EDM again:

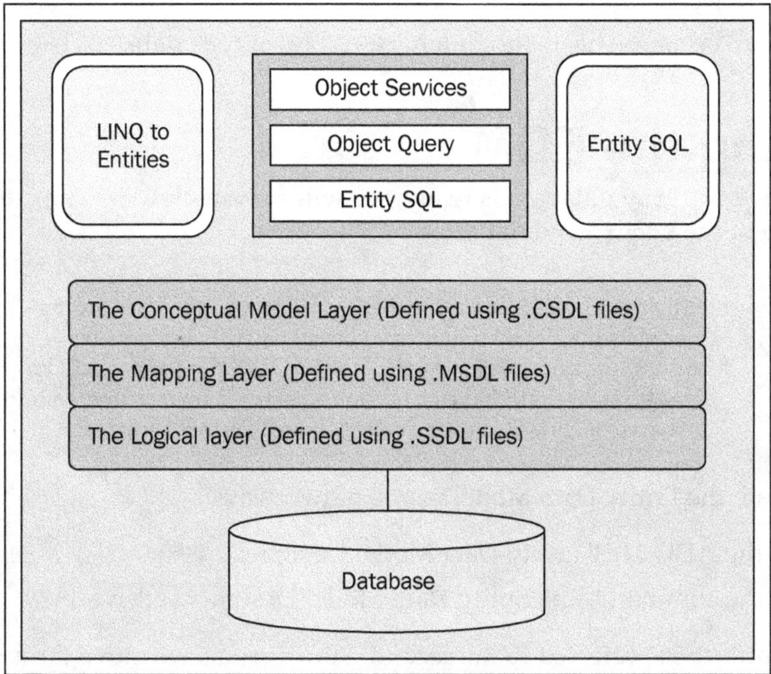

As you can see in this diagram, our application needs to interact with the CSDL layer. The SSDL layer will connect to the database (the `Security` database in our example), and the mapping layer will map these two layers so that they can communicate.

The `Security` database comprises of a list of the following tables:

- `Users`: This table contains the user details.
- `UsersAuthentication`: This table contains the user authentication details.
- `UserAuthenticationTypes`: This table contains user authentication type data. User authentication type can be `Windows`, `Forms`, `Passport`, and `Anonymous`.

- `UsersLoginHistory`: This table contains data related to user login history; that is, the user login history data of the user.
- `UserRoles`: This table contains the user role details.
- `Roles`: This table contains the role details.
- `Controls`: This table contains an entry per control (note that each control is an object).
- `ControlTypes`: This table contains the control type data.

Creating the EDM

Now that the `Security` database is ready, we will explore how we can create an EDM on top of the `Security` database.

Note that, before Entity Framework 7, there were two storage models – the EDMX file format based on XML schema or code. With Entity Framework 7, the EDMX file format will be dropped – we will have only the code-based format. Interestingly, this approach is also termed the "code-first only" approach.

You can create the Entity Data Model in one of two ways:

- Use the ADO.NET Entity Data Model Designer
- Use the command-line Entity Data Model Designer called `EdmGen.exe`

The first approach is preferred to the second. However, as we move through the chapters of the book, we will explore how we can follow the code-first approach to implement the model for our application that uses Entity Framework.

We will first take a look at how we can design an EDM using the ADO.NET Entity Data Model Designer.

Creating the Entity Data Model using the ADO.NET Entity Data Model Designer

To create an EDM using the ADO.NET Entity Data Model Designer, follow these simple steps:

1. Open Visual Studio.NET 2013 IDE, create a solution for a new web application project as follows, and save it with a name.
2. Switch to the **Solution Explorer**, and navigate to **Add** | **New Item...** to create a new Entity Data Model using **Entity Data Model Wizard**.
3. Next, select **ADO.NET Entity Data Model** from the list of templates displayed, as shown in the following screenshot:

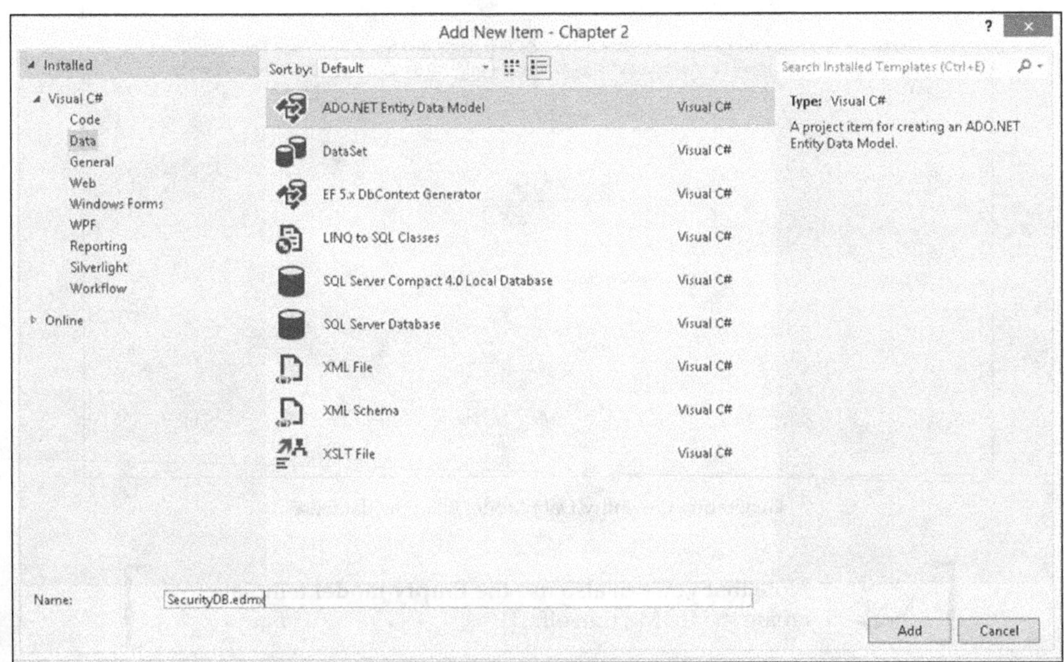

Creating a new ADO.NET Entity Data Model

4. Name the Entity Data Model `SecurityDB`, and click on **Add**.

5. Select **Generate from database** from **Entity Data Model Wizard**, as shown in the following screenshot:

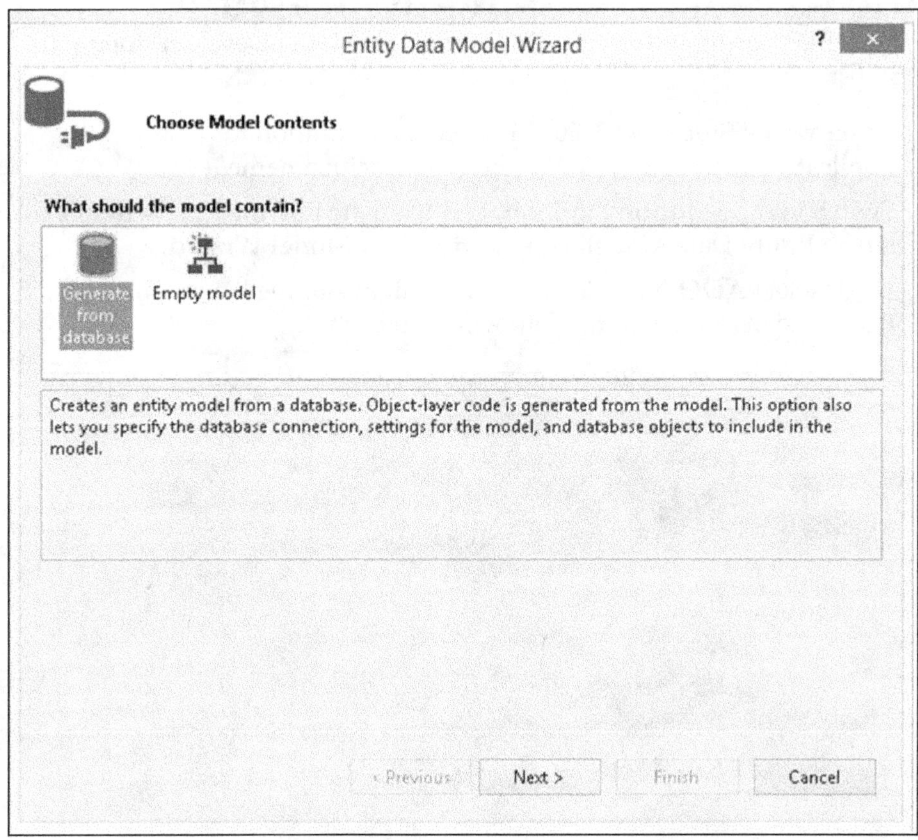

Generating the Entity Data Model from the database

Note that you can also use the **Empty model** template to create the EDM yourself.

If you select the **Empty model** template and click on **Next**, the following screen appears:

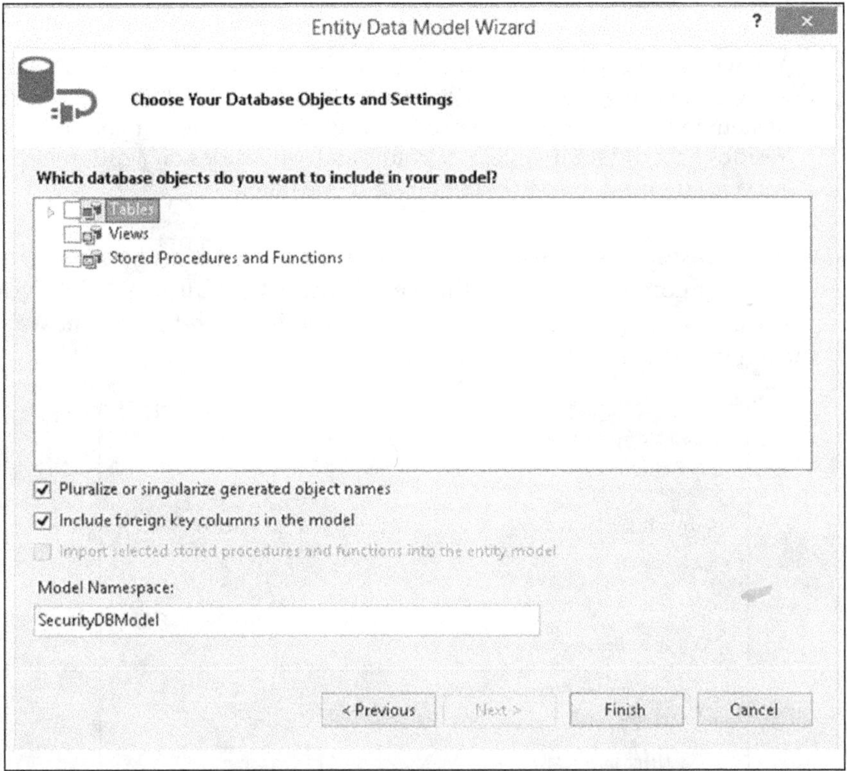

Empty Entity Data Model Wizard

As you can see from the previous screenshot, you can use this template to create the EDM yourself.

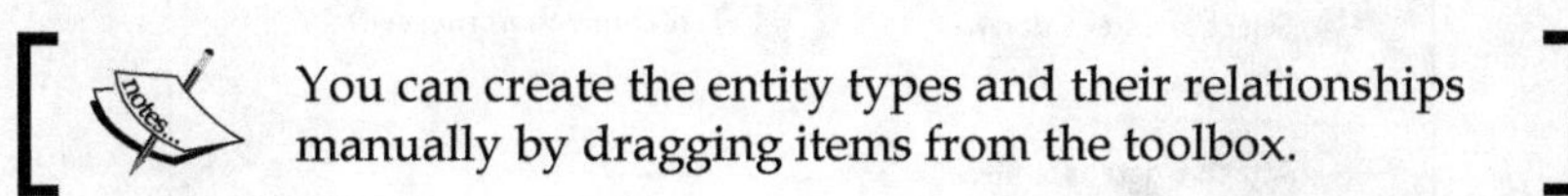

You can create the entity types and their relationships manually by dragging items from the toolbox.

We will not use this template in our discussion here, so let's get to the next step.

6. Click on **Next** in the **Entity Data Model Wizard** window shown earlier.
7. The modal dialog box will now appear and prompt you to choose your connection.

8. Click on **New Connection**. Now you will need to specify the connection properties and parameters for the database to connect to. In our example, the database is `Security`.

> We will use a dot to specify the database server name. This implies that we will be using the database server of the localhost, which is the current system in use. You can also specify the server name here if your database resides on a different system. If your database resides on a different server, you need to specify the server name here.

9. After you specify the necessary user name, password, and server name, you can test your connection using the **Test Connection** button. When you do so, the message **Test connection succeeded** gets displayed in the message box, as shown in the following screenshot:

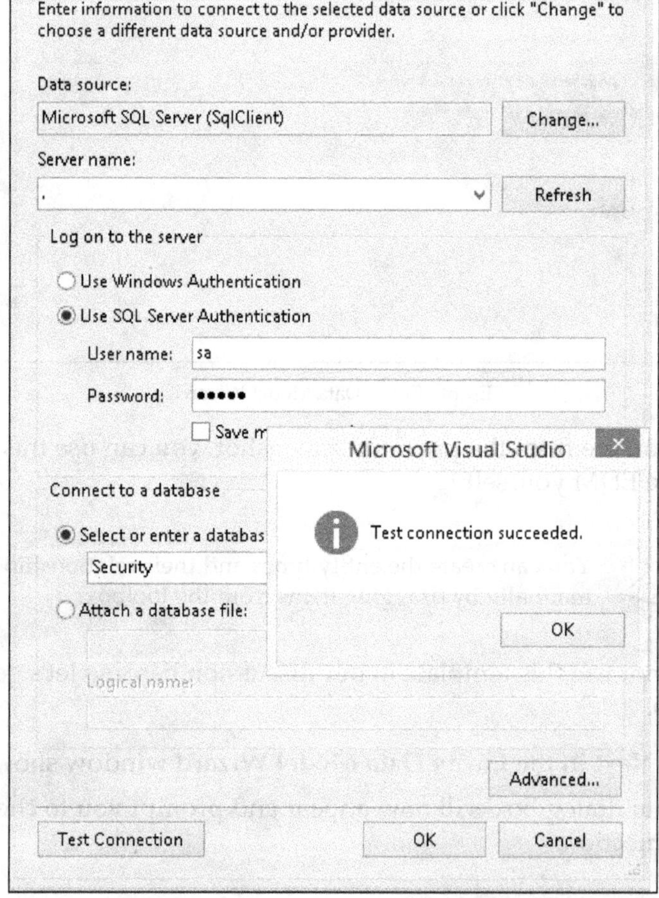

Testing the database connection

> Note that the entity connection string is generated automatically. This connection string will be saved in the `ConnectionStrings` section of your application's `web.config` file. This is what it will look like:

```
<connectionStrings>
    <add name="SecurityDBEntities"
connectionString="metadata=res://*/SecurityDB.
csdl|res:/
/*/SecurityDB.ssdl|res://*/SecurityDB.
msl;provider=Syste
m.Data.SqlClient;provider connection string=&quot;data
source=.;initial catalog=SecurityDB;user
id=sa;password=sa1@3;MultipleActiveResultSets=True;App=
EntityFramework&quot;"
providerName="System.Data.EntityClient" />
  </connectionStrings>
```

10. Now, click on **Next** and specify the database objects you would like to have in your model from the **Choose Your Database Objects and Settings** window that is shown next:

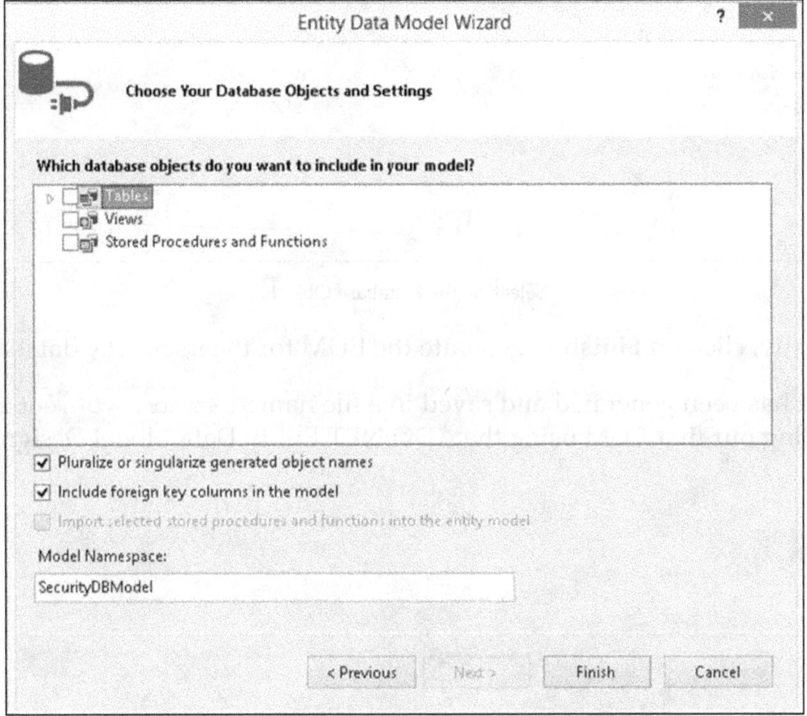

Choosing the database objects to be used in the model

We will select all the tables of the `Security` database now. Refer to the following screenshot:

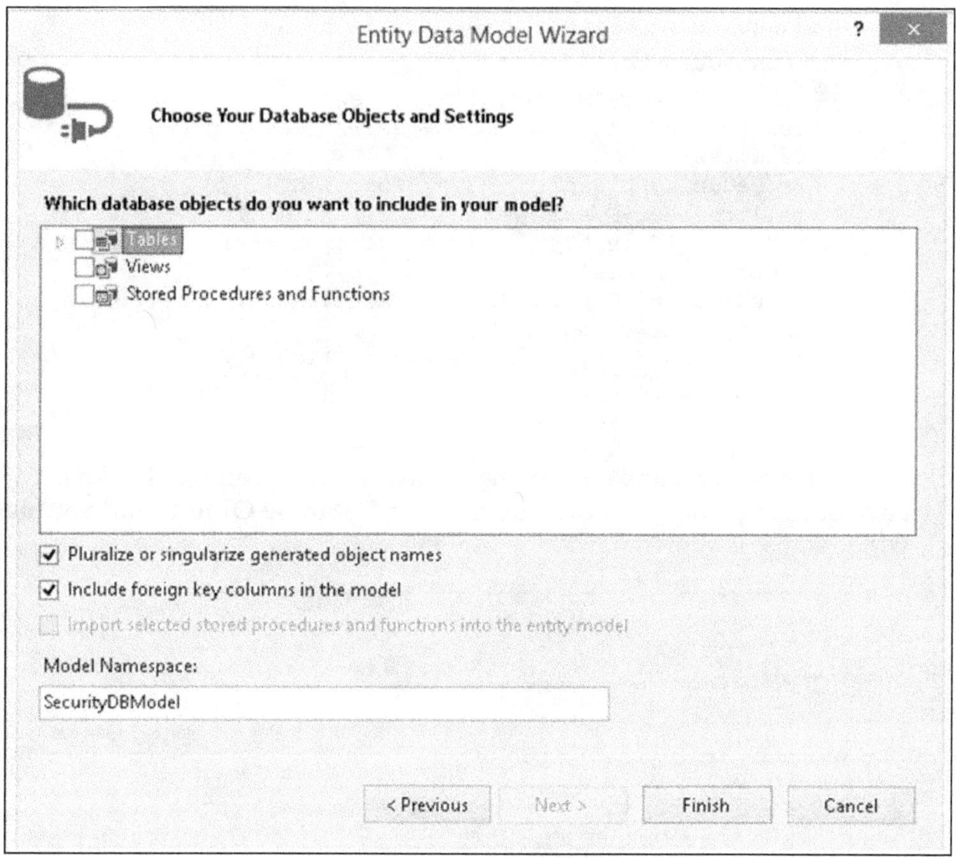

Selecting the Database Objects

11. Lastly, click on **Finish** to generate the EDM for the `Security` database.

Your EDM has been generated and saved in a file named `SecurityDB.edmx`. We are done creating our first EDM using the ADO.NET Entity Data Model Designer tool.

When you open `SecurityDB.edmx` that we just created in the designer view, it will appear as shown in the following image:

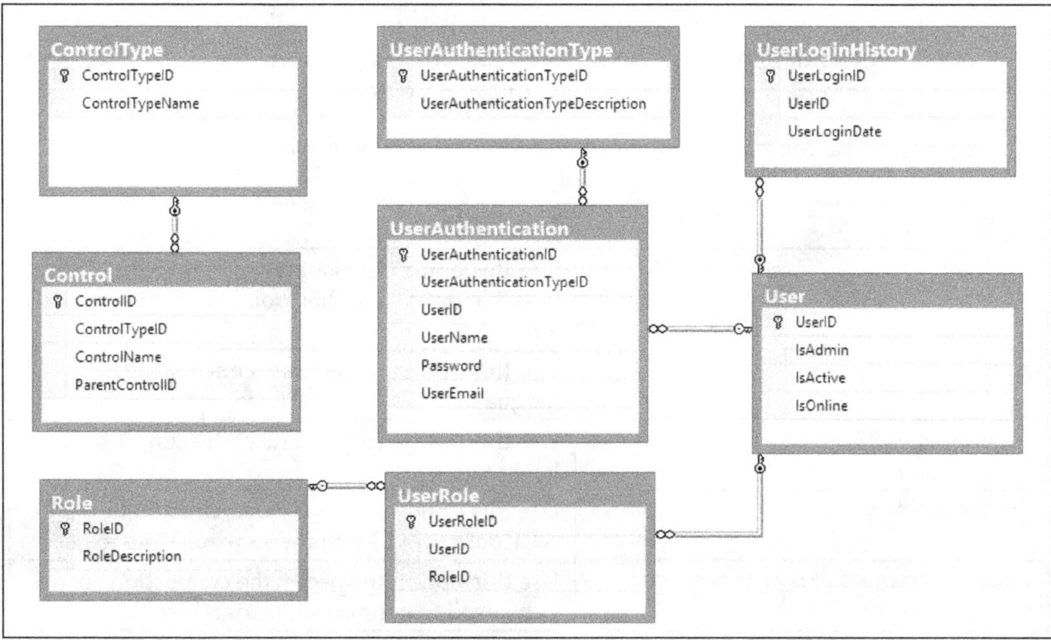

The SecurityDB Entity Data Model

In the next section, we will learn to create an EDM using the `EdmGen.exe` command-line tool.

Creating Entity Data Model using the EdmGen tool

We will now take a look at how to create a data model using the EDM generation tool called **EdmGen**.

The `EdmGen.exe` command-line tool can be used to do one or more of the following:

- Generate the `.cdsl`, `.msl`, and `.ssdl` files as part of the EDM
- Generate object classes from a `.csdl` file
- Validate an EDM

The `EdmGen.exe` command-line tool generates the EDM as a set of three files: `.csdl`, `.msl`, and `.ssdl`. If you have used the ADO.NET Entity Data Model Designer to generate your EDM, the `.edmx` file generated will contain the CSDL, MSL, and the SSDL sections. You will have a single `.edmx` file that bundles all of these sections into it. On the other hand, if you use the `EdmGen.exe` tool to generate the EDM, you will find three separate files with `.csdl`, `.msl`, or `.ssdl` extensions.

Here is a list of the major options of the `EdmGen.exe` command-line tool:

Option	**Description**
`/help`	Use this option to display help on all the possible options of this tool. The short form is `/?`
`/language:CSharp`	Use this option to generate code using C# language
`/language:VB`	Use this option to generate code using VB language
`/provider:<string>`	Use this option to specify the name of the ADO.NET data provider that you would like to use
`/connectionstring:<connection string>`	Use this option to specify the connection string to be used to connect to the database
`/namespace:<string>`	Use this option to specify the name of the namespace
`/mode:FullGeneration`	Use this option to generate your CSDL, MSL, and SSDL objects from the database schema
`/mode:EntityClassGeneration`	Use this option to generate your entity classes from a given CSDL file
`/mode:FromSsdlGeneration`	Use this option to generate MSL, CSDL, and entity classes from a given SSDL file
`/mode:ValidateArtifacts`	Use this option to validate the CSDL, SSDL, and MSL files
`/mode:ViewGeneration`	Use this option to generate mapping views from the CSDL, SSDL, and MSL files
`/entitycontainer:<string>`	Use this option to specify the name of the Entity Container to be used in the conceptual model
`/project:<string>`	Use this option to specify the base name to be used for all the artifact files (`.csdl`, `.msl`, and `.ssdl`) to be generated. The short form of this option is `/p`

Note that you need to pass the connection string, and specify the mode and the project name of the artifact files (the `.csdl`, `.msl`, and `.ssdl` files) to be created. To create the EDM for our database, open a Visual Studio command window and type in the following:

```
edmgen /mode:fullgeneration /c:"Data Source=.;Initial
Catalog=SecurityDB;User ID=sa;Password=sa1@3;" /p:SecurityDB
```

This will create a full Entity Data Model for our database. The output is shown in the following screenshot:

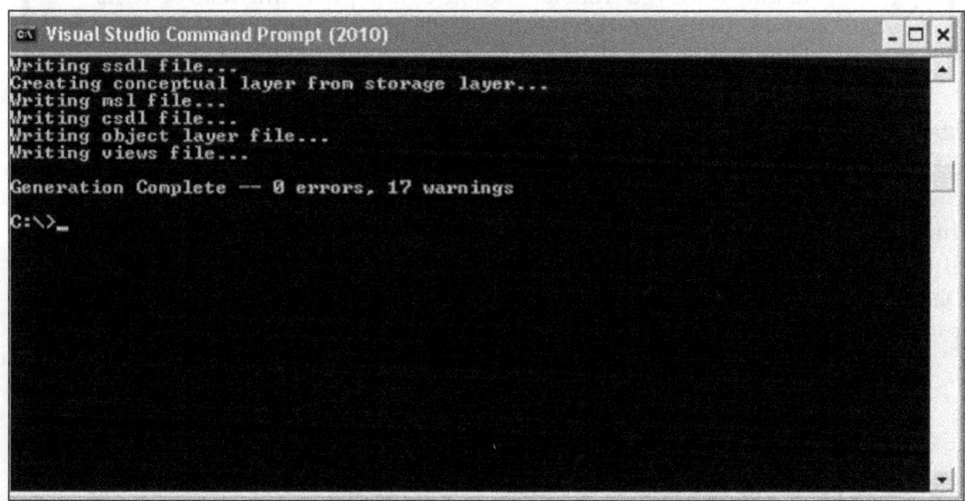

Generating the Entity Data Model from the command line

You can also validate the `SecurityDB` model that was just created, using the `ValidateArtifacts` option of the EdmGen command-line tool, as follows:

```
EdmGen /mode:ValidateArtifacts /inssdl:SecurityDB.ssdl
/inmsl:SecurityDB.msl /incsdl:SecurityDB.csdl
```

When you execute the preceding command, the output will be similar to what is shown in the previous screenshot.

As you can see in the previous screenshot, there are no warnings or errors displayed. So, our EDM is perfect.

The section that follows discusses the DataSource controls included in ASP.NET and also the new EntityDataSource control, which was first introduced as part of the Visual Studio.NET 2008 SP1 release. Note that the EntityDataSource control is included as part of Visual Studio 2010 and onward.

The DataSource controls

The DataSource controls are those that can be bound to data from external data sources. These data sources may include databases, XML files, or even flat files. ASP.NET 2.0 introduced some DataSource controls with a powerful data binding technique, so the need for writing lengthy code for binding data-to-data controls has been eliminated.

In ASP.NET, the term **data binding** implies binding the controls to data retrieved from a data source and providing read or write connectivity between these controls and the data that they are bound to.

A DataSource control acts like a layer in between your data source and the data bound control. Data bound controls can be any control that actually interacts with the end user while consuming the data services provided by the DataSource control to which it is bound. It defines certain methods and properties that perform data-specific operations like insert, delete, update, and select over the data exposed by the DataSource control while at the same time abstracting the data source.

In the sections that follow, we will discuss these controls with special emphasis on the EntityDataSource control.

The ObjectDataSource control

The `ObjectDataSource` control works with in-memory collections. It defines properties like `InsertMethod`, `DeleteMethod`, `UpdateMethod`, and `SelectMethod`, which perform basic data storage and retrieval operations. Appropriate methods must be created and mapped to the properties that perform the required task. When one of these properties is used, the `ObjectDataSource` control actually creates an instance, invokes the appropriate method, and destroys as soon as it completes its execution phase. `ObjectDataSource` are usually used in the business layer in your application, which helps you to directly bind to the data bound controls at the presentation layer.

The SqlDataSource control

The `SqlDataSource` control allows you to perform standard data operations, like insert, update, delete, and select on the data persisting in you relation database. The `SqlDataSource` control is not meant only for the SQL Server database; it can work with any managed ADO.NET provider, which means that you can use the `SqlDataSource` control with different relational data sources. The `SqlDataSource` control defines properties like `InsertCommand`, `DeleteCommand`, `UpdateCommand`, and `SelectCommand`, for performing standard data operations, like insert, delete, update, and select, over the data. The command properties need appropriate queries to be set before using them. When updates are performed on a data control that connects to a `SqlDataSource` control, the `SqlDataSource` control creates update parameters for all columns, even though few columns are updated. The control also supports caching capabilities, which assist in improving the performance of the application. For further reading on this topic, please refer to this link: `http://msdn.microsoft.com/en-us/library/system.web.ui.webcontrols.sqldatasource(v=vs.110).aspx`.

The SiteMapDataSource control

The `SiteMapDataSource` control allows you to bind the site map of your website. The site map can represent a hierarchical structure. The `SiteMapDataSource` control needs an appropriate root node to be specified in a given hierarchy. The `SiteMapDataSource` control contains properties that allow you to specify the node locations. Primarily, the `SiteMapDataSource` control is used for the data navigation purpose, which means that you cannot perform standard data operations, like inserts, updates, deletes, sorting, and paging of the data.

The XMLDataSource control

The `XmlDataSource` control is another kind of DataSource control. It basically represents the data, which is in the form of XML. You can access the XML data from the `XmlDataSource` control by connecting to a XML file or to XML data embedded as a string within the DataSource control. Caching in the `XmlDataSource` control is enabled by default for increasing the performance. You can perform standard data operations like insert, delete, update, and select over the XML data that is represented by the `XmlDataSource` control. However, operations like sorting and paging are not supported by the `XmlDataSource` control. The control also provides support for applying XML transformations through a XML style sheet.

The LinqDataSource control

The `LinqDataSource` control is a new control that has been introduced in ASP.NET 3.5. It extends the DataSource control and resides in the `System.Web.UI.WebControls` namespace. It provides a new approach for binding LINQ models to web controls in your ASP.NET applications. The `LinqDataSource` control provides properties and events, using which you can perform operations like selecting, filtering, grouping, and ordering against `LinqDataSource`. The `LinqDataSource` data control provides a flexible mechanism to build a data control with wizard-based workflow. It allows you to perform CRUD operations on the data over a LINQ model with minimal need to write SQL queries.

The EntityDataSource control

The EntityDataSource control is an example of a data control that was first included as part of the Visual Studio 2008 SP1 release, and can be used to bind data retrieved from an EDM to the data bound controls of ASP.NET.

For further reading on this topic, please refer to this link: `http://blogs.msdn.com/b/webdev/archive/2014/01/30/announcing-preview-of-dynamic-data-provider-and-entitydatasource-control-for-entity-framework-6.aspx`.

Implementing our first application using the Entity Framework

In this section, we will learn how to use the EDM and the EntityDataSource control to implement our first program using the Entity Framework. We will use a GridView control to display bound data.

Let's first have the environment ready. I will run you through the steps to download and install Entity Framework 6 now.

In the **Solution Explorer**, right-click on the project and select **EntityFramework** from the list of NuGet packages, as shown in the following screenshot:

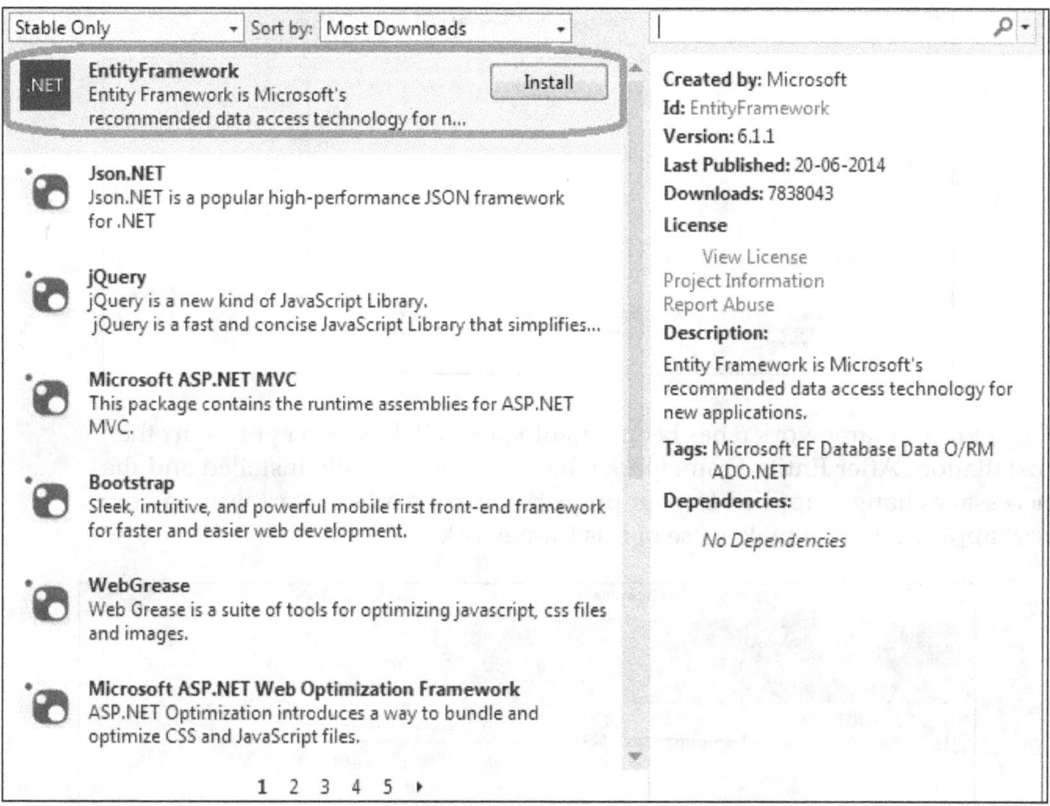

Click on **Install** to start downloading and installing Entity Framework 6:

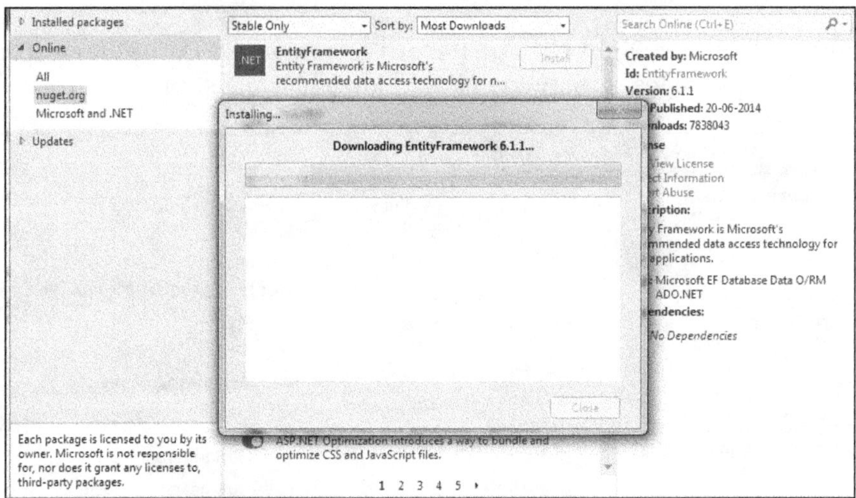

Once Entity Framework 6 has been downloaded, click on **Accept** to start the installation. After Entity Framework 6 has been successfully installed and the necessary changes applied to your project, you are ready to start writing your first application that makes use of this framework.

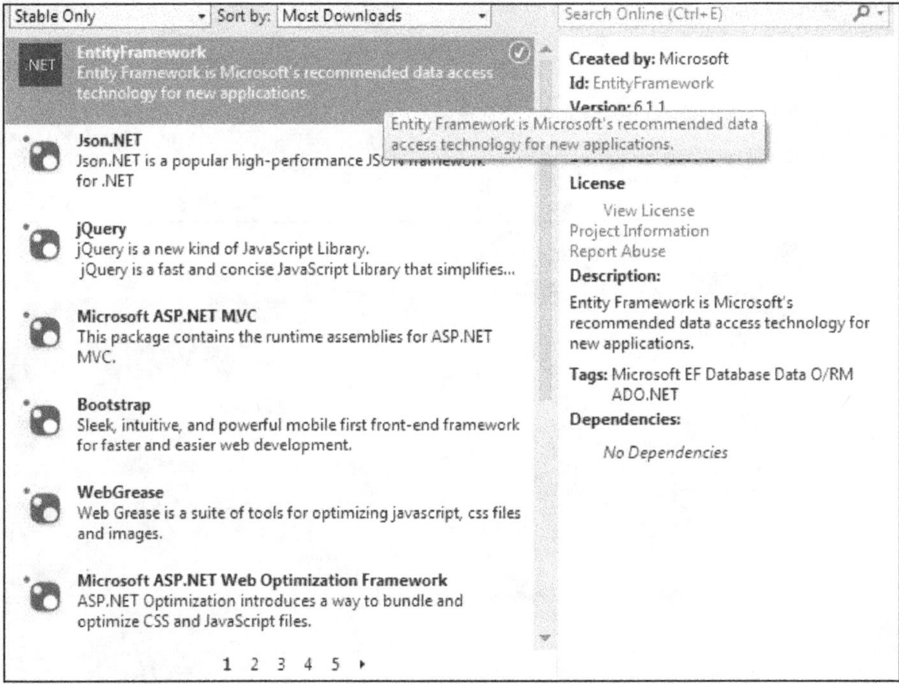

Refer to the solution we created earlier using the Entity Data Model Designer. Now follow these steps:

1. Drag and drop an **EntityDataSource** control from the toolbox onto your `Default.aspx` web form:

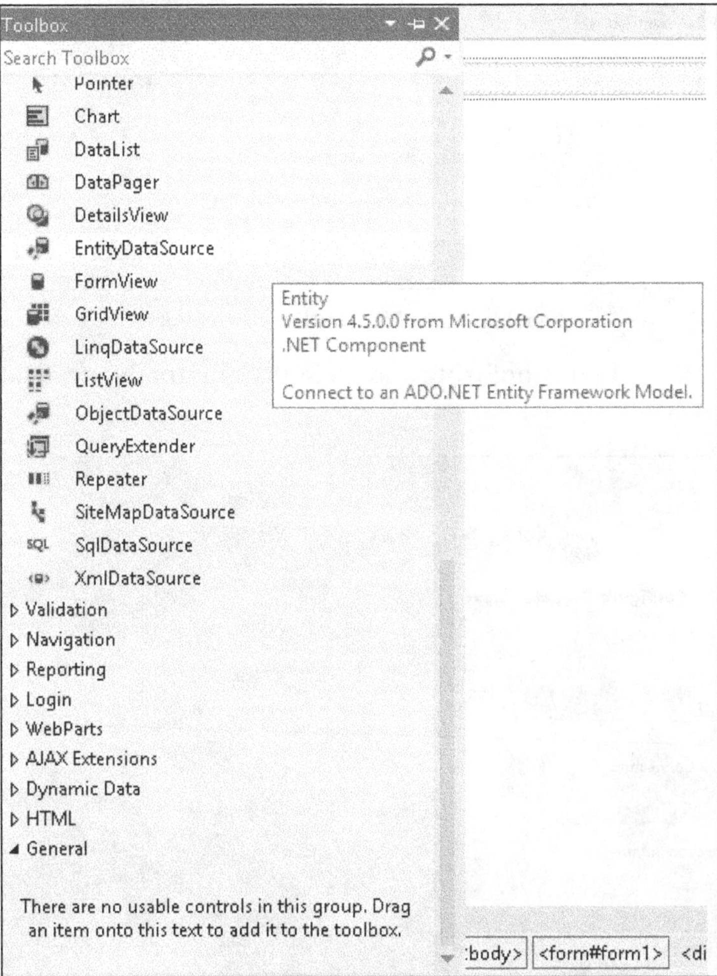

The EntityDataSource Control

2. Now click on the **Configure Data Source...** option to specify the data source. Refer to the following screenshot:

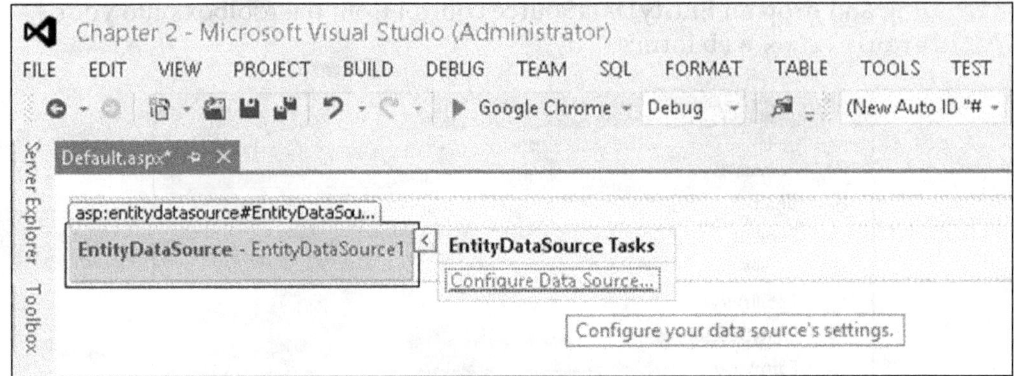

Configuring the EntityDataSource Control

3. Specify the **ConnectionString** and **DefaultContainerName** fields, and then click on **Next**:

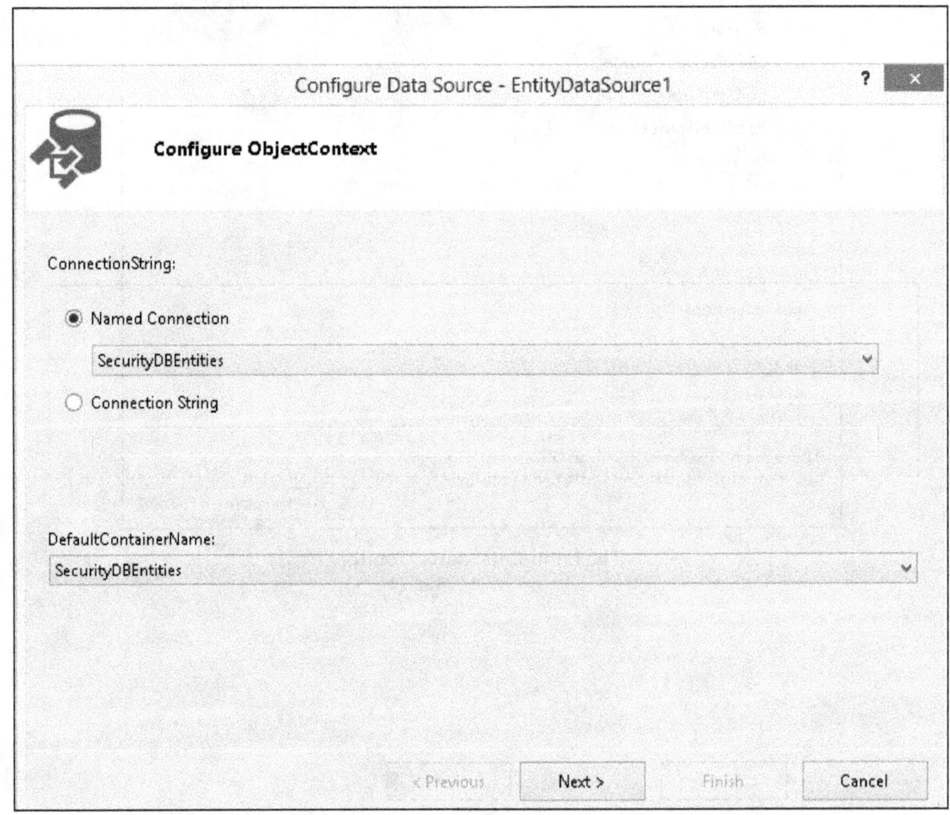

4. Specify the fields you want to retrieve from the database table, and click on **Finish** when done:

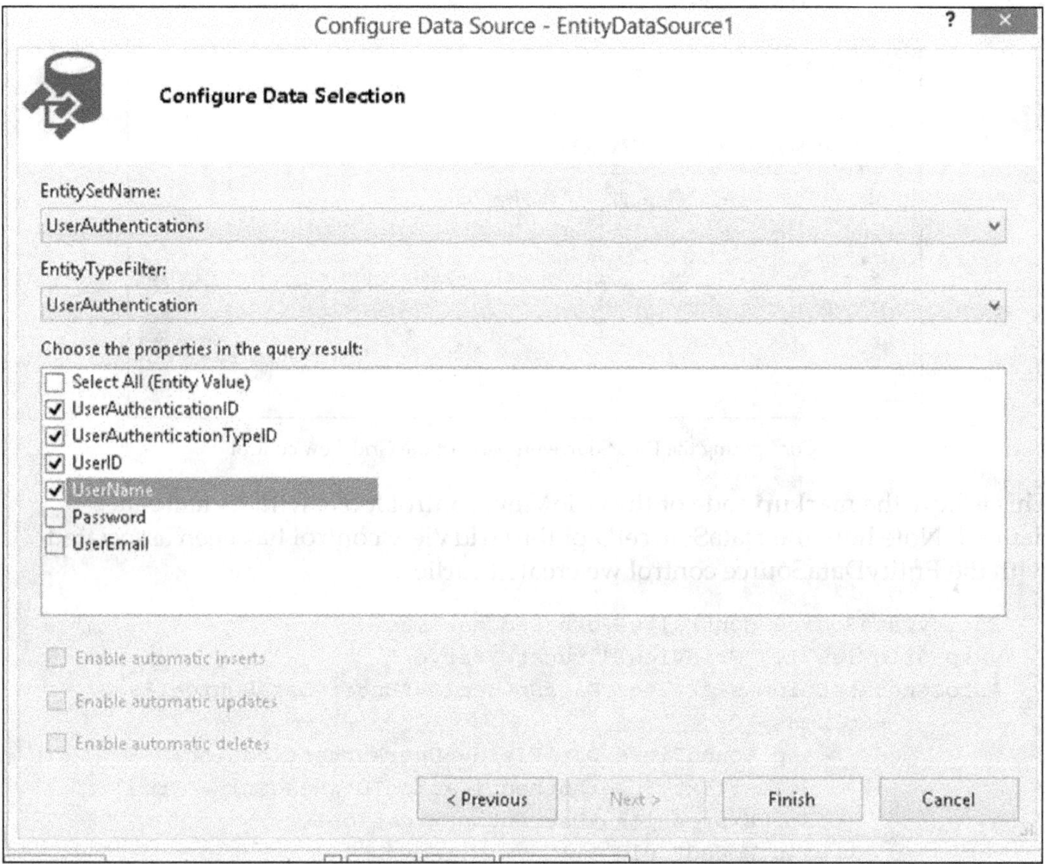

Configuring the data selection

5. Now drag and drop a GridView control from the toolbox onto the `Default.aspx` web form.

6. Next, use the **Choose Data Source** option of the GridView control to associate its data source with the EntityDataSource control we created earlier. Refer to the following screenshot:

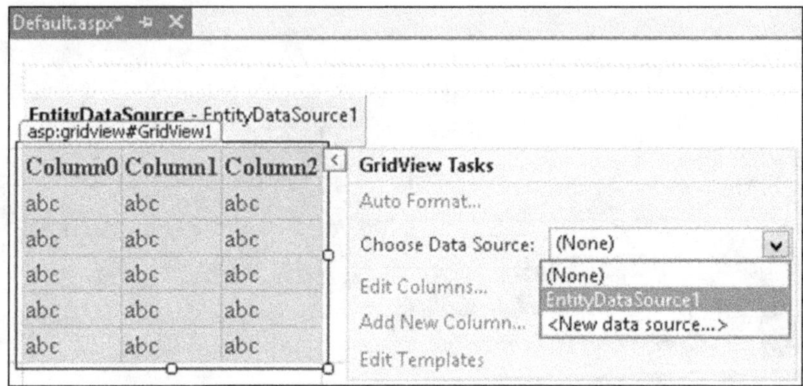

Configuring the Data Source property of the GridView control

This is how the markup code of the GridView control looks with its templates defined. Note how the DataSourceID of the GridView control has been associated with the EntityDataSource control we created earlier.

```
EntityDataSource control we created earlier.
<asp:GridView ID="GridView1" runat="server"
AutoGenerateColumns="False" DataSourceID="EntityDataSource1">
        <Columns>
            <asp:BoundField DataField="UserAuthenticationID"
             HeaderText="UserAuthenticationID" ReadOnly="True"
             SortExpression="UserAuthenticationID" />
            <asp:BoundField
             DataField="UserAuthenticationTypeID"
             HeaderText="UserAuthenticationTypeID"
             ReadOnly="True"
             SortExpression="UserAuthenticationTypeID" />
            <asp:BoundField DataField="UserID"
             HeaderText="UserID" ReadOnly="True"
             SortExpression="UserID" />
            <asp:BoundField DataField="UserName"
             HeaderText="UserName" ReadOnly="True"
             SortExpression="UserName" />
        </Columns>
</asp:GridView>
```

The markup code of the EntityDataSource control looks like the following:

```
<asp:EntityDataSource ID="EntityDataSource1" runat="server"
ConnectionString="name=SecurityDBEntities"
DefaultContainerName="SecurityDBEntities" EnableFlattening="False"
EntitySetName="UserAuthentications"
EntityTypeFilter="UserAuthentication"
Select="it.[UserAuthenticationID], it.[UserAuthenticationTypeID],
it.[UserID], it.[UserName]">
</asp:EntityDataSource>
```

This is what the complete markup code of the `Default.aspx` web page looks like:

```
<!DOCTYPE html>

<html xmlns="http://www.w3.org/1999/xhtml">
<head runat="server">
<title></title>
</head>
<body>
<form id="form1" runat="server">
    <asp:EntityDataSource ID="EntityDataSource1"
     runat="server" ConnectionString="name=SecurityDBEntities"
     DefaultContainerName="SecurityDBEntities"
     EnableFlattening="False"
     EntitySetName="UserAuthentications"
     EntityTypeFilter="UserAuthentication"
     Select="it.[UserAuthenticationID],
     it.[UserAuthenticationTypeID],
     it.[UserID], it.[UserName]">
    </asp:EntityDataSource>
    <asp:GridView ID="GridView1" runat="server"
     AutoGenerateColumns="False"
     DataSourceID="EntityDataSource1">
        <Columns>
            <asp:BoundField DataField="UserAuthenticationID"
             HeaderText="UserAuthenticationID" ReadOnly="True"
             SortExpression="UserAuthenticationID" />
            <asp:BoundField
             DataField="UserAuthenticationTypeID"
             HeaderText="UserAuthenticationTypeID"
             ReadOnly="True"
             SortExpression="UserAuthenticationTypeID" />
            <asp:BoundField DataField="UserID"
             HeaderText="UserID" ReadOnly="True"
             SortExpression="UserID" />
```

```
                <asp:BoundField DataField="UserName"
                 HeaderText="UserName" ReadOnly="True"
                 SortExpression="UserName" />
            </Columns>
        </asp:GridView>
    </form>
    </body>
    </html>
```

When you execute the application, your output should be similar to what is shown in the following image:

UserAuthenticationID	UserAuthenticationTypeID	UserID	UserName
1	1	1	Joydip
3	1	2	Udal
4	1	3	Santosh
9	1	4	Sanjeeb

Data exposed by the Entity Data Model is displayed in the GridView control

Summary

In this chapter, we discussed how we can get started with Entity Framework. You learned how to create an EDM and use it along with the EntityDataSource control, to bind data to a GridView data control. In this chapter, we created the `UserAuthentication` database and an EDM that exposed this database. We also explored the EntityDataSource control and used it to bind data in our first application that leverages Entity Framework 6.

In the next chapter, we will continue to explore the EDM including each of its sections and will learn how they are related to each other.

3

Entities, Relationships, and the Entity Data Model

In the last chapter, you learned how we can get started using Entity Framework. As I mentioned in the earlier chapter, Entity Framework 7 is not yet released at the time of writing. So, we will discuss Entity Framework 6.x in this book and highlight the features of Entity Framework 7 wherever applicable.

In this chapter, you will learn about the Entity Data Model and its components. The Entity Data Model is a conceptual model that can be used to design the data access layer of your application. We will revisit the `Security` EDM we created in the previous chapter and discuss each of the sections. Specifically, we will discuss the following points:

- Entities, entity types, and relationships
- Introducing the Entity Data Model (EDM)
- The goals of EDM
- CSDL, MSL, and SSDL
- Customizing entities
- Customizing the EDM
- Exception handling with Entity Framework

In this chapter, we will discuss each of the sections of the EDM in detail. We will start our discussion with our understanding of entities and their relationships. We will then move ahead and discuss how they are mapped in the EDM using XML.

Entities, entity types, and relationships in the EDM

The EDM is an implementation of the Entity-Relationship model (commonly called the E-R model). It depicts entities and their relationships. The EDM is a view of the data store that your application will use.

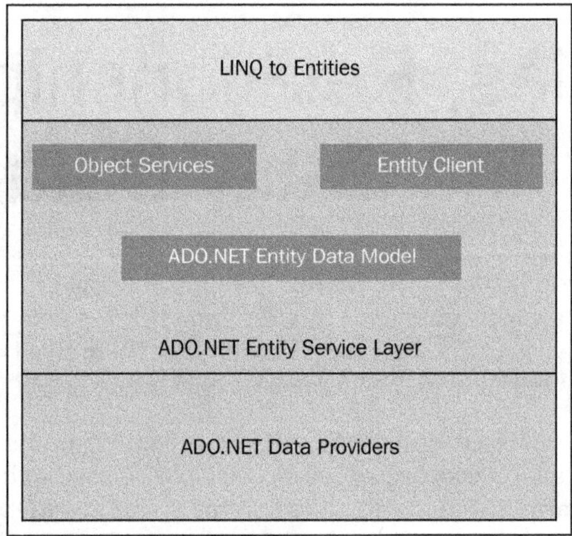

Before we explore deeper into our `Security` DataModel, let's discuss entities, entity types, relationships, and how these are all represented.

What is an entity?

An **entity** essentially models individual, real-world objects such as employees and customers. Such objects contain information pertaining to the entity. An entity is something that is uniquely definable, distinctly identifiable, and can have one or more of the following properties:

- It should be identifiable easily through the data that it holds
- It should have properties that can hold scalar values that represent the entity's data
- It should only contain data, not methods or operations on the data
- It can have entity relationship information such as how one entity is related to another

An entity refers to an instance of an EntityType, such as an employee, a customer, or a product. The type of an entity is defined using an EntityType. An EntityType is used to represent a particular type of data in the conceptual model—an employee, a customer, order, or anything that is relevant to an application.

As an example, an employee belongs to a particular department, a product belongs to a particular group, a customer buys a particular product, and so on. Each and every EntityType is uniquely identified by a unique key also called the **EntityKey**.

The names of the nodes in the EDM, such as EntityKey and EntityType, should not have any space in the middle. This is the convention for the XML syntax used in EDM.

Any two entities can be related to each other using relationships. These relationships are actually instances of **Relationship Types**. Such relationships can either be an **Association** or **Containment**. The following code snippet illustrates how this is defined in the EDM:

```
<Association Name="PublisherBook">
       <End Type="Publisher" Multiplicity="1">
       <End Type="Book" Multiplicity="*">
       <OnDelete Action="Cascade" />
      </End>
</Association>
```

Defining entity sets in the EDM

An **EntitySet** may be defined as a logical group of similar entities. In other words, all the entities contained within an EntitySet are of the same, or derived from the same EntityType. Here is how an `EntitySet` attribute is defined in the EDM:

```
<EntitySet Name="Controls" EntityType="SecurityDBModel.Control" />
<EntitySet Name="ControlTypes"
EntityType="SecurityDBModel.ControlType" />
<EntitySet Name="Roles" EntityType="SecurityDBModel.Role" />
<EntitySet Name="Users" EntityType="SecurityDBModel.User" />
<EntitySet Name="UserAuthentications"
EntityType="SecurityDBModel.UserAuthentication" />
<EntitySet Name="UserAuthenticationTypes"
EntityType="SecurityDBModel.UserAuthenticationType" />
<EntitySet Name="UserLoginHistories"
EntityType="SecurityDBModel.UserLoginHistory" />
<EntitySet Name="UserRoles" EntityType="SecurityDBModel.UserRole"
/>
```

Note that the EntityType for the EntitySets are defined using the `EntityType` attribute. Fine, but what does an `EntityType` attribute contain? An `EntityType` attribute consists of one or more properties and a key. These properties can be non-nullable, which implies that they are mandatory fields in the database.

Here is how the `EntityType` attributes are defined in the EDM:

```
<EntityType Name="Control">
    <Key>
      <PropertyRef Name="ControlID" />
    </Key>
    <Property Name="ControlID" Type="Int32" Nullable="false"
     p1:StoreGeneratedPattern="Identity" />
          <Property Name="ControlTypeID" Type="Int32"
           Nullable="false" />
          <Property Name="ControlName" Type="String"
           Nullable="false" MaxLength="Max" Unicode="true"
           FixedLength="false" />
          <Property Name="ParentControlID" Type="Int32"
           Nullable="false" />
          <NavigationProperty Name="ControlType"
           Relationship="SecurityDBModel.FK_Control_ControlType"
           FromRole="Control" ToRole="ControlType" />
        </EntityType>
        <EntityType Name="ControlType">
          <Key>
            <PropertyRef Name="ControlTypeID" />
          </Key>
          <Property Name="ControlTypeID" Type="Int32"
           Nullable="false" p1:StoreGeneratedPattern="Identity" />
          <Property Name="ControlTypeName" Type="String"
           Nullable="false" MaxLength="Max" Unicode="true"
           FixedLength="false" />
          <NavigationProperty Name="Controls"
           Relationship="SecurityDBModel.FK_Control_ControlType"
           FromRole="ControlType" ToRole="Control" />
        </EntityType>
        <EntityType Name="Role">
          <Key>
            <PropertyRef Name="RoleID" />
          </Key>
          <Property Name="RoleID" Type="Int32" Nullable="false"
           p1:StoreGeneratedPattern="Identity" />
```

```
    <Property Name="RoleDescription" Type="String"
     Nullable="false" MaxLength="Max" Unicode="true"
     FixedLength="false" />
  </EntityType>
```

The following code snippet illustrates how the EntityType `User` is defined:

```
  <EntityType Name="User">
    <Key>
      <PropertyRef Name="UserID" />
    </Key>
    <Property Name="UserID" Type="Int32" Nullable="false"
     p1:StoreGeneratedPattern="Identity" />
    <Property Name="IsAdmin" Type="Boolean" />
    <Property Name="IsActive" Type="Boolean" />
    <Property Name="IsOnline" Type="Boolean" />
    <NavigationProperty Name="UserAuthentications"
     Relationship="SecurityDBModel.
     FK_UserAuthentication_User" FromRole="User"
     ToRole="UserAuthentication" />
    <NavigationProperty Name="UserLoginHistories"
     Relationship="SecurityDBModel.FK_UserLoginHistory_User"
     FromRole="User" ToRole="UserLoginHistory" />
    <NavigationProperty Name="UserRoles"
     Relationship="SecurityDBModel.FK_UserRole_Role"
     FromRole="User" ToRole="UserRole" />
  </EntityType>
```

The following code snippet illustrates how the entities `UserAuthentication` and `UserAuthenticationType` are defined:

```
  <EntityType Name="UserAuthentication">
    <Key>
      <PropertyRef Name="UserAuthenticationID" />
    </Key>
    <Property Name="UserAuthenticationID" Type="Int32"
     Nullable="false" p1:StoreGeneratedPattern="Identity" />
    <Property Name="UserAuthenticationTypeID" Type="Int32"
     Nullable="false" />
    <Property Name="UserID" Type="Int32" Nullable="false" />
    <Property Name="UserName" Type="String" Nullable="false"
     MaxLength="Max" Unicode="true" FixedLength="false" />
    <Property Name="Password" Type="String" Nullable="false"
     MaxLength="Max" Unicode="true" FixedLength="false" />
```

```
    <Property Name="UserEmail" Type="String" MaxLength="Max"
     Unicode="true" FixedLength="false" />
    <NavigationProperty Name="User"
     Relationship="SecurityDBModel.
     FK_UserAuthentication_User"
     FromRole="UserAuthentication" ToRole="User" />
    <NavigationProperty Name="UserAuthenticationType"
     Relationship="SecurityDBModel.
     FK_UserAuthentication_User
     AuthenticationType" FromRole="UserAuthentication"
     ToRole="UserAuthenticationType" />
  </EntityType>
  <EntityType Name="UserAuthenticationType">
    <Key>
      <PropertyRef Name="UserAuthenticationTypeID" />
    </Key>
    <Property Name="UserAuthenticationTypeID" Type="Int32"
     Nullable="false" p1:StoreGeneratedPattern="Identity" />
    <Property Name="UserAuthenticationTypeDescription"
     Type="String" Nullable="false" MaxLength="Max"
     Unicode="true"
     FixedLength="false" />
    <NavigationProperty Name="UserAuthentications"
     Relationship="SecurityDBModel.
     FK_UserAuthentication_User
     AuthenticationType" FromRole="UserAuthenticationType"
     ToRole="UserAuthentication" />
  </EntityType>
```

The `UserLoginHistory` table in the `Security` database stores the login history of the users who have logged in to the system. Refer to the following code:

```
  <EntityType Name="UserLoginHistory">
    <Key>
      <PropertyRef Name="UserLoginID" />
    </Key>
    <Property Name="UserLoginID" Type="Int32"
     Nullable="false" p1:StoreGeneratedPattern="Identity" />
    <Property Name="UserID" Type="Int32" Nullable="false" />
    <Property Name="UserLoginDate" Type="DateTime"
     Nullable="false" Precision="3" />
    <NavigationProperty Name="User"
     Relationship="SecurityDBModel.FK_UserLoginHistory_User"
     FromRole="UserLoginHistory" ToRole="User" />
  </EntityType>
```

The `UserRole` entity defines the roles for each user:

```
        <EntityType Name="UserRole">
          <Key>
            <PropertyRef Name="UserRoleID" />
          </Key>
          <Property Name="UserRoleID" Type="Int32"
           Nullable="false" p1:StoreGeneratedPattern="Identity" />
          <Property Name="UserID" Type="Int32" Nullable="false" />
          <Property Name="RoleID" Type="Int32" Nullable="false" />
          <NavigationProperty Name="User"
           Relationship="SecurityDBModel.FK_UserRole_Role"
           FromRole="UserRole" ToRole="User" />
</EntityType>
```

Note how the `Name` attribute and the `Key` element of the EntityType are defined. The property names of the entity are defined using the `Property` elements. Each of these properties has specified types such as `Integer` or `String` types The `Nullable` attribute is used to denote whether or not the property can accept null values. It is a `Boolean` attribute and accepts either a true or false value. `NavigationProperty` is one that defines the end points of a relationship.

If you look at the preceding code snippet that illustrates the `UserRole` EntityType, you will find a navigation property called `User`.

Extending the existing entity types to create derived entity types

The EDM allows you to derive (inheritance) a type from a base type. The derived type extends an existing entity type to add additional information specific to the type. The EDM also allows you to specify multiple derived types, also called sub types, from a common base type. Note that entity types may have scalar, complex, and navigation properties.

Properties are the fundamental building blocks of entity types and complex types in Entity Framework. A scalar property is one whose actual value is contained in the entity. As an example, the entity `Employee` contains scalar properties such as `EmployeeId`, `FirstName`, `LastName`, and so on. Navigation properties are used to navigate from one entity to another—this is similar to foreign key relationships in your database. As an example, the entity `Employee` can be mapped to the entity `Department`. A complex type is a non-scalar property that allows you to group related properties. As an example, `Address` is a complex property.

Let's start with an example. Both `Employee` and `Customer` can derive from the base type called `Person`. These sub types then in turn become the base types for other entities. So, the `Employee` type can in turn be the base type for `Manager`, and so on.

Here is how you can extend an existing `EntityType` to specify your own derived EntityType:

```
<EntityType Name="Manager" BaseType="Employee">
    <Property Name="Role" Type="System.String"
Size="max" />
</EntityType>
```

In the EDM, you can specify inheritance in three ways:

- **Table-per-Hierarchy Model (TPH)**
- **Table-per-Type Model (TPT)**
- **Table-per-Concrete Class (TPC)**

In the TPH, the base types and the derived types are all specified using the same database table. In the TPT, the base type is in one table while the derived types are spread across other tables. In the TPC type of inheritance, each derived entity is mapped to a particular physical database table. In essence, data for the entity is stored in a separate table.

Consider the following POCO classes:

```
public abstract class User
{
 public int UserID { get; set; }
 public string UserName { get; set; }
}

public class UserLoginHistory : User
{
 public DateTime LoginTime { get; set; }
}
```

For TPT type of inheritance, mapping is specified as follows:

```
modelBuilder.Entity<User>().ToTable("User");
modelBuilder.Entity<UserLoginHistory>().ToTable("UserLoginHistory"
);
```

Here is how mapping is specified in TPH:

```
modelBuilder.Entity<User>()
  .Map<UserLoginHistory>(m =>
m.Requires("Type").HasValue("UserLoginHistory"));
```

And, here is how TPC inheritance is mapped in an Entity Framework:

```
modelBuilder.Entity<UserLoginHistory>().Map(m =>
{
 m.MapInheritedProperties();
 m.ToTable("UserLoginHistory");
});
```

We will discuss more on how we can implement inheritance in Entity Framework 6 later in this book. You can refer to this link for further studies on this topic: `http://msdn.microsoft.com/en-us/library/vstudio/cc716702(v=vs.100).aspx`.

Association sets, associations, containment, and multiplicity

A relationship represents the logical connection between two or more entities. The EDM supports both unary and binary relationships. The association type of relationship models the peer to peer connection between entities. In other words, it links two or more entities. It has a name and some elements that define the endpoints of the association.

The figure given next illustrates how a `Batch` entity and a `Student` entity are related—one batch can have one or more students.

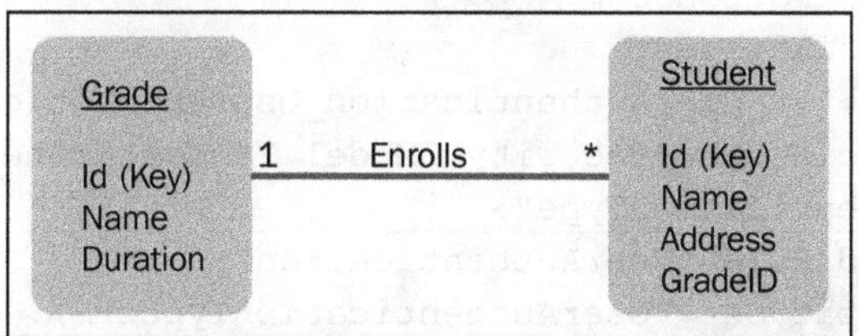

An `AssociationSet` attribute is a set of associations. In essence, an association set may be defined as a logical container of one or more associations of the same type. An association defines the relationship between entity types.

While an association and an entity represent the types, an `AssociationSet` attribute and an `EntitySet` attribute represent the storage location of those types. It is to be noted that `Association` and `AssociationSet` attributes act as building blocks to the pre-runtime library that is created.

Here is how `AssociationSet` is defined in the EDM:

```
<AssociationSet Name="FK_Control_ControlType"
Association="SecurityDBModel.FK_Control_ControlType">
            <End Role="ControlType" EntitySet="ControlTypes" />
            <End Role="Control" EntitySet="Controls" />
          </AssociationSet>
          <AssociationSet Name="FK_UserAuthentication_User"
           Association="SecurityDBModel.
           FK_UserAuthentication_User">
            <End Role="User" EntitySet="Users" />
            <End Role="UserAuthentication"
             EntitySet="UserAuthentications" />
          </AssociationSet>
          <AssociationSet Name="FK_UserLoginHistory_User"
           Association="SecurityDBModel.FK_UserLoginHistory_User">
            <End Role="User" EntitySet="Users" />
            <End Role="UserLoginHistory"
             EntitySet="UserLoginHistories" />
          </AssociationSet>
          <AssociationSet Name="FK_UserRole_Role"
           Association="SecurityDBModel.FK_UserRole_Role">
            <End Role="User" EntitySet="Users" />
            <End Role="UserRole" EntitySet="UserRoles" />
          </AssociationSet>
          <AssociationSet
           Name="FK_UserAuthentication_UserAuthenticationType"
           Association="SecurityDBModel.FK_UserAuthentication_User
           AuthenticationType">
            <End Role="UserAuthenticationType"
             EntitySet="UserAuthenticationTypes" />
            <End Role="UserAuthentication"
             EntitySet="UserAuthentications" />
          </AssociationSet>
```

Containment is a type of bidirectional relationship with the multiplicity as *1* to *0..N*. A containment relation can be used to represent inheritance between entities. Here is an example of how a containment relationship is defined in the EDM. A parent can have one or more or zero children:

```
<Containment Name="Parent_Child">
   <End Type="Parent" role="Parent" />
   <End Type="Child" Multiplicity="*" role="Children" />
</Containment>
```

Multiplicity is used to define the number of entity instances that are related to the other. Based on multiplicity, relationships between entities can be one of the following:

- One-to-one
- One-to-many
- Many-to-many

The figure given next illustrates how multiplicity is defined:

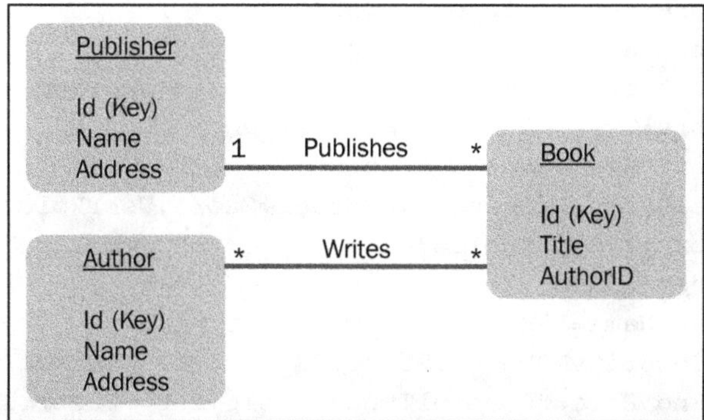

The `Multiplicity` attribute as shown in the preceding code snippet, is used to define one-to-one, one-to-many, or many-to-many relations among the entities.

What are entity containers?

An entity set is defined as a logical container for entities of a particular type and its subtypes. All EntitySets and AssociationSets are defined within the context of the entity container, which is a logical grouping of EntitySets and RelationshipSets. Here is an example of how an `EntityContainer` attribute is defined in the EDM:

```
<EntityContainer Name="SecurityDBModelStoreContainer">
          <EntitySet Name="Control"
           EntityType="SecurityDBModel.Store.Control"
           store:Type="Tables"
           Schema="dbo" />
          <EntitySet Name="ControlType"
           EntityType="SecurityDBModel.Store.ControlType"
           store:Type="Tables" Schema="dbo" />
          <EntitySet Name="Role"
           EntityType="SecurityDBModel.Store.Role"
           store:Type="Tables"
           Schema="dbo" />
```

```
            <EntitySet Name="User"
             EntityType="SecurityDBModel.Store.User"
             store:Type="Tables"
             Schema="dbo" />
            <EntitySet Name="UserAuthentication"
             EntityType="SecurityDBModel.Store.UserAuthentication"
             store:Type="Tables" Schema="dbo" />
            <EntitySet Name="UserAuthenticationType"
             EntityType="SecurityDBModel.Store.
             UserAuthenticationType"
             store:Type="Tables" Schema="dbo" />
            <EntitySet Name="UserLoginHistory"
             EntityType="SecurityDBModel.Store.UserLoginHistory"
             store:Type="Tables" Schema="dbo" />
            <EntitySet Name="UserRole"
             EntityType="SecurityDBModel.Store.UserRole"
             store:Type="Tables"
             Schema="dbo" />
  <AssociationSet Name="FK_Control_ControlType"
  Association="SecurityDBModel.Store.FK_Control_ControlType">
              <End Role="ControlType" EntitySet="ControlType" />
              <End Role="Control" EntitySet="Control" />
            </AssociationSet>
            <AssociationSet Name="FK_UserAuthentication_User"
             Association="SecurityDBModel.Store.
             FK_UserAuthentication_User">
              <End Role="User" EntitySet="User" />
              <End Role="UserAuthentication"
               EntitySet="UserAuthentication" />
            </AssociationSet>
            <AssociationSet
             Name="FK_UserAuthentication_UserAuthenticationType"
             Association="SecurityDBModel.Store.
             FK_UserAuthentication_User
             AuthenticationType">
              <End Role="UserAuthenticationType"
               EntitySet="UserAuthenticationType" />
              <End Role="UserAuthentication"
               EntitySet="UserAuthentication" />
            </AssociationSet>
            <AssociationSet Name="FK_UserLoginHistory_User"
             Association="SecurityDBModel.Store.
             FK_UserLoginHistory_User">
              <End Role="User" EntitySet="User" />
```

```
              <End Role="UserLoginHistory"
               EntitySet="UserLoginHistory" />
            </AssociationSet>
            <AssociationSet Name="FK_UserRole_Role"
             Association="SecurityDBModel.Store.FK_UserRole_Role">
              <End Role="User" EntitySet="User" />
              <End Role="UserRole" EntitySet="UserRole" />
            </AssociationSet>
  </EntityContainer>
```

In the next section, we will revisit the `Security` EDM and take a look at its components (the CSDL, MSL, and SSDL sections).

Exploring the Security EDM

The EDM allows the application to have its own view of the application's data. Consider the following EDM created using the Visual Studio 2015 ADO.NET EDM Wizard:

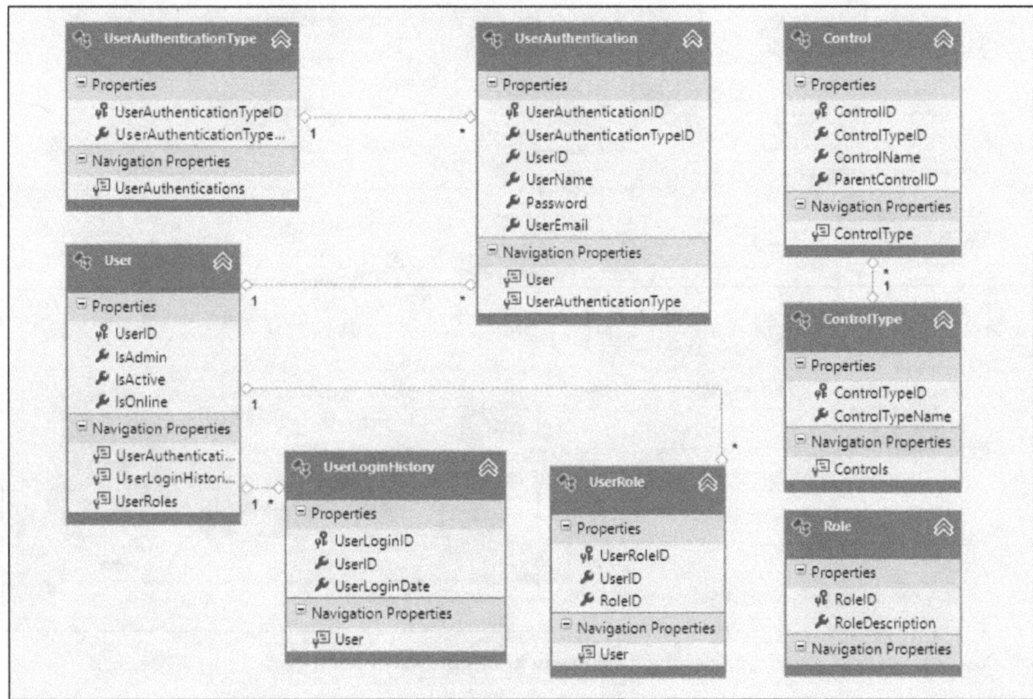

The Security Entity Data Model

Note that the relationships and the respective fields are displayed along with their multiplicity. You can also see the scalar and navigation properties. While the **Scalar Properties** section lists the attributes or the fields of the entity, the **Navigation Properties** are those that denote the associations of a particular entity with other entities.

As an example, the `UserRole` entity uses the `User` and the `Role` entities to relate its foreign keys `UserID` and `RoleID` respectively. This is also called a **join table** and facilitates a many-to-many relationship.

The Mapping Details window

Now we will take a look at the mappings details. That is, how the properties of the entities are mapped to the underlying database.

To do this, select any entity in the `Security` DataModel in the design view, right-click on it, and then click on the **Show in Model Browser** option, as shown in the following figure:

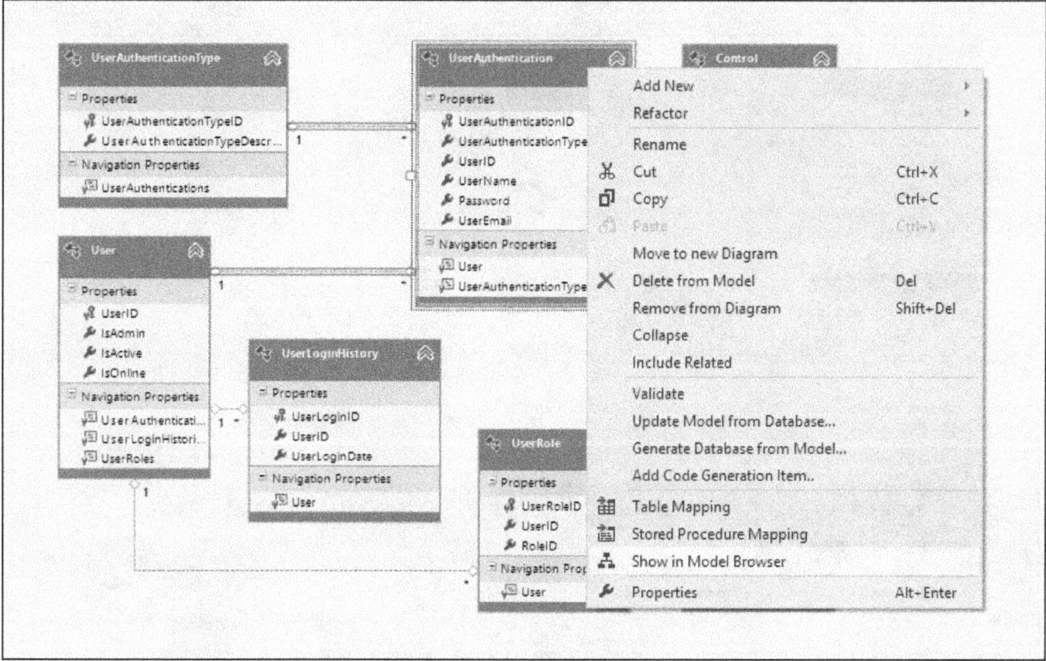

Selecting the Show in Model Browser option

The following screenshot shows the **Model Browser** window:

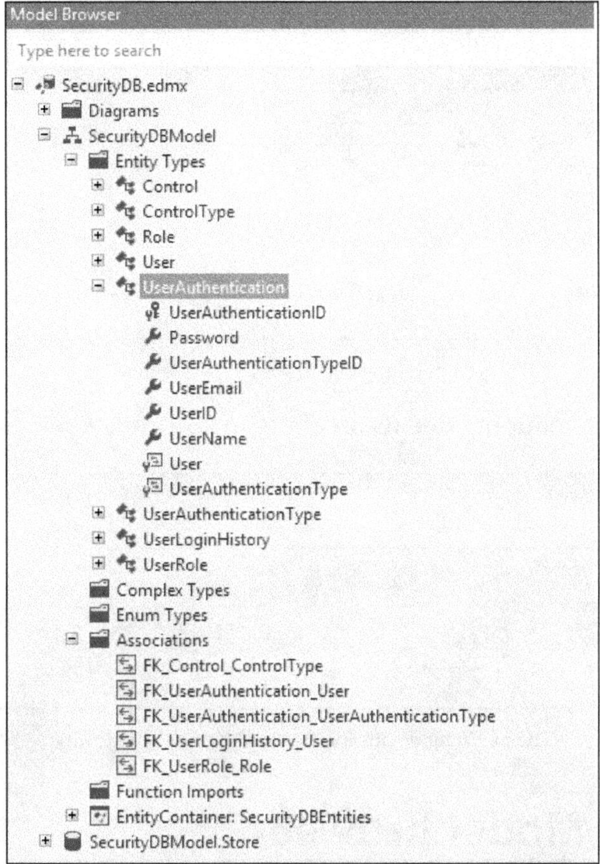

The Model Browser window

This is what the mapping details of the `UserAuthentication` entity looks like:

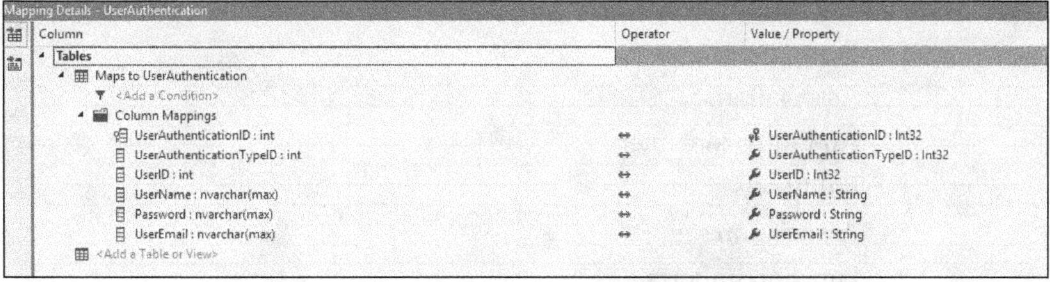

The mapping details for the UserAuthentication Entity

Following the same steps, you can view the table mapping details for all other entities in the EDM. As an example, this is what the mapping details for the `User` entity looks like:

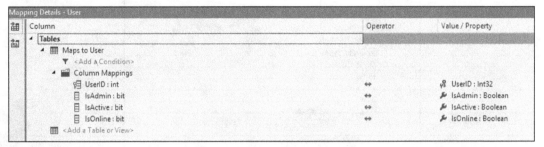

The mapping details for the User entity

And this is what the mapping details for the `UserLoginHistory` table looks like:

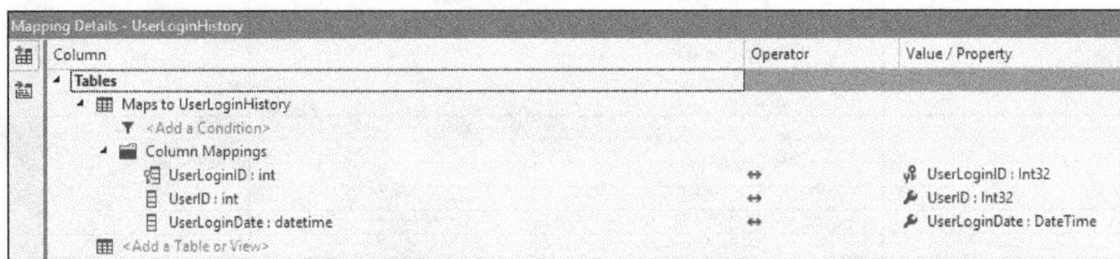

The mapping details for the UserLoginHistory Entity

The Entity Model browser

The Entity Model browser shows the conceptual and storage models of your EDM in a diagram view. When you open an EDM in the **Model Browser** window, you can see the following:

- The Conceptual Model
  - Entity types
  - Associations
  - An Entity container
  - Entity sets
  - Association sets
  - Function imports

- The Storage Model
    - Tables
    - Views
    - Stored procedures
    - Constraints

This is what the `Security` DataModel looks like when opened in the **Model Browser** window:

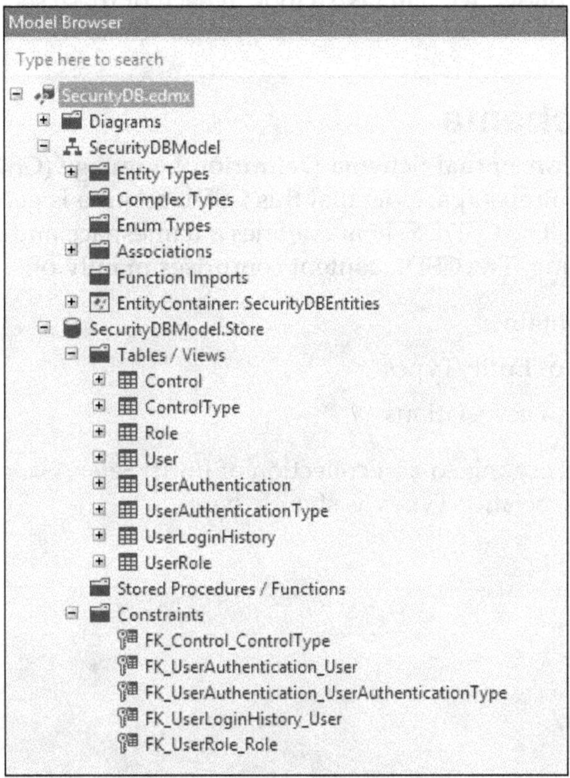

The Security EDM in the Model Browser

As you can see from the preceding figure, we have the EDM and its entity types, the associations, and also the store where we have our database tables, views, stored procedures, and constraints.

The EDM layers

To see the EDM layers, you can right-click on the `.edmx` file in the solution explorer and open it in XML editor. Now, when you open our `Security` DataModel file in its XML view, you can see three major sections including:

- The Conceptual Model (CSDL)
- The Storage Model (SSDL)
- The Mapping Layer (MSL)

In the sections that follow, we will take a look at each of these sections of our Security DataModel.

The CSDL schema

The EDM uses the **Conceptual Schema Definition Language (CSDL)** to define entities and their relationships. Note that this CSDL schema is generated when the `.edmx` file is created. The CSDL Schema defines a namespace and an alias that can be used for referencing. The CSDL content comprises mainly of:

- An entity container
- A collection of EntityTypes
- A collection of associations

The CSDL schema is organized as a collection of EntitySets, AssociationSets, EntityTypes, and AssociationTypes as shown here:

```
<EntityContainer>
    <EntitySet>
    <EntitySet/>

    <EntitySet>
    <EntitySet/>

    <AssociationSet>
    </AssociationSet>

    <AssociationSet>
    </AssociationSet>

</EntityContainer>

<EntityType>
</EntityType>
```

```
<EntityType>
</EntityType>

<Association>
</Association>
<Association>
</Association>
```

We have an `EntityContainer` attribute called `SecurityDBModelStoreContainer`, a collection of EntitySets including `Control`, `ControlType`, `Role`, `User`, `UserAuthentication`, `UserAuthenticationType`, `UserLoginHistory`, and `UserRole`.

Here is how the EntitySets are organized:

```
<EntitySet Name="Control"
 EntityType="SecurityDBModel.Store.Control" store:Type="Tables"
 Schema="dbo" />
        <EntitySet Name="ControlType"
         EntityType="SecurityDBModel.Store.ControlType"
         store:Type="Tables"
         Schema="dbo" />
        <EntitySet Name="Role"
         EntityType="SecurityDBModel.Store.Role"
         store:Type="Tables" Schema="dbo" />
        <EntitySet Name="User"
         EntityType="SecurityDBModel.Store.User"
         store:Type="Tables" Schema="dbo" />
        <EntitySet Name="UserAuthentication"
         EntityType="SecurityDBModel.Store.UserAuthentication"
         store:Type="Tables" Schema="dbo" />
        <EntitySet Name="UserAuthenticationType"
         EntityType="SecurityDBModel.Store.
         UserAuthenticationType" store:Type="Tables"
         Schema="dbo" />
        <EntitySet Name="UserLoginHistory"
         EntityType="SecurityDBModel.Store.UserLoginHistory"
         store:Type="Tables" Schema="dbo" />
        <EntitySet Name="UserRole"
         EntityType="SecurityDBModel.Store.UserRole"
         store:Type="Tables" Schema="dbo" />
...
</<EntityContainer>
```

We also have a collection of `EntityType` attributes with their properties and navigation properties defined. An entity type is defined as a logical specification for a data type that includes a key and a named set of properties.

The following code snippet illustrates how the entity types `Control` and `ControlType` are defined:

```
<EntityType Name="Control">
  <Key>
    <PropertyRef Name="ControlID" />
  </Key>
  <Property Name="ControlID" Type="int" Nullable="false"
   StoreGeneratedPattern="Identity" />
  <Property Name="ControlTypeID" Type="int"
   Nullable="false" />
  <Property Name="ControlName" Type="nvarchar(max)"
   Nullable="false" />
  <Property Name="ParentControlID" Type="int"
   Nullable="false" />
</EntityType>
<EntityType Name="ControlType">
  <Key>
    <PropertyRef Name="ControlTypeID" />
  </Key>
  <Property Name="ControlTypeID" Type="int"
   Nullable="false" StoreGeneratedPattern="Identity" />
  <Property Name="ControlTypeName" Type="nvarchar(max)"
   Nullable="false" />
</EntityType>
```

The following code snippet illustrates how the entity types `Role` and `User` are defined:

```
<EntityType Name="Role">
  <Key>
    <PropertyRef Name="RoleID" />
  </Key>
  <Property Name="RoleID" Type="int" Nullable="false"
   StoreGeneratedPattern="Identity" />
  <Property Name="RoleDescription" Type="nvarchar(max)"
   Nullable="false" />
</EntityType>
<EntityType Name="User">
  <Key>
    <PropertyRef Name="UserID" />
```

```
    </Key>
    <Property Name="UserID" Type="int" Nullable="false"
     StoreGeneratedPattern="Identity" />
    <Property Name="IsAdmin" Type="bit" />
    <Property Name="IsActive" Type="bit" />
    <Property Name="IsOnline" Type="bit" />
  </EntityType>
  <EntityType Name="UserAuthentication">
    <Key>
      <PropertyRef Name="UserAuthenticationID" />
    </Key>
    <Property Name="UserAuthenticationID" Type="int"
     Nullable="false" StoreGeneratedPattern="Identity" />
    <Property Name="UserAuthenticationTypeID" Type="int"
     Nullable="false" />
    <Property Name="UserID" Type="int" Nullable="false" />
    <Property Name="UserName" Type="nvarchar(max)"
     Nullable="false" />
    <Property Name="Password" Type="nvarchar(max)"
     Nullable="false" />
    <Property Name="UserEmail" Type="nvarchar(max)" />
  </EntityType>
```

The following code snippet shows how the other entity types of the `Security` Entity DataModel is defined:

```
  <EntityType Name="UserAuthenticationType">
    <Key>
      <PropertyRef Name="UserAuthenticationTypeID" />
    </Key>
    <Property Name="UserAuthenticationTypeID" Type="int"
     Nullable="false" StoreGeneratedPattern="Identity" />
    <Property Name="UserAuthenticationTypeDescription"
     Type="nvarchar(max)" Nullable="false" />
  </EntityType>
  <EntityType Name="UserLoginHistory">
    <Key>
      <PropertyRef Name="UserLoginID" />
    </Key>
    <Property Name="UserLoginID" Type="int" Nullable="false"
     StoreGeneratedPattern="Identity" />
    <Property Name="UserID" Type="int" Nullable="false" />
    <Property Name="UserLoginDate" Type="datetime"
     Nullable="false" />
```

```
</EntityType>
<EntityType Name="UserRole">
  <Key>
    <PropertyRef Name="UserRoleID" />
  </Key>
  <Property Name="UserRoleID" Type="int" Nullable="false"
   StoreGeneratedPattern="Identity" />
  <Property Name="UserID" Type="int" Nullable="false" />
  <Property Name="RoleID" Type="int" Nullable="false" />
</EntityType>
```

Next we have several associations as shown here:

```
<Association Name="FK_Control_ControlType">
  <End Role="ControlType"
   Type="SecurityDBModel.Store.ControlType"
   Multiplicity="1" />
  <End Role="Control" Type="SecurityDBModel.Store.Control"
   Multiplicity="*" />
  <ReferentialConstraint>
    <Principal Role="ControlType">
      <PropertyRef Name="ControlTypeID" />
    </Principal>
    <Dependent Role="Control">
      <PropertyRef Name="ControlTypeID" />
    </Dependent>
  </ReferentialConstraint>
</Association>
<Association Name="FK_UserAuthentication_User">
  <End Role="User" Type="SecurityDBModel.Store.User"
   Multiplicity="1" />
  <End Role="UserAuthentication"
   Type="SecurityDBModel.Store.UserAuthentication"
   Multiplicity="*"
   />
  <ReferentialConstraint>
    <Principal Role="User">
      <PropertyRef Name="UserID" />
    </Principal>
    <Dependent Role="UserAuthentication">
      <PropertyRef Name="UserID" />
    </Dependent>
  </ReferentialConstraint>
</Association>
```

```
<Association
 Name="FK_UserAuthentication_UserAuthenticationType">
  <End Role="UserAuthenticationType"
   Type="SecurityDBModel.Store.UserAuthenticationType"
   Multiplicity="1" />
  <End Role="UserAuthentication"
   Type="SecurityDBModel.Store.UserAuthentication"
   Multiplicity="*"
   />
  <ReferentialConstraint>
    <Principal Role="UserAuthenticationType">
      <PropertyRef Name="UserAuthenticationTypeID" />
    </Principal>
    <Dependent Role="UserAuthentication">
      <PropertyRef Name="UserAuthenticationTypeID" />
    </Dependent>
  </ReferentialConstraint>
</Association>
<Association Name="FK_UserLoginHistory_User">
  <End Role="User" Type="SecurityDBModel.Store.User"
   Multiplicity="1" />
  <End Role="UserLoginHistory"
   Type="SecurityDBModel.Store.UserLoginHistory"
   Multiplicity="*" />
  <ReferentialConstraint>
    <Principal Role="User">
      <PropertyRef Name="UserID" />
    </Principal>
    <Dependent Role="UserLoginHistory">
      <PropertyRef Name="UserID" />
    </Dependent>
  </ReferentialConstraint>
</Association>
<Association Name="FK_UserRole_Role">
  <End Role="User" Type="SecurityDBModel.Store.User"
   Multiplicity="1" />
  <End Role="UserRole"
   Type="SecurityDBModel.Store.UserRole" Multiplicity="*"
    />
  <ReferentialConstraint>
    <Principal Role="User">
      <PropertyRef Name="UserID" />
    </Principal>
```

```
          <Dependent Role="UserRole">
            <PropertyRef Name="UserID" />
          </Dependent>
        </ReferentialConstraint>
      </Association>
```

You also have the `AssociationSet` elements that comprise a set of association definitions with each association depicting a foreign key relation. Note that the `End Role` attribute of the `AssociationSet` element defines the end point of the foreign key relation.

Here is the how the `AssociationSet` attributes are defined in our `Security DataModel`:

```
<AssociationSet Name="FK_Control_ControlType"
Association="SecurityDBModel.Store.FK_Control_ControlType">
            <End Role="ControlType" EntitySet="ControlType" />
            <End Role="Control" EntitySet="Control" />
          </AssociationSet>
          <AssociationSet Name="FK_UserAuthentication_User"
           Association="SecurityDBModel.Store.
           FK_UserAuthentication_User">
            <End Role="User" EntitySet="User" />
            <End Role="UserAuthentication"
             EntitySet="UserAuthentication" />
          </AssociationSet>
          <AssociationSet
           Name="FK_UserAuthentication_UserAuthenticationType"
           Association="SecurityDBModel.Store.
           FK_UserAuthentication_User
           AuthenticationType">
            <End Role="UserAuthenticationType"
             EntitySet="UserAuthenticationType" />
            <End Role="UserAuthentication"
             EntitySet="UserAuthentication" />
          </AssociationSet>
          <AssociationSet Name="FK_UserLoginHistory_User"
           Association="SecurityDBModel.Store.
           FK_UserLoginHistory_User">
            <End Role="User" EntitySet="User" />
            <End Role="UserLoginHistory"
             EntitySet="UserLoginHistory" />
          </AssociationSet>
          <AssociationSet Name="FK_UserRole_Role"
```

```
            Association="SecurityDBModel.Store.FK_UserRole_Role">
             <End Role="User" EntitySet="User" />
             <End Role="UserRole" EntitySet="UserRole" />
</AssociationSet>
```

As you can see from the preceding code snippet, the `AssociationSet` attribute called `FK_UserRole_Role` defines a foreign key relation between the `User` and `UserRole` entities. In the next section, we will take a look at the SSDL section in the `Security` DataModel.

The SSDL schema

The schema definition for the Store Schema Definition Language or SSDL (automatically generated by Visual Studio when the `.edmx` file is created) section is similar to its CSDL counterpart. In addition to what we have just seen in the CSDL schema, we have field types, field lengths, and identity properties that specify whether a particular column in the database table is an identity column.

The SSDL schema is also organized much the same as CSDL with the relational schema information of the database in use. Here is how the entities are represented in SSDL:

```
<EntityType Name="Control">
          <Key>
            <PropertyRef Name="ControlID" />
          </Key>
          <Property Name="ControlID" Type="int" Nullable="false"
           StoreGeneratedPattern="Identity" />
          <Property Name="ControlTypeID" Type="int"
           Nullable="false" />
          <Property Name="ControlName" Type="nvarchar(max)"
           Nullable="false" />
          <Property Name="ParentControlID" Type="int"
           Nullable="false" />
        </EntityType>
        <EntityType Name="ControlType">
          <Key>
            <PropertyRef Name="ControlTypeID" />
          </Key>
          <Property Name="ControlTypeID" Type="int"
           Nullable="false" StoreGeneratedPattern="Identity" />
          <Property Name="ControlTypeName" Type="nvarchar(max)"
           Nullable="false" />
        </EntityType>
```

```
<EntityType Name="Role">
  <Key>
    <PropertyRef Name="RoleID" />
  </Key>
  <Property Name="RoleID" Type="int" Nullable="false"
   StoreGeneratedPattern="Identity" />
  <Property Name="RoleDescription" Type="nvarchar(max)"
   Nullable="false" />
</EntityType>
<EntityType Name="User">
  <Key>
    <PropertyRef Name="UserID" />
  </Key>
  <Property Name="UserID" Type="int" Nullable="false"
   StoreGeneratedPattern="Identity" />
  <Property Name="IsAdmin" Type="bit" />
  <Property Name="IsActive" Type="bit" />
  <Property Name="IsOnline" Type="bit" />
</EntityType>
<EntityType Name="UserAuthentication">
  <Key>
    <PropertyRef Name="UserAuthenticationID" />
  </Key>
  <Property Name="UserAuthenticationID" Type="int"
   Nullable="false" StoreGeneratedPattern="Identity" />
  <Property Name="UserAuthenticationTypeID" Type="int"
   Nullable="false" />
  <Property Name="UserID" Type="int" Nullable="false" />
  <Property Name="UserName" Type="nvarchar(max)"
   Nullable="false" />
  <Property Name="Password" Type="nvarchar(max)"
   Nullable="false" />
  <Property Name="UserEmail" Type="nvarchar(max)" />
</EntityType>
<EntityType Name="UserAuthenticationType">
  <Key>
    <PropertyRef Name="UserAuthenticationTypeID" />
  </Key>
  <Property Name="UserAuthenticationTypeID" Type="int"
   Nullable="false" StoreGeneratedPattern="Identity" />
  <Property Name="UserAuthenticationTypeDescription"
   Type="nvarchar(max)" Nullable="false" />
</EntityType>
```

```
        <EntityType Name="UserLoginHistory">
          <Key>
            <PropertyRef Name="UserLoginID" />
          </Key>
          <Property Name="UserLoginID" Type="int" Nullable="false"
           StoreGeneratedPattern="Identity" />
          <Property Name="UserID" Type="int" Nullable="false" />
          <Property Name="UserLoginDate" Type="datetime"
           Nullable="false" />
        </EntityType>
        <EntityType Name="UserRole">
          <Key>
            <PropertyRef Name="UserRoleID" />
          </Key>
          <Property Name="UserRoleID" Type="int" Nullable="false"
           StoreGeneratedPattern="Identity" />
          <Property Name="UserID" Type="int" Nullable="false" />
          <Property Name="RoleID" Type="int" Nullable="false" />
</EntityType>
```

The MSL schema

We will now take a look at the Mapping Specification Language or MSL schema (automatically generated by Visual Studio when the `.edmx` file is produced) that defines the C-S mapping, which maps the Conceptual Model to the Relational Store. Here is the MSL schema for our `Security` DataModel:

```
<EntityContainerMapping
StorageEntityContainer="SecurityDBModelStoreContainer"
CdmEntityContainer="SecurityDBEntities">
          <EntitySetMapping Name="Controls">
            <EntityTypeMapping TypeName="SecurityDBModel.Control">
              <MappingFragment StoreEntitySet="Control">
                <ScalarProperty Name="ControlID"
                 ColumnName="ControlID" />
                <ScalarProperty Name="ControlTypeID"
                 ColumnName="ControlTypeID" />
                <ScalarProperty Name="ControlName"
                 ColumnName="ControlName" />
                <ScalarProperty Name="ParentControlID"
                 ColumnName="ParentControlID" />
              </MappingFragment>
            </EntityTypeMapping>
          </EntitySetMapping>
```

```
<EntitySetMapping Name="ControlTypes">
  <EntityTypeMapping
   TypeName="SecurityDBModel.ControlType">
    <MappingFragment StoreEntitySet="ControlType">
      <ScalarProperty Name="ControlTypeID"
       ColumnName="ControlTypeID" />
      <ScalarProperty Name="ControlTypeName"
      ColumnName="ControlTypeName" />
    </MappingFragment>
  </EntityTypeMapping>
</EntitySetMapping>
<EntitySetMapping Name="Roles">
  <EntityTypeMapping TypeName="SecurityDBModel.Role">
    <MappingFragment StoreEntitySet="Role">
      <ScalarProperty Name="RoleID" ColumnName="RoleID"
       />
      <ScalarProperty Name="RoleDescription"
       ColumnName="RoleDescription" />
    </MappingFragment>
  </EntityTypeMapping>
</EntitySetMapping>
<EntitySetMapping Name="Users">
  <EntityTypeMapping TypeName="SecurityDBModel.User">
    <MappingFragment StoreEntitySet="User">
      <ScalarProperty Name="UserID" ColumnName="UserID"
       />
      <ScalarProperty Name="IsAdmin"
       ColumnName="IsAdmin" />
      <ScalarProperty Name="IsActive"
       ColumnName="IsActive" />
      <ScalarProperty Name="IsOnline"
       ColumnName="IsOnline" />
    </MappingFragment>
  </EntityTypeMapping>
</EntitySetMapping>
<EntitySetMapping Name="UserAuthentications">
  <EntityTypeMapping
   TypeName="SecurityDBModel.UserAuthentication">
    <MappingFragment
     StoreEntitySet="UserAuthentication">
      <ScalarProperty Name="UserAuthenticationID"
       ColumnName="UserAuthenticationID" />
      <ScalarProperty Name="UserAuthenticationTypeID"
       ColumnName="UserAuthenticationTypeID" />
```

```
            <ScalarProperty Name="UserID" ColumnName="UserID"
             />
            <ScalarProperty Name="UserName"
             ColumnName="UserName" />
            <ScalarProperty Name="Password"
             ColumnName="Password" />
            <ScalarProperty Name="UserEmail"
             ColumnName="UserEmail" />
          </MappingFragment>
        </EntityTypeMapping>
      </EntitySetMapping>
      <EntitySetMapping Name="UserAuthenticationTypes">
        <EntityTypeMapping
         TypeName="SecurityDBModel.UserAuthenticationType">
          <MappingFragment
           StoreEntitySet="UserAuthenticationType">
            <ScalarProperty Name="UserAuthenticationTypeID"
             ColumnName="UserAuthenticationTypeID" />
            <ScalarProperty
             Name="UserAuthenticationTypeDescription"
             ColumnName="UserAuthenticationTypeDescription" />
          </MappingFragment>
        </EntityTypeMapping>
      </EntitySetMapping>
      <EntitySetMapping Name="UserLoginHistories">
        <EntityTypeMapping
         TypeName="SecurityDBModel.UserLoginHistory">
          <MappingFragment StoreEntitySet="UserLoginHistory">
            <ScalarProperty Name="UserLoginID"
             ColumnName="UserLoginID" />
            <ScalarProperty Name="UserID" ColumnName="UserID"
             />
            <ScalarProperty Name="UserLoginDate"
             ColumnName="UserLoginDate" />
          </MappingFragment>
        </EntityTypeMapping>
      </EntitySetMapping>
      <EntitySetMapping Name="UserRoles">
        <EntityTypeMapping
         TypeName="SecurityDBModel.UserRole">
          <MappingFragment StoreEntitySet="UserRole">
            <ScalarProperty Name="UserRoleID"
             ColumnName="UserRoleID" />
            <ScalarProperty Name="UserID" ColumnName="UserID"
```

```
                    />
                    <ScalarProperty Name="RoleID" ColumnName="RoleID"
                    />
                  </MappingFragment>
                </EntityTypeMapping>
              </EntitySetMapping>
            </EntityContainerMapping>
          </Mapping>
      </edmx:Mappings>
```

As you can see in the MSL schema just mentioned, the `EntityContainerMapping` attribute is used to indicate that the `StorageEntityContainer` attribute is mapped to the conceptual model container.

But how is this mapping achieved? Entity Framework does this by mapping each `EntitySet` and `AssociationSet` attributes to the corresponding elements in the data store. As an example, it uses the `StoreEntitySet` attribute to map a particular EntityType to the corresponding database table. There are also many `ScalarProperty` attributes that define how a particular property is mapped to its corresponding column name in the database table.

Here is how the mapping information for the `UserRoles` entity set is represented:

```
<EntitySetMapping Name="UserRoles">
            <EntityTypeMapping
             TypeName="SecurityDBModel.UserRole">
              <MappingFragment StoreEntitySet="UserRole">
                <ScalarProperty Name="UserRoleID"
                 ColumnName="UserRoleID" />
                <ScalarProperty Name="UserID" ColumnName="UserID"
                 />
                <ScalarProperty Name="RoleID" ColumnName="RoleID"
                 />
              </MappingFragment>
            </EntityTypeMapping>
</EntitySetMapping>
```

The `EntityTypeMapping` attribute in the preceding code snippet is used to specify the type of the entity being represented. The MSL schema maps the CSDL and SSDL sections of the EDM.

Entity classes

These are .NET classes that are automatically generated from the CSDL definition. You can create POCO classes from `.edmx` files using Entity Framework DbContext Fluent Generator. When you do this, T4 templates will be automatically added to your project. You can download the DbContext Fluent Generator from `https://visualstudiogallery.msdn.microsoft.com/5d663b99-ed3b-481d-b7bc-b947d2457e3c`.

These are similar to business entities and can be used to populate data and pass instances of these classes across the layers of the application. Note that whenever the CSDL definition changes, these classes are automatically updated to reflect the changes. Also, these classes are partial classes and hence you can extend them to create your own custom classes too. These are also partial because you want to keep your extensions in a separate file so they are not overridden if the class is regenerated—this facilitates extensibility and also convenience.

The following code snippet shows what the `Control` and `ControlType` entity classes look like:

```
public partial class Control
    {
        public int ControlID { get; set; }
        public int ControlTypeID { get; set; }
        public string ControlName { get; set; }
        public int ParentControlID { get; set; }

        public virtual ControlType ControlType { get; set; }
    }

public partial class ControlType
    {
        public ControlType()
        {
            this.Controls = new HashSet<Control>();
        }

        public int ControlTypeID { get; set; }
        public string ControlTypeName { get; set; }

        public virtual ICollection<Control> Controls { get; set; }
    }
```

Note the use of the `virtual` keyword in the `ControlType` class. This is used to promote lazy loading. The `virtual` keyword is used to facilitate lazy loading—if the `virtual` keyword is not there, the property would be eager loaded. The usage of the `virtual` keyword also helps in efficient change tracking. The `Role` and `User` entity classes are given as follows:

```
public partial class Role
    {
        public int RoleID { get; set; }
        public string RoleDescription { get; set; }
    }

public partial class User
    {
        public User()
        {
            this.UserAuthentications = new
            HashSet<UserAuthentication>();
            this.UserLoginHistories = new
            HashSet<UserLoginHistory>();
            this.UserRoles = new HashSet<UserRole>();
        }

        public int UserID { get; set; }
        public Nullable<bool> IsAdmin { get; set; }
        public Nullable<bool> IsActive { get; set; }
        public Nullable<bool> IsOnline { get; set; }

        public virtual ICollection<UserAuthentication>
        UserAuthentications { get; set; }
        public virtual ICollection<UserLoginHistory>
        UserLoginHistories { get; set; }
        public virtual ICollection<UserRole> UserRoles { get; set;
  }
    }
```

Note the use of `HashSet` in the `User` class. `HashSet` is used to ensure that the collection contains one instance (no duplicates) of an instance. The `UserAuthentication` and `UserAuthenticationType` entity classes are shown as follows:

```
public partial class UserAuthentication
    {
        public int UserAuthenticationID { get; set; }
        public int UserAuthenticationTypeID { get; set; }
        public int UserID { get; set; }
        public string UserName { get; set; }
```

```
        public string Password { get; set; }
        public string UserEmail { get; set; }

        public virtual User User { get; set; }
        public virtual UserAuthenticationType
        UserAuthenticationType { get; set; }
    }

public partial class UserAuthenticationType
    {
        public UserAuthenticationType()
        {
            this.UserAuthentications = new
            HashSet<UserAuthentication>();
        }

        public int UserAuthenticationTypeID { get; set; }
        public string UserAuthenticationTypeDescription { get;
        set; }

        public virtual ICollection<UserAuthentication>
        UserAuthentications { get; set; }
    }
```

Here is the code of the `UserLoginHistory` entity class:

```
public partial class UserLoginHistory
    {
        public int UserLoginID { get; set; }
        public int UserID { get; set; }
        public System.DateTime UserLoginDate { get; set; }

        public virtual User User { get; set; }
    }
```

And, the following code snippet illustrates the `UserRole` entity class:

```
public partial class UserRole
    {
        public int UserRoleID { get; set; }
        public int UserID { get; set; }
        public int RoleID { get; set; }

        public virtual User User { get; set; }
    }
```

Summary

The EDM comprises a storage schema, a conceptual schema, and a mapping schema together with the entity classes. In this chapter, we took a detailed look at the EDM and how each of its sections relate to each other. We discussed each of the sections of our `Security` DataModel and how they are related.

In the next chapter, we will explore the use of stored procedures with the EDM.

4

Working with Stored Procedures in the Entity Data Model

The Entity Framework is an extended Object Relational Mapping (ORM) technology from Microsoft that abstracts the object model of an application from its relational or logical model. The newer versions of this framework provide you with many exciting features – model-first development being one of these things. In this chapter, we will explore how we can work with stored procedures in Entity Framework 6.

We will discuss the following points:

- Creating a database using model-first development
- Creating stored procedures for the database
- Mapping stored procedures to functions in the EDM
- Using the stored procedures in the Object Layer
- Mapping stored procedures that return custom entity types
- Adding stored procedures to the EDM
- Mapping stored procedures to functions in the EDM
- Mapping stored procedures that return custom entity types

Note that as of this writing, support for stored procedures is not yet included in Entity Framework 7. However, you can do it using plain ADO.NET statements, as shown in the code snippet that follows:

```
var connection =
(SqlConnection)context.Database.AsSqlServer().
Connection .DbConnection;
var command = connection.CreateCommand();
command.CommandType = CommandType.StoredProcedure;
command.CommandText = "DeleteEmployee";
command.Parameters.AddWithValue("@EmployeeId", 1);
command.ExecuteNonQuery();
```

Creating a database using model-first development

One of the most interesting new features and enhancements introduced in Entity Framework 6 is its ability to generate a database from an existing object model. This approach provides you with better control over your design and promotes **domain-driven design (DDD)**. In this approach, you can design your domain model based on the business requirements first and then generate the database from it.

Before we explore this further, let's take a quick tour of the modeling approaches that are supported. The domain modeling approaches in Entity Framework include the following:

- **Code-first**: In this approach, the domain model is first defined using the POCO classes and then the database is created from these classes. This approach is popular and provides much more control over your code—you just need to define the database mappings and leave the creating of the database entirely to Entity Framework. Note that as your code drives the database, manual changes to the database are not preferred in this approach.
- **Model-first**: In the model-first approach you create your entities, relationships, and the inheritance hierarchies directly on the design surface of the EDM Designer in Visual Studio, and then generate the database from the model designed. If you need additional features, you can use partial classes. In essence, in this approach, the model drives and defines the database. This is also known as a model-driven approach. This approach is good for small projects, but with complex databases and large projects, this is not a preferred approach as you don't have much control over the database and making manual changes to the database schema is also not preferred.

- **Database-first**: In this approach, the database is first designed and then the model is generated from the database. In this approach, you can make manual changes to the database and then regenerate the model from the database.

Microsoft has planned to retire the Visual Design tool for the Entity Framework from version 7 of the framework. As a result, you will only have the code-first approach to build your entity classes. This is also known as the *code-first only* approach.

In this section, we will explore how we can make use of Entity Framework to create a database using Visual Studio 2015 and Entity Framework.

Follow these steps:

1. Open Visual Studio 2015, create a blank new ASP.NET project, and save it with a name.
2. Right-click on the project created in the **Solution Explorer** window and select **Add | New Item...**, as shown in the following screenshot:

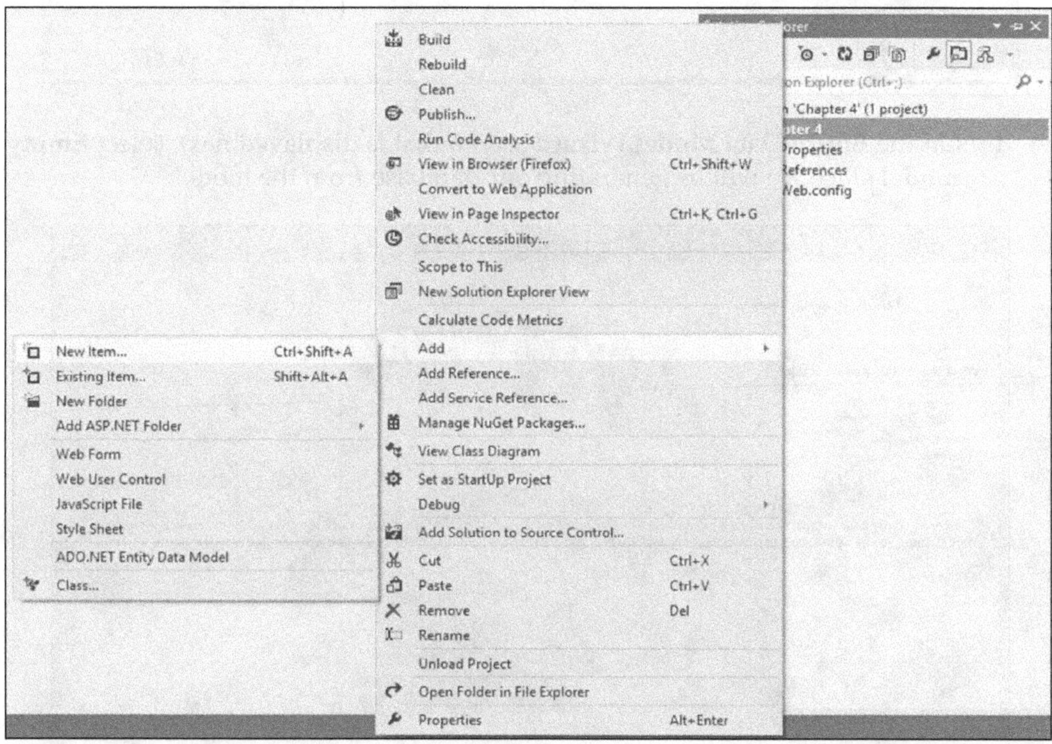

3. Select **ADO.NET Entity Data Model** from the list of the templates displayed and provide the name, `Payroll`. Then, click on **Add**:

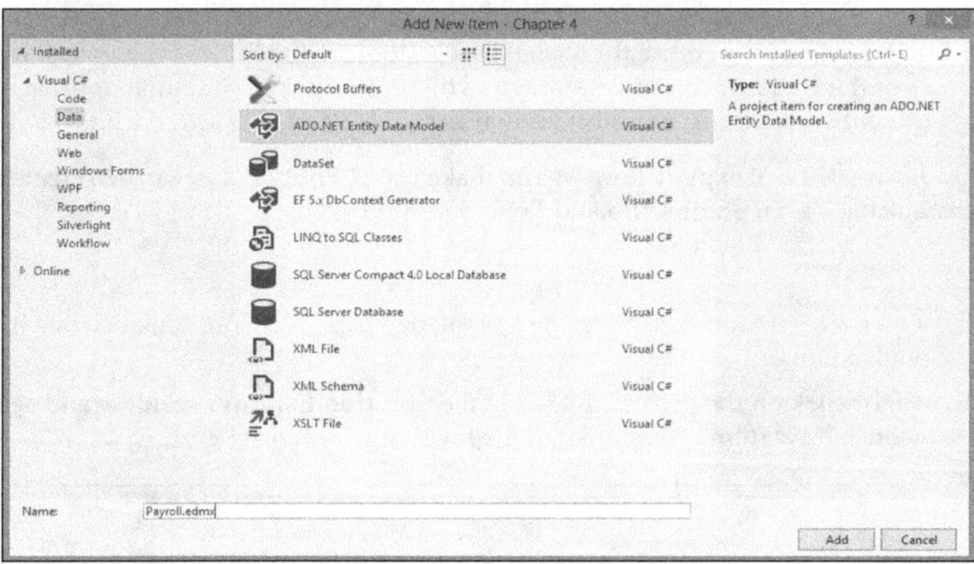

4. On the **Entity Data Model Wizard** screen that is displayed next, select **Empty model** since we will be generating our database from the model:

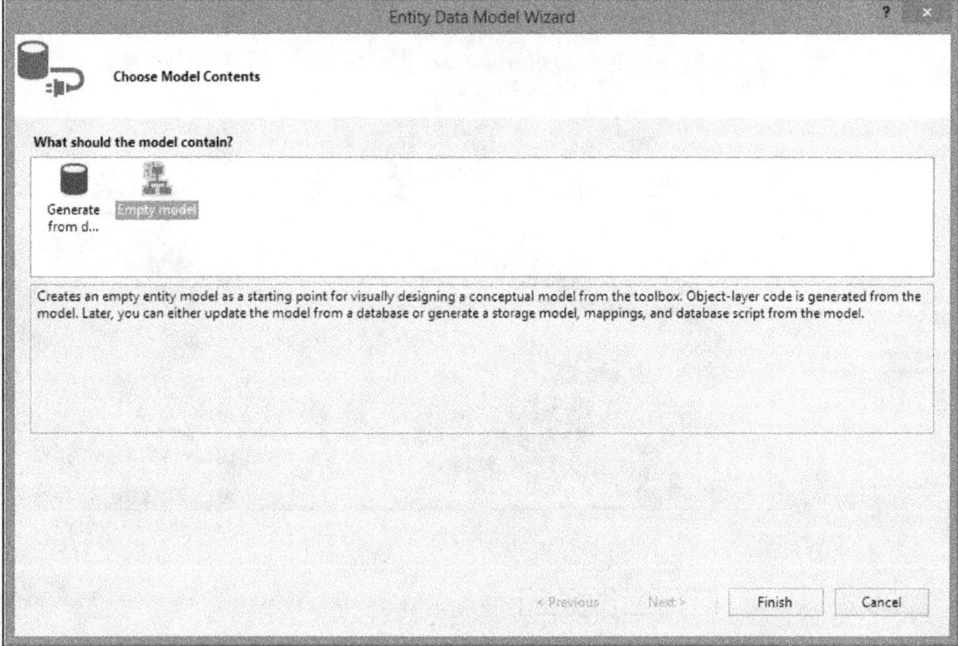

5. Click on **Finish**.

   The `Payroll.edmx` file will be created and added to the project. The EDM we just created looks like the following screenshot:

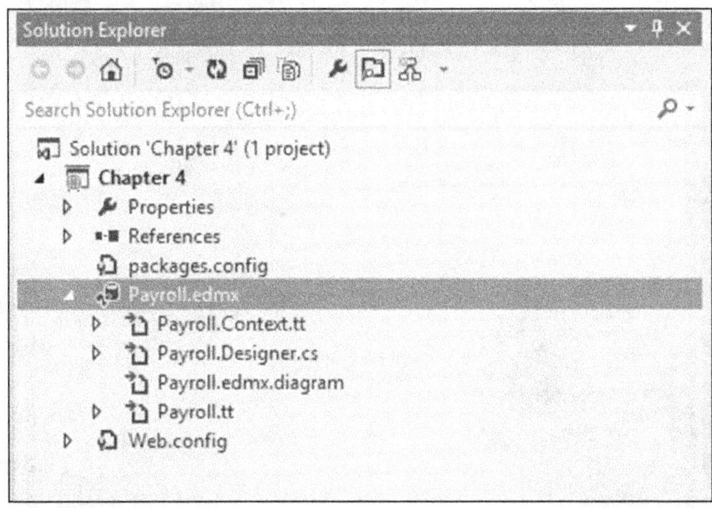

The next step is to create entities and associations. To do this, follow these steps:

1. Right-click on the **Entity Data Model Designer** and navigate to **Add New** | **Entity...** from the pop-up menu displayed:

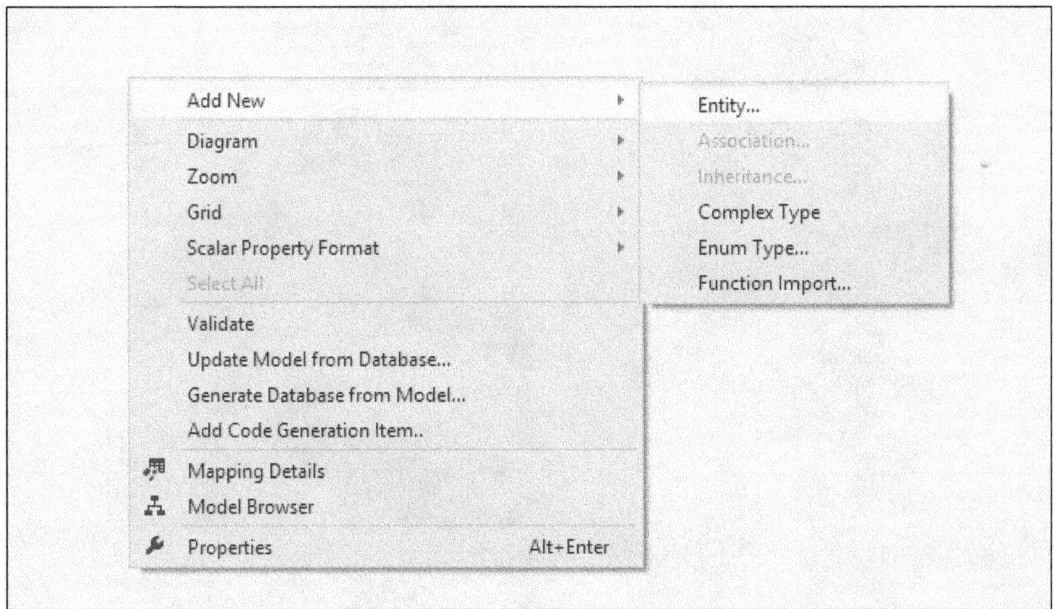

2. Provide the name of the entity as `Employee` and specify the key property name as `EmployeeID`, as shown here:

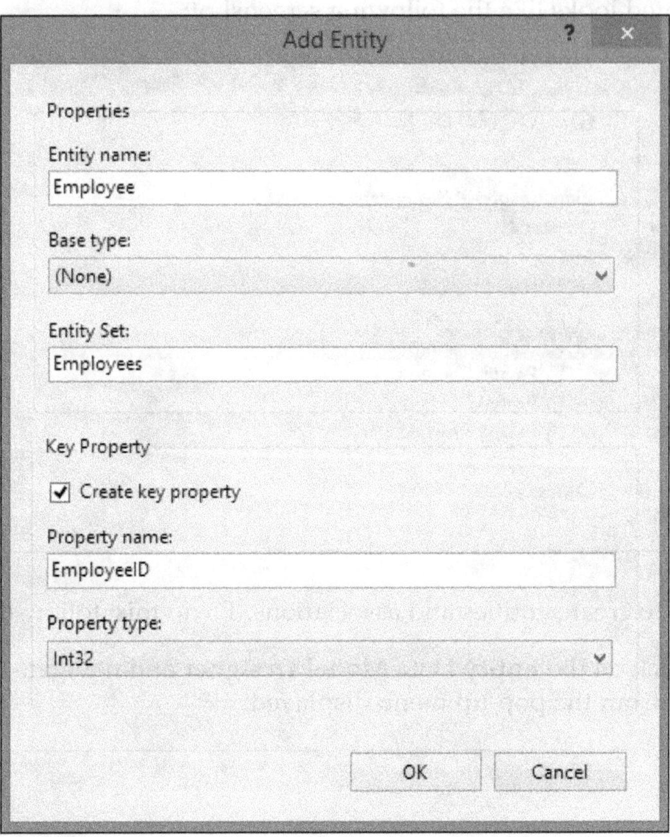

The next step is to create the properties for the entity we just created.

1. To create a scalar property for the `Employee` entity, right-click on the entity in the **Entity Data Model Designer** and navigate to **Add New | Scalar Property**:

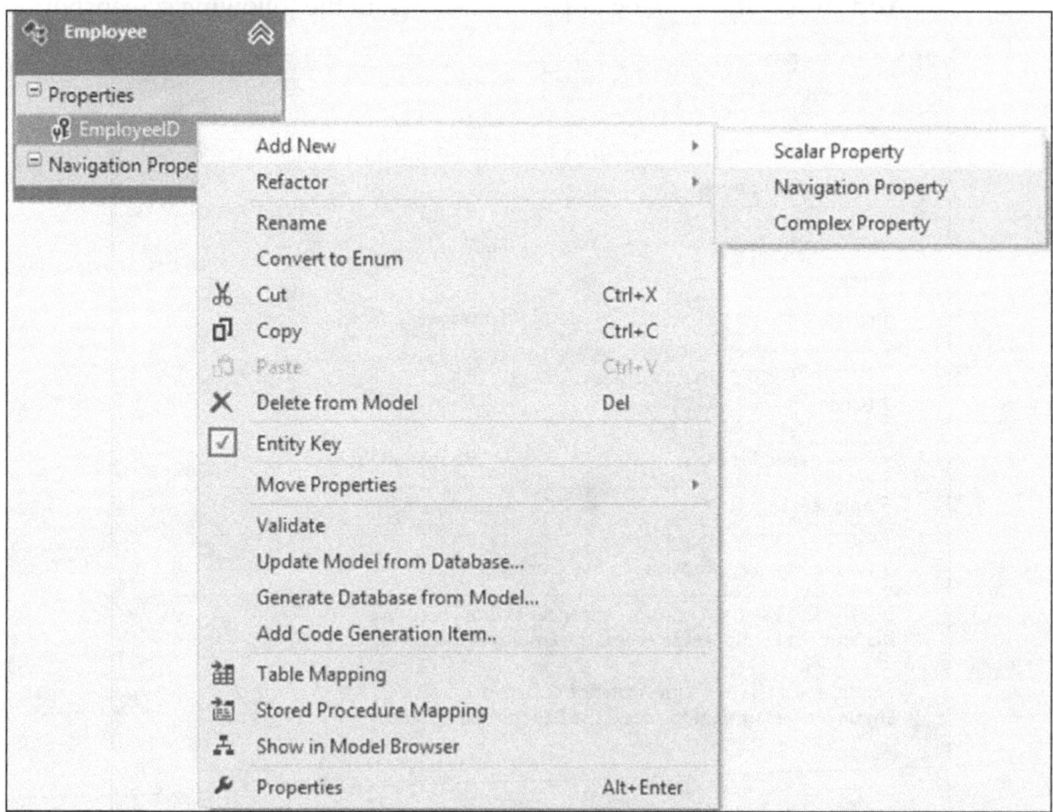

2. Specify the name, length, and type of the scalar property.
3. Repeat the same for all the properties you need for the `Employee` entity.
4. Now, create the `Department` entity and its properties by using the same procedure you followed for the `Employee` entity.

So, we have two entities, namely `Employee` and `Department`, created. The next step is to associate these entities.

1. To create an association between the entities, select the `Department` entity in the designer and navigate to **Add** | **Association**.
2. The **Add Association** dialog appears as shown in the following screenshot:

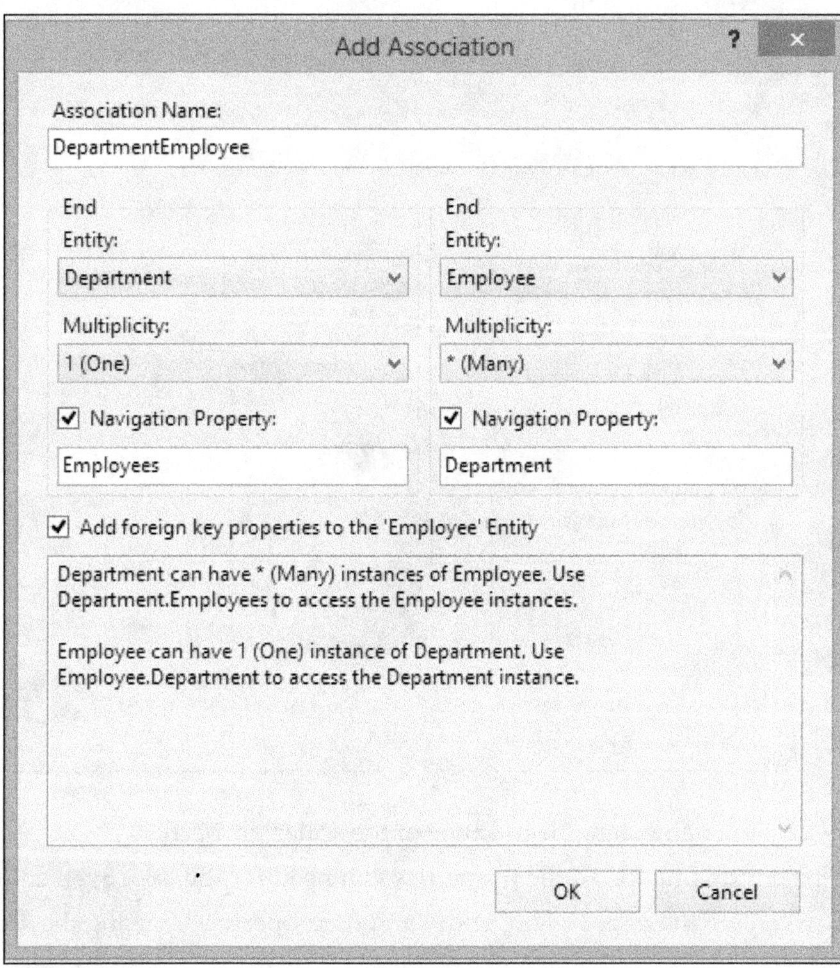

3. You can specify the variations in the association by using the multiplicity drop-down controls, as shown in the preceding screenshot. In this example, we will go ahead with the default association. So, click on **OK** to save the association. The following screenshot illustrates what the EDM now looks like in the **Model Browser** window:

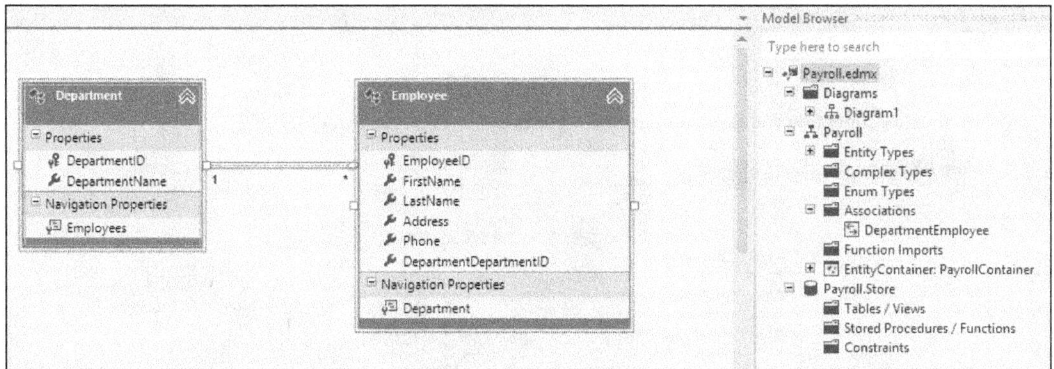

Now that the entity, its properties, and associations have been created, we can go ahead and generate our database from the model we created:

1. To do this, right-click on the designer and select **Generate Database from Model...**, as shown in the screenshot that follows:

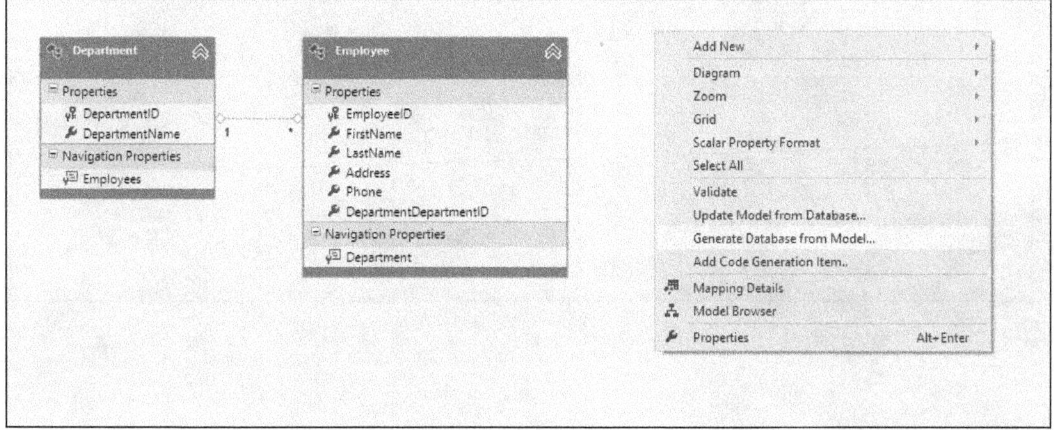

2. In the **Generate Database Wizard** window that appears next, select **New Connection...** and specify the connection properties:

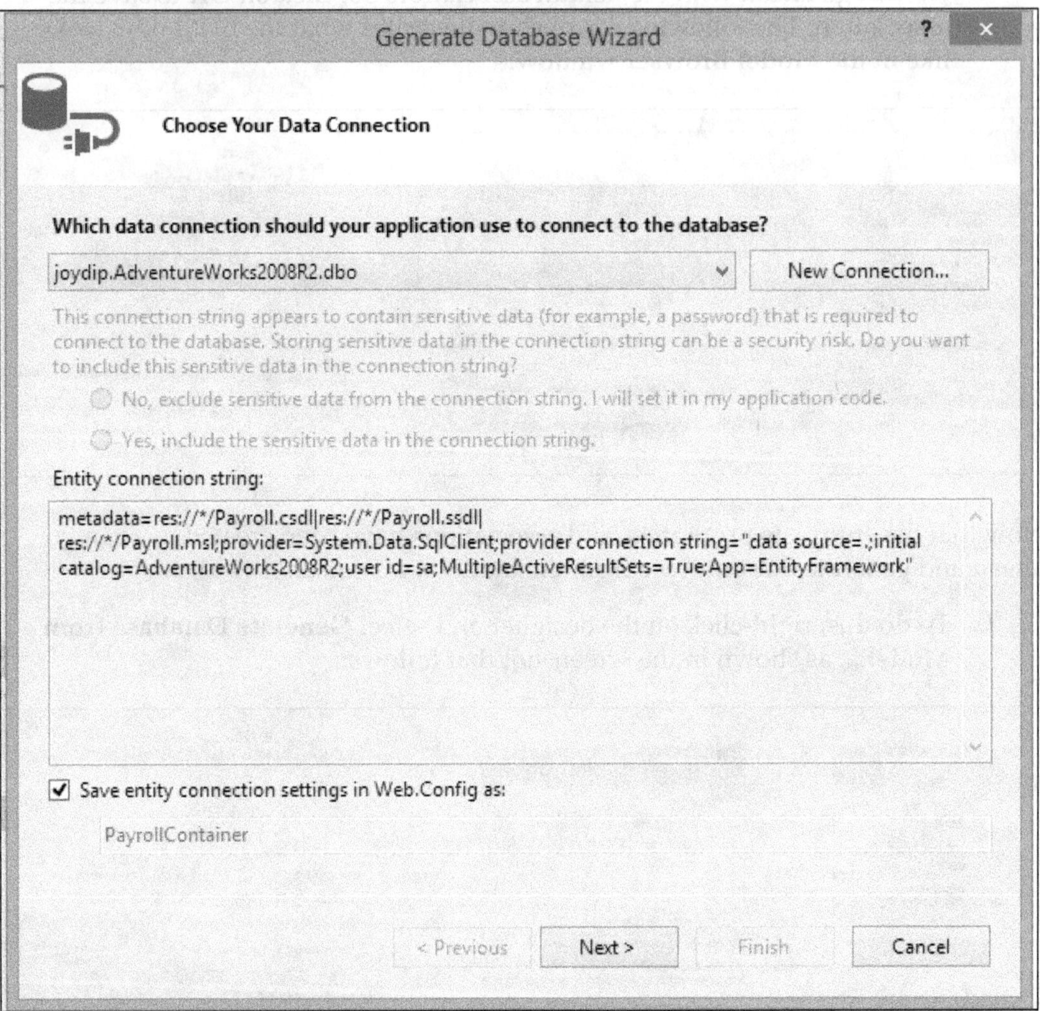

3. Specify the database name as `Payroll` and click on **OK**:

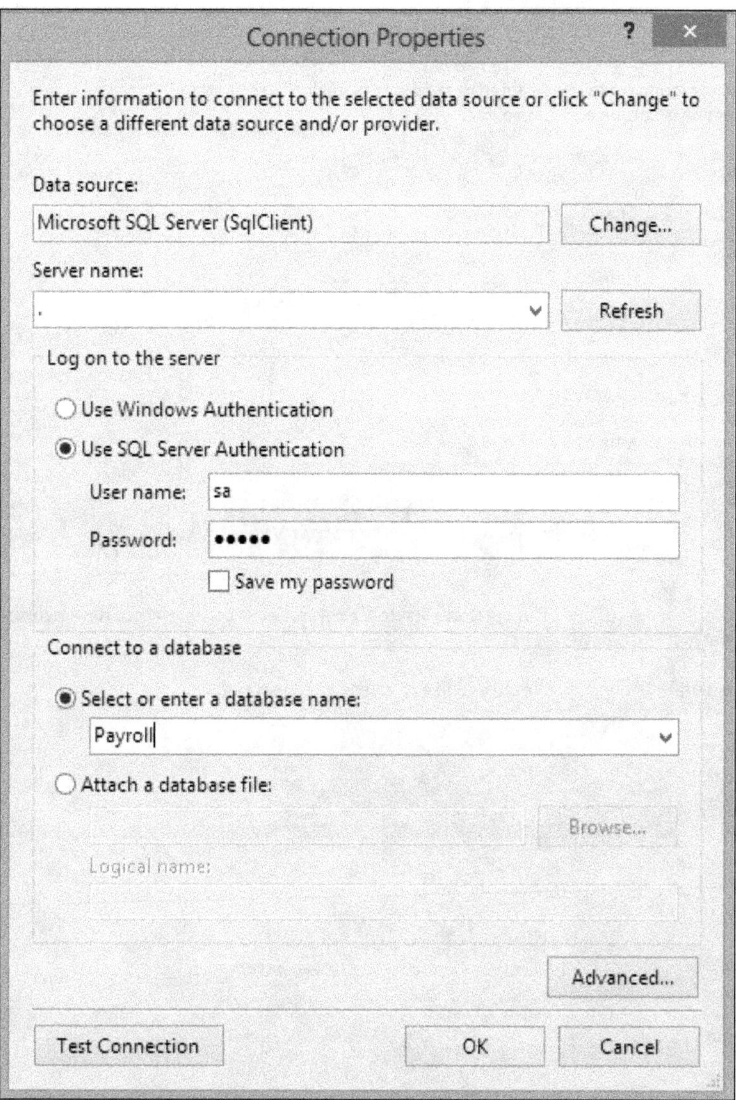

4. You will be prompted to create a new database as none exist with this name:

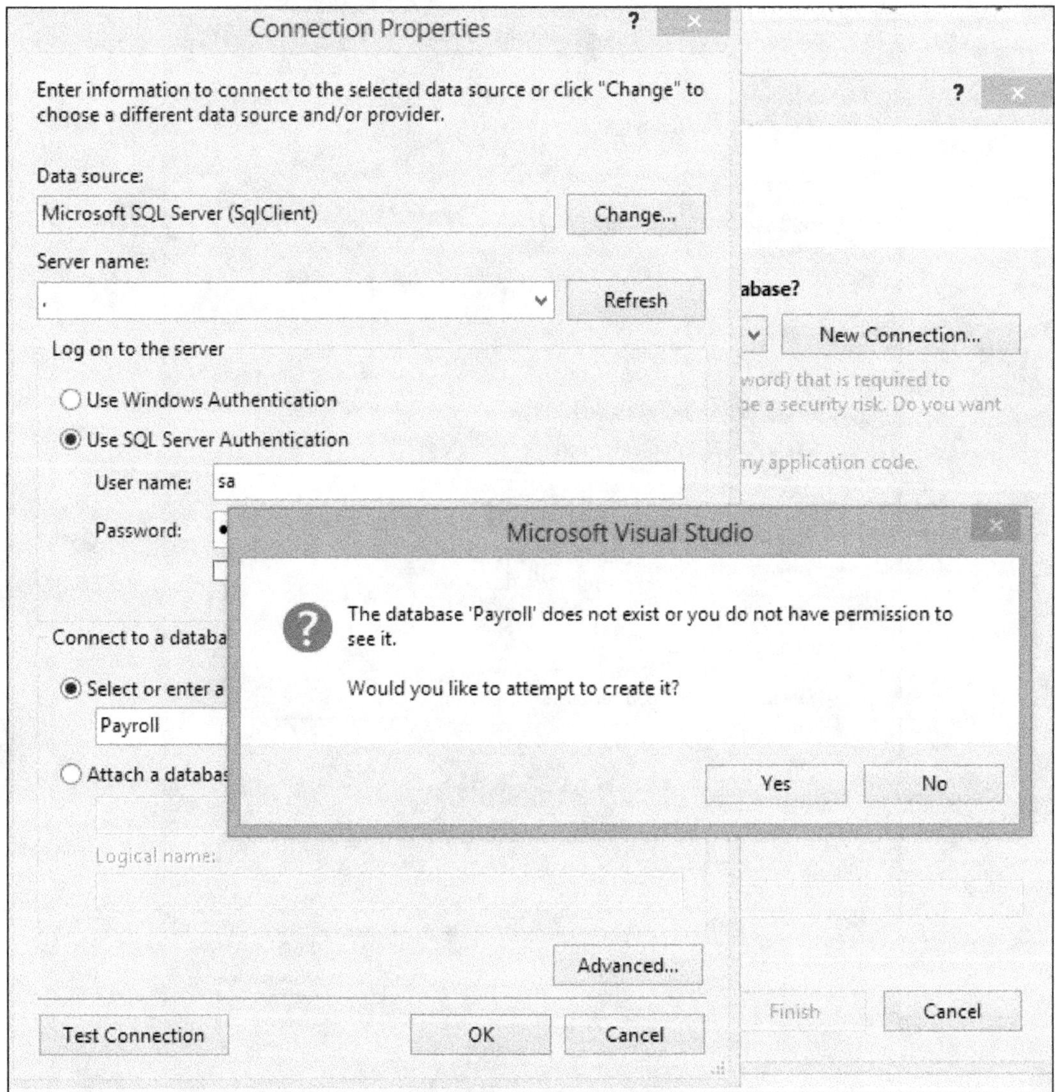

5. Click on **Yes**.
6. You'll be returned to the **Generate Database Wizard** dialog again. Now, select the checkbox and the second radio button and click on **Next**, as shown in the screenshot that follows:

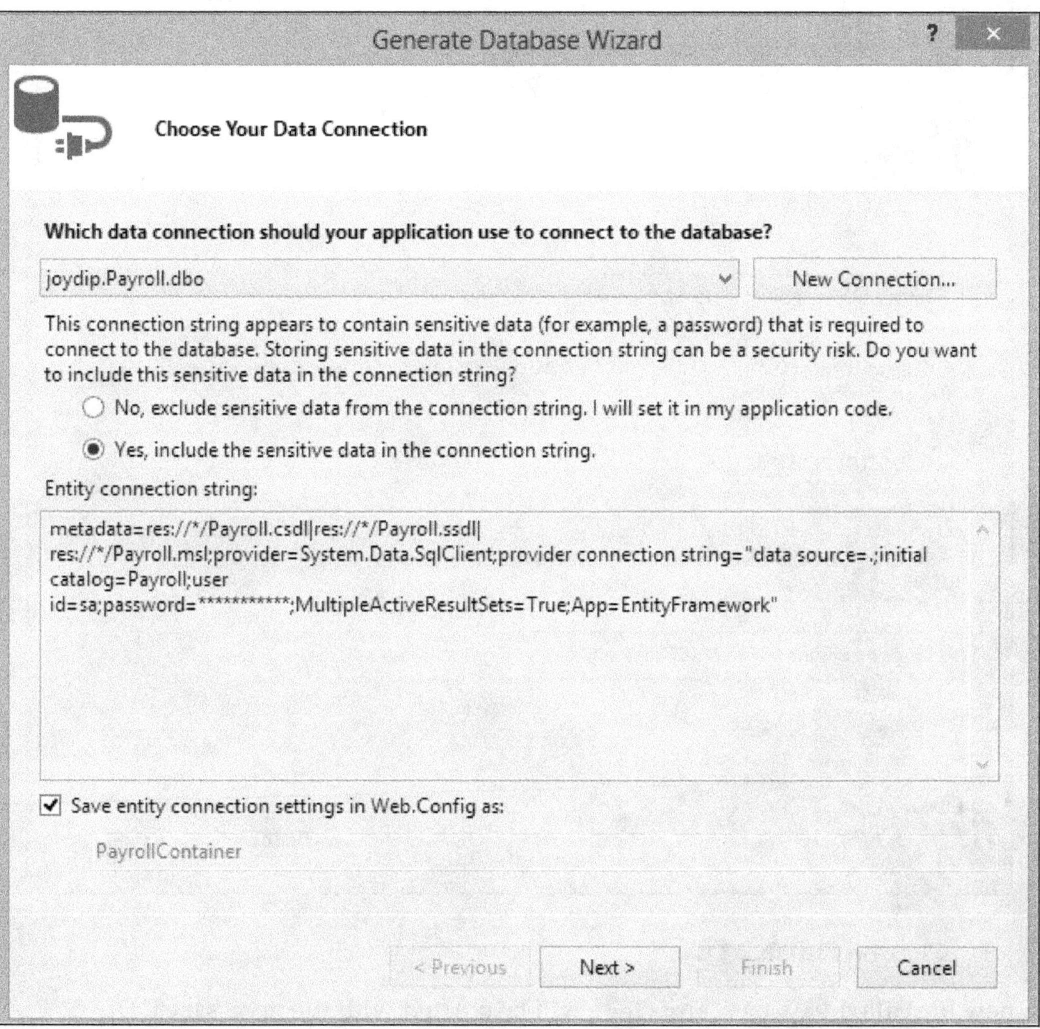

7. The **Generate Database Wizard** dialog will now generate the necessary DDL statements to create the database.

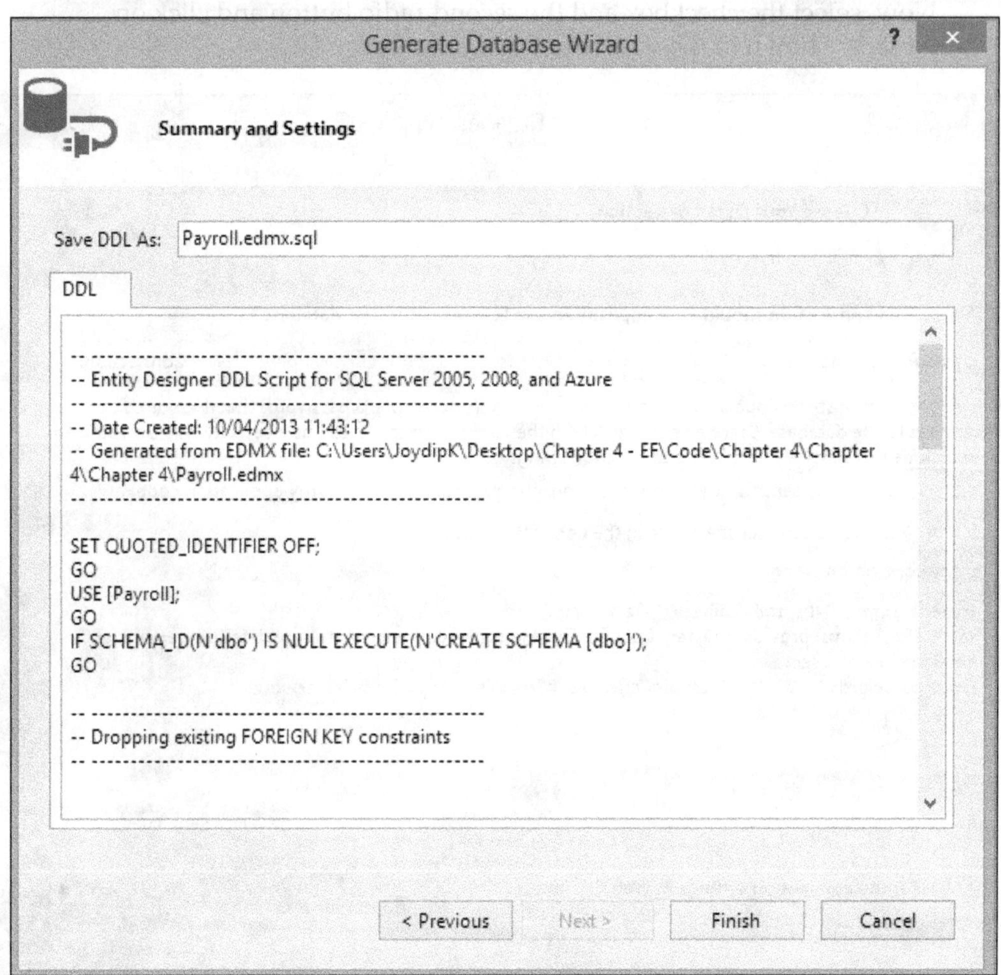

8. Click on **Finish**.

A new file called `Payroll.edmx.sql` will be created with the necessary DDL statements to create the database from the model we created earlier in this chapter.

Here's how the content of this file will look:

```
SET QUOTED_IDENTIFIER OFF;
GO
USE [Payroll];
GO
```

```
IF SCHEMA_ID(N'dbo') IS NULL EXECUTE(N'CREATE SCHEMA [dbo]');
GO

-- --------------------------------------------------
-- Dropping existing FOREIGN KEY constraints
-- --------------------------------------------------


-- --------------------------------------------------
-- Dropping existing tables
-- --------------------------------------------------


-- --------------------------------------------------
-- Creating all tables
-- --------------------------------------------------

-- Creating table 'Employees'
CREATE TABLE [dbo].[Employees] (
    [EmployeeID] int IDENTITY(1,1) NOT NULL,
    [FirstName] nvarchar(50)  NOT NULL,
    [LastName] nvarchar(50)  NOT NULL,
    [Address] nvarchar(200)  NOT NULL,
    [Phone] nvarchar(20)  NOT NULL,
    [JoiningDate] datetime  NOT NULL,
    [DepartmentDepartmentID] int  NOT NULL,
    [CreatedDate_DateCreated] datetime  NOT NULL
);
GO

-- Creating table 'Departments'
CREATE TABLE [dbo].[Departments] (
    [DepartmentID] int IDENTITY(1,1) NOT NULL,
    [DepartmentName] nvarchar(100)  NOT NULL,
    [CreatedDate_DateCreated] datetime  NOT NULL
);
GO

-- --------------------------------------------------
-- Creating all PRIMARY KEY constraints
-- --------------------------------------------------

-- Creating primary key on [EmployeeID] in table 'Employees'
ALTER TABLE [dbo].[Employees]
```

```
ADD CONSTRAINT [PK_Employees]
    PRIMARY KEY CLUSTERED ([EmployeeID] ASC);
GO

-- Creating primary key on [DepartmentID] in table 'Departments'
ALTER TABLE [dbo].[Departments]
ADD CONSTRAINT [PK_Departments]
    PRIMARY KEY CLUSTERED ([DepartmentID] ASC);
GO

-- --------------------------------------------------
-- Creating all FOREIGN KEY constraints
-- --------------------------------------------------

-- Creating foreign key on [DepartmentDepartmentID] in table
'Employees'
ALTER TABLE [dbo].[Employees]
ADD CONSTRAINT [FK_DepartmentEmployee]
    FOREIGN KEY ([DepartmentDepartmentID])
    REFERENCES [dbo].[Departments]
        ([DepartmentID])
    ON DELETE NO ACTION ON UPDATE NO ACTION;

-- Creating non-clustered index for FOREIGN KEY
'FK_DepartmentEmployee'
CREATE INDEX [IX_FK_DepartmentEmployee]
ON [dbo].[Employees]
    ([DepartmentDepartmentID]);
GO

-- --------------------------------------------------
-- Script has ended
-- --------------------------------------------------
```

Note that the database tables haven't been created yet—you will need to actually execute this script to have the necessary database tables created in the database. To do this, follow these steps:

1. Open the `Payroll.edmx.sql` file.
2. Right-click on it and then select **Execute SQL** from the pop-up menu.
3. Specify the connection properties for the database server and click on **Connect**.
4. If the connection is successful, the database and the tables will be created.

Creating stored procedures

A stored procedure is a group of one or more Transact-SQL statements stored in the database data dictionary and compiled as a single execution plan. We will create stored procedures that we will use to select, insert, update, and delete data from the `Employee` and `Department` tables we just created. Here is a list of the stored procedures that we will create for our `Payroll` database:

- `Employee_Select`
- `Employee_Insert`
- `Employee_Update`
- `Employee_Delete`
- `Department_Select`
- `Department_Insert`
- `Department_Update`
- `Department_Delete`

The following code shows the complete scripts for each of the stored procedures for the `Employee` and `Department` tables:

```
Create Procedure Employee_Select
as
Select EmployeeID, FirstName, LastName, Address,Phone,
DepartmentDepartmentID, JoiningDate,CreatedDate_DateCreated
from Employees
Go

Create Procedure Employee_Insert
@FirstName varchar(50), @LastName varchar(50), @Address
varchar(200),
@Phone varchar(20), @DepartmentID int, @JoiningDate datetime,
@DateCreated datetime
as
Insert into Employees(FirstName, LastName, Address,Phone,
DepartmentDepartmentID, JoiningDate,CreatedDate_DateCreated)
values (@FirstName, @LastName, @Address, @Phone,
@DepartmentID,@JoiningDate, @DateCreated)
Go

Create Procedure Employee_Update
@EmployeeID int, @FirstName varchar(50), @LastName varchar(50),
```

```
@Address varchar(200), @Phone varchar(20)
as
Update Employees Set @FirstName = @FirstName, LastName =
LastName, Address = @Address, Phone = @Phone Where EmployeeID =
@EmployeeID
Go

Create Procedure Employee_Delete
@EmployeeID int
as
Delete from Employees where EmployeeID = @EmployeeID
Go

Create Procedure Department_Select
as
Select DepartmentID, DepartmentName, CreatedDate_DateCreated
from Departments
Go

Create Procedure Department_Insert
@DepartmentName varchar(100), @CreatedDate datetime
as
Insert into Departments (DepartmentName, CreatedDate_DateCreated)
values (@DepartmentName, @CreatedDate)
Go

Create Procedure Department_Update
@DepartmentID int,@DepartmentName varchar(100)
as
Update Departments Set DepartmentName = @DepartmentName where
DepartmentID = @DepartmentID
Go

Create Procedure Department_Delete
@DepartmentID int
as
Delete from Departments where DepartmentID = @DepartmentID
Go
```

Once you are done creating the stored procedures, select the EDM in the designer, right-click on it, and select **Update Model from Database...** to update the EDM with the changes (new stored procedures created) we just made.

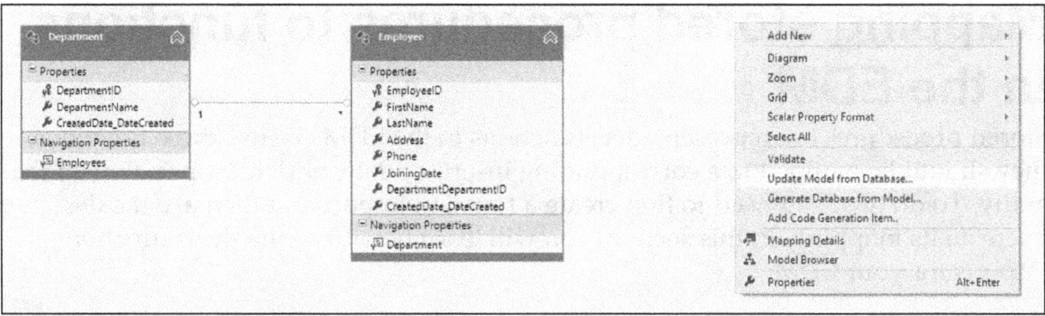

In the **Update Wizard** that shows up next, select the database objects (this time we will select the stored procedures we created) you need, and then click on **Finish**.

The following screenshot shows how the `Payroll` EDM now looks in the **Model Browser** window:

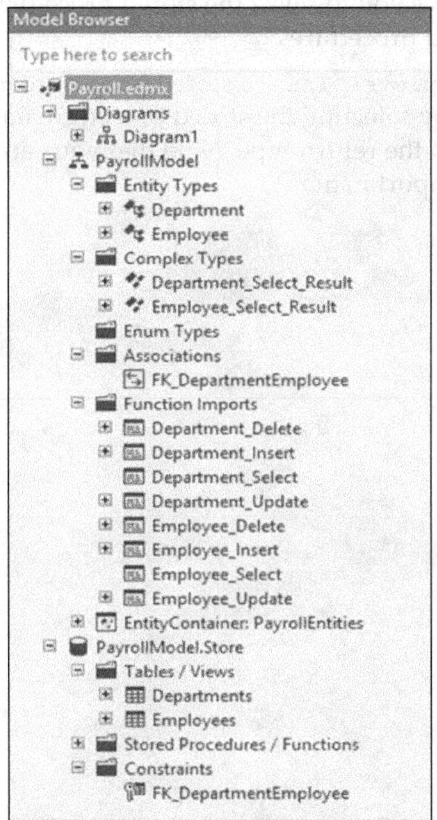

Note that the stored procedures have been listed.

Mapping stored procedures to functions in the EDM

Stored procedures are represented as functions in the EDM. To use these functions, they should be mapped to a corresponding insert, update, or delete operation on the entity. To do this, you need to first create a function import and then use the designer to create its mapping. In this section, you will learn how to create these function imports for your EDM.

To begin, let's refer to the EDM we created earlier in this chapter. To create function imports, follow these steps:

1. Switch to the **Model Browser** of the `Payroll` Entity Data Model.
2. Expand the **Entity Container** and right-click on **Function Imports**.
3. When you select **Create Function Import**, the **New Function Import** dialog appears and allows you to select the stored procedure you want from the list of available stored procedures.
4. Now, map the `Employee_Insert` stored procedure to a corresponding function import by selecting the stored procedure name, the function import name, and the return type. Note that you can specify any name as the function import name.

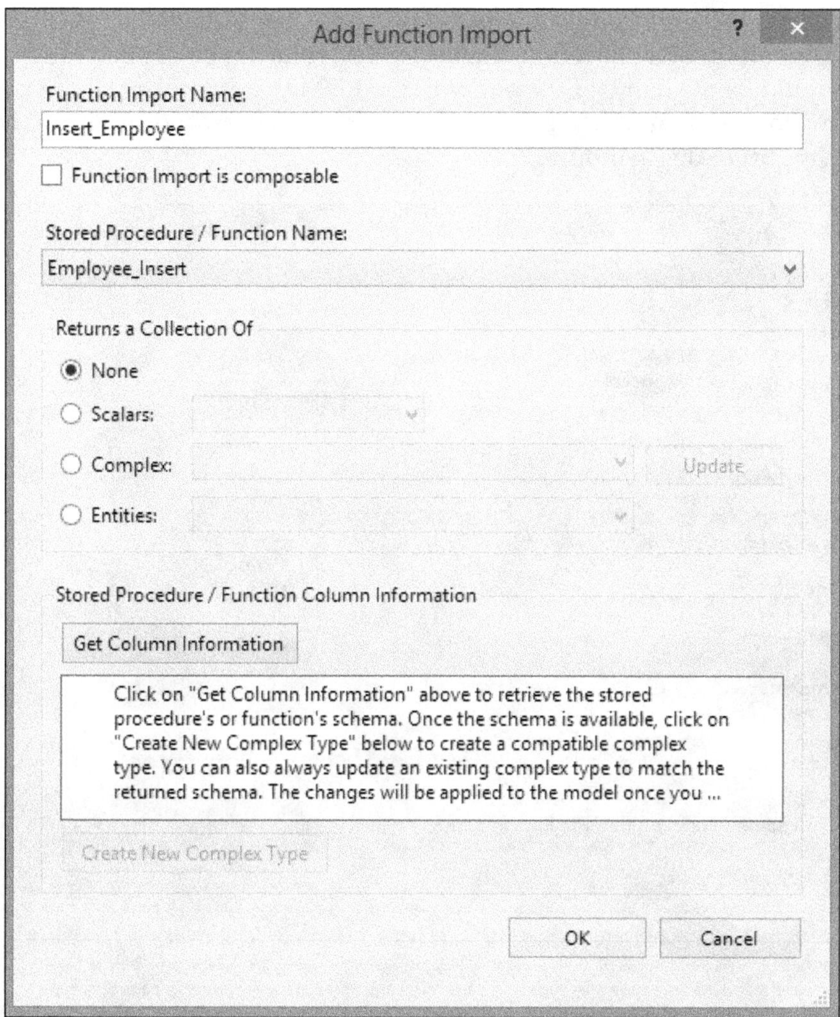

5. Repeat the aforementioned steps to map the remaining procedures to their corresponding functions.

You can use the same procedure to map your select procedures, that is, procedures that return an entity or a collection of entities. The return type of such function imports should be the name of the entity in the EDM that it returns. As an example, here is how you can map the `Department_Select` stored procedure using the **New Function Import** dialog window:

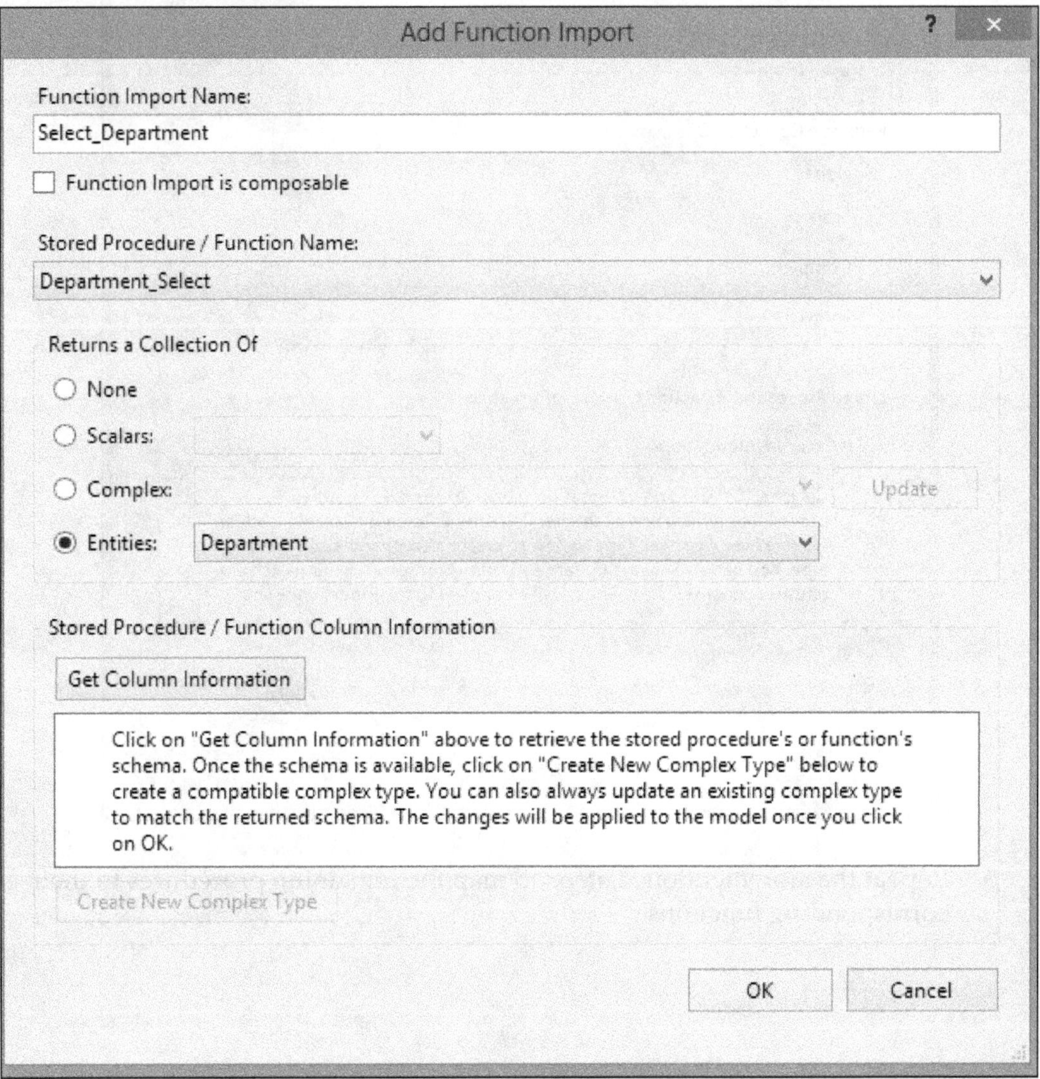

Once you are done mapping the procedures you need, you can see the complete list in the **Model Browser** dialog:

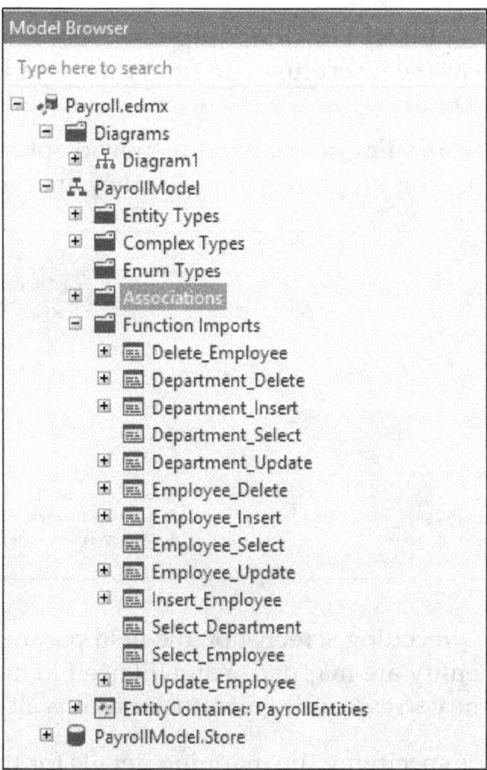

Now that the function imports have been created, you need to map them to the corresponding insert, update, and delete operations on the entity using the designer.

Mapping the create, update, and delete functions to entities in the EDM

In this section, we will explore how to map the functions we just created to the corresponding entities of our EDM. Note that we only need to map the CUD functions.

Now, follow these steps:

1. Select the **Employee** entity in the designer, right-click on it, and select **Show** in **Mapping Details**.
2. Click on **Map Entities to Functions** to map the CUD functions of the `Employee` entity.

3. The **Mapping Details-Employee** window for the `Employee` entity appears where you can specify the insert, update, and delete functions for the `Employee` entity.
4. Click on the **Select Insert Function** drop-down list to select the `Employee_Insert` function as the insert function from the list of available functions for the `Employee` entity.
5. The **Mapping Details-Employee** window now displays the parameters and the corresponding properties to which they are bound:

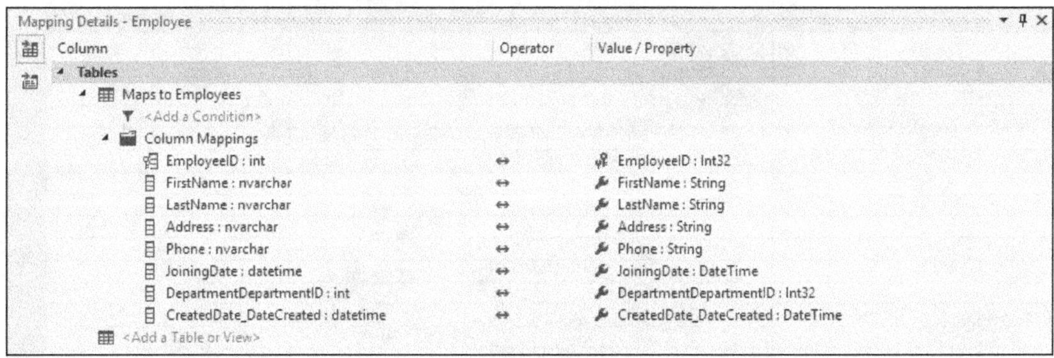

As you can see from the preceding screenshot, the field parameters and the field names of the `Employee` entity are mapped. You will need to manually map the `DepartmentID` field to the corresponding parameter as it is an association mapping.

Repeat the same steps for specifying the mapping details for the `Department` entity. Once the mapping details for the `Department` entity have all been specified, here's how it would look in the **Mapping Details-Department** window:

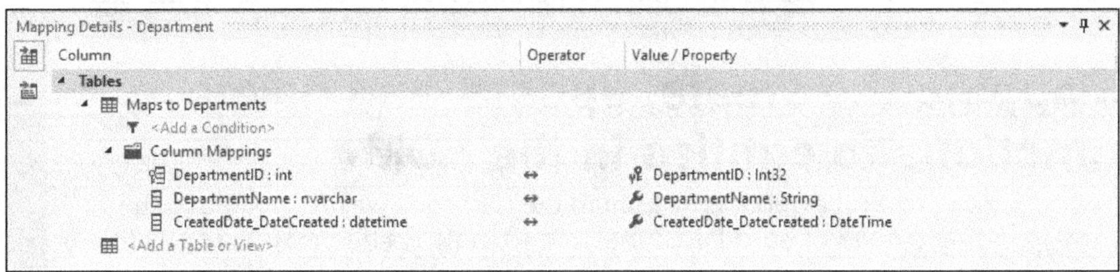

Mapping stored procedures with no entity set

In the earlier version of Entity Framework, the ADO.NET Entity Data Model code generator doesn't include code for functions that return scalar types. That is, the import functions that don't have any EntitySets. In essence, if your stored procedure returns a single value while not returning an entity or a collection of entities, you will not find code for the function in the generated code. The stored procedures that we used to map to the corresponding function imports don't have a return type.

You can easily map stored procedures that return an existing entity type or a collection of entity types. To map a stored procedure that doesn't return an entity type and enable the code generator to generate code for you, just create a dummy table in your database and an entity type from that table in the EDM Designer. You can now designate this entity type as the return type for the function imports in your EDM that doesn't return entity types. The other alternative is to use the entity client to invoke stored procedures and perform the CUD operations though the EDM.

Executing stored procedures using the EDM

Let's now discuss how we can use the entity client to insert the `Department` data. To do this, follow these simple steps:

1. Create an instance of the `EntityConnection` class as follows:

   ```
   EntityConnection conn = new EntityConnection
                           ("Name=PayrollContainer");
   ```

2. Open the connection by using the `EntityConnection` instance:

   ```
   conn.Open();
   ```

3. Create an `EntityCommand` instance and specify the `CommandText` and `CommandType` properties:

   ```
   EntityCommand cmd = conn.CreateCommand();
   cmd.CommandText = "PayrollEntities.Insert_Department";
   cmd.CommandType = CommandType.StoredProcedure;
   ```

4. Add parameters using the `AddWithValue` method of the `Parameters` collection of the `EntityCommand` instance:

   ```
   cmd.Parameters.AddWithValue
   ("DepartmentName", "Finance");
   ```

5. Next, execute the procedure by using the `ExecuteNonQuery` method:

   ```
   cmd.ExecuteNonQuery();
   ```

Here is the complete code listing:

```
using (EntityConnection conn = new EntityConnection("Name=
PayrollContainer "))
{
    try
    {
        conn.Open();
        EntityCommand cmd = conn.CreateCommand();
        cmd.CommandText = "PayrollEntities.Insert_Department";
        cmd.CommandType = CommandType.StoredProcedure;
        cmd.Parameters.AddWithValue
        ("DepartmentName", "Finance");
        ("CreatedDate_DateCreated", DateTime.Now);

        cmd.ExecuteNonQuery();
    }
    catch (Exception ex)
    {
         Response.Write(ex.ToString());
    }
}
```

Mapping stored procedures that return custom entity types

In this section, we will discuss how we can use the EDM to map stored procedures that return miscellaneous bits of data. Let's consider a scenario where we need to create an entity that returns the `EmployeeID`, `FirstName`, and `LastName` of all employees who are no longer working in the organization.

To do this, follow these steps:

1. Add a new field of the `DateTime` type called `LeavingDate` to the `Employee` table in the `Payroll` database.
2. Create a stored procedure called `OldEmployees`. Here is the script:

   ```
   Create procedure OldEmployees
   as
   Select EmployeeID, FirstName, LastName from Employee
 where LeavingDate is not null
   ```

3. Create an entity called `OldEmployees` in the EDM with the property names matching the corresponding field names of the stored procedure.
4. Create an EntityType called `OldEmployees` in the CSDL:

```
<EntityType Name="OldEmployees">
        <Key>
          <PropertyRef Name="EmployeeID" />
        </Key>
          <Property Name="EmployeeID" Type="Int32"
           Nullable="false" />
          <Property Name="FirstName" Type="Int32"
           Nullable="true" />
          <Property Name="LastName" Type="Int32"
           Nullable="true" />
</EntityType>
```

5. Create an EntitySet called `OldEmployeesSet` in the CSDL:

```
<EntitySet Name="OldEmployeesSet"
EntityType="PayrollModel. OldEmployees" />
```

6. Create an EntityType called `OldEmployees` in the SSDL:

```
<EntityType Name=" OldEmployees">
          <Key>
            <PropertyRef Name="EmployeeID" />
          </Key>
          <Property Name="EmployeeID" Type="int"
           Nullable="false" />
          <Property Name="FirstName" Type="varchar"
           Nullable="false" MaxLength="50" />
          <Property Name="LastName" Type="varchar"
           Nullable="false" MaxLength="50" />
</EntityType>
```

7. Create an EntitySet called `OldEmployeesSet` in the SSDL:

```
<EntitySet Name="OldEmployeesSet"
EntityType="PayrollModel.Store.
OldEmployees" Schema="dbo"/>
```

8. Create an import function in the CSDL:

```
<FunctionImport Name="GetOldEmployees"
EntitySet="OldEmployee"
ReturnType="Collection(Self.OldEmployees)" />
```

9. Now, specify the CSDL-MSL mappings in the Mapping Layer (MSL) to map the Entity in the Conceptual Layer (CSDL) to the entity in the Storage Layer (SSDL).

That's it. You are done!

Summary

In this chapter, you learned how to map stored procedures in the EDM and use them in your applications. We have also discussed how we can map stored procedures that return custom entities.

In the next chapter, we will discuss Entity SQL and Entity Client. We will also see how we can use them to perform CRUD operations against the EDM.

5
Working with Entity Client and Entity SQL

Entity Framework contains a powerful client-side query engine that allows you to execute queries against the conceptual model of data, irrespective of the underlying data store in use. This query engine works with a rich functional language called **Entity SQL** (or **E-SQL** for short), a derivative of **Transact SQL** (**T-SQL**), that enables you to query entities or a collection of entities.

In this chapter, we will take a look at both Entity Client and E-SQL and learn how to use them in our applications.

We will discuss the following areas:

- An overview of the E-SQL language
- Differences between E-SQL and T-SQL
- When to choose E-SQL over LINQ
- Working with the Entity Client
- Transaction management in Entity Framework
- Deferred loading and eager loading

Before we get started with Entity Client, we should have a proper understanding of E-SQL. This is a T-SQL-like query language used by the Entity Client provider. We will start this chapter with a discussion on the E-SQL language, and then discuss how we can work with the Entity Client provider.

An overview of the E-SQL language

Entity Framework allows you to write programs against the EDM and also add a level of abstraction on top of the relational model. This isolation of the logical view of data from the Object Model is accomplished by expressing queries in terms of abstractions using an enhanced query language called E-SQL. This language is specially designed to query data from the EDM. E-SQL was designed to address the need for a language that can query data from its conceptual view, rather than its logical view.

From T-SQL to E-SQL

SQL is the primary language that has been in use for years for querying databases. Remember, SQL is a standard and not owned by any particular database vendor. SQL-92 is a standard, and is the most popular SQL standard currently in use. This standard was released in 1992. The 92 in the name reflects this fact. Different database vendors implemented their own flavors of the SQL-92 standard.

The T-SQL language was designed by Microsoft as an SQL Server implementation of the SQL-92 standard. Similar to other SQL languages implemented by different database vendors, the E-SQL language is Entity Framework implementation of the SQL-92 standard that can be used to query data from the EDM.

E-SQL is a text-based, provider independent, query language used by Entity Framework to express queries in terms of EDM abstractions and to query data from the conceptual layer of the EDM.

One of the major differences between E-SQL and T-SQL is in nested queries. Note that you should always enclose your nested queries in E-SQL using parentheses as seen here:

```
SELECT d, (SELECT DEREF (e) FROM NAVIGATE (d,
PayrollEntities.FK_Employee_Department) AS e) AS Employees FROM
PayrollEntities.Department AS d;
```

The `Select VALUE...` statement is used to retrieve singleton values. It is also used to retrieve values that don't have any column names. However, the `Select ROW...` statement is used to select one or more rows. As an example, if you want a value as a collection from an entity without the column name, you can use the `VALUE` keyword in the `SELECT` statement as shown here:

```
SELECT VALUE emp.EmployeeName FROM PayrollEntities.Employee as emp
```

The preceding statement will return the employee names from the `Employee` entity as a collection of strings.

In T-SQL, you can have the `ORDER BY` clause at the end of the last query when using `UNION ALL`.

```
SELECT EmployeeID, EmployeeName
From Employee
UNION ALL
SELECT EmployeeID, Basic, Allowances
FROM Salary
ORDER BY EmployeeID
```

On the contrary, you do not have the `ORDER BY` clause in the `UNION ALL` operator in E-SQL.

Why E-SQL when I already have LINQ to Entities?

LINQ to Entities is a new version of LINQ, well suited for Entity Framework. But why do you need E-SQL when you already have LINQ to Entities available to you? LINQ to Entities queries are verified at the time of compilation. Therefore, it is not at all suited for building and executing dynamic queries. On the contrary, E-SQL queries are verified at runtime, so they can be used for building and executing dynamic queries.

You now have a new ADO.NET provider in E-SQL, which is a sophisticated query engine that can be used to query your data from the conceptual model. It should be noted, however, that both LINQ and E-SQL queries are converted into canonical command trees that are in turn translated into database-specific query statements based on the underlying database provider in use, as shown in the following diagram:

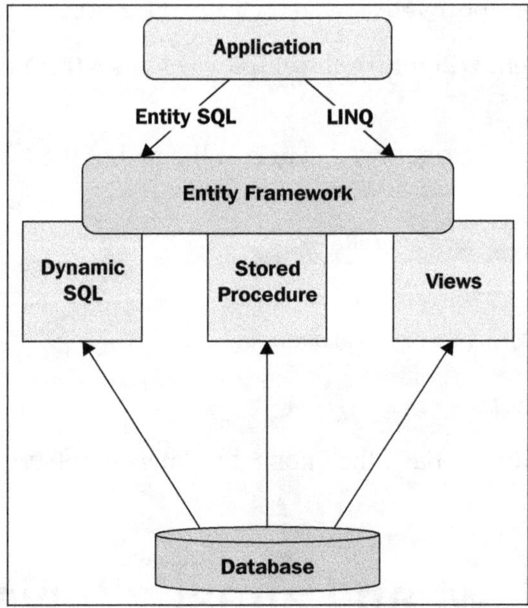

We will now take a quick look at the features of E-SQL before we delve deep into this language.

Features of E-SQL

These are the features of E-SQL:

- **Provider neutrality**: E-SQL is independent of the underlying ADO.NET data provider in use because it works on top of the conceptual model.
- **SQL like**: The syntax of E-SQL statements resemble T-SQL.
- **Expressive with support for entities and types**: You can write your E-SQL queries in terms of EDM abstractions.
- **Composable and orthogonal**: You can use a subquery wherever you have support for an expression of that type. The subqueries are all treated uniformly regardless of where they have been used.

In the sections that follow, we will take a look at the E-SQL language in depth. We will discuss the following points:

- Operators
- Expressions
- Identifiers
- Variables
- Parameters
- Canonical functions

Operators in E-SQL

An operator is one that operates on a particular operand to perform an operation. Operators in E-SQL can broadly be classified into the following categories:

- **Arithmetic operators**: These are used to perform arithmetic operations.
- **Comparison operators**: You can use these to compare the values of two operands.
- **Logical operators**: These are used to perform logical operations.
- **Reference operators**: These act as logical pointers to a particular entity belonging to a particular entity set.
- **Type operators**: These can operate on the type of an expression.
- **Case operators**: These operate on a set of Boolean expressions.
- **Set operators**: These operate on set operations.

Arithmetic operators

Here is an example of an arithmetic operator:

```
SELECT VALUE s FROM PayrollEntities.Salary AS s
    where s.Basic = 5000 + 1000
```

The following arithmetic operators are available in E-SQL:

- + (add)
- - (subtract)
- / (divide)
- % (modulo)
- * (multiply)

Comparison operators

Here is an example of a comparison operator:

```
SELECT VALUE e FROM PayrollEntities.Employee
    AS e where e.EmployeeID = 1
```

The following is a list of the comparison operators available in E-SQL:

- = (equals)
- != (not equal to)
- <> (not equal to)
- > (greater than)
- < (less than)
- >= (greater than or equal to)
- <= (less than or equal to)

Logical operators

Here is an example of using logical operators in E-SQL:

```
SELECT VALUE s FROM PayrollEntities.Salary
    AS s where s.Basic > 5000 && s.Allowances > 3000
```

This is a list of the logical operators available in E-SQL:

- && (And)
- ! (Not)
- || (Or)

Reference operators

The following is an example of how you can use a reference operator in E-SQL:

```
SELECT VALUE REF(e).FirstName FROM PayrollEntities.Employee
 as e
```

The following is a list of the reference operators available in E-SQL:

- Key
- Ref

- CreateRef
- DeRef

Type operators

Here is an example of a type operator that returns a collection of employees from a collection of persons:

```
SELECT VALUE e FROM
    OFTYPE(PayrollEntities.Person, PayrollEntities.Employee) AS e
```

The following is a list of the type operators available in E-SQL:

- OfType
- Cast
- Is [Not] Of
- Treat

Set operators

This is an example of how you can use a set operator in E-SQL:

```
(Select VALUE e from PayrollEntities.Employee
    as e where e.FirstName Like 'J%') Union All
    ( select VALUE s from PayrollEntities.Employee
    as s where s.DepartmentID = 1)
```

Here is a list of the set operators available in E-SQL:

- Set
- Union
- Element
- AnyElement
- Except
- [Not] Exists
- [Not] In
- Overlaps
- Intersect

Operator precedence

When you have multiple operators operating in a sequence, the order in which the operators will be executed will be determined by the operator precedence. The following table shows the operator, operator type, and their precedence levels in E-SQL language:

<table>
<tr><th>Operators</th><th>Operator type</th><th>Precedence level</th></tr>
<tr><td>. , [] ()</td><td>Primary</td><td>Level 1</td></tr>
<tr><td>! not</td><td>Unary</td><td>Level 2</td></tr>
<tr><td>* / %</td><td>Multiplicative</td><td>Level 3</td></tr>
<tr><td>+ and -</td><td>Additive</td><td>Level 4</td></tr>
<tr><td>< > <= >=</td><td>Relational</td><td>Level 5</td></tr>
<tr><td>= != <></td><td>Equality</td><td>Level 6</td></tr>
<tr><td>&&</td><td>Conditional And</td><td>Level 7</td></tr>
<tr><td>||</td><td>Conditional Or</td><td>Level 8</td></tr>
</table>

Expressions in E-SQL

Expressions are the building blocks of the E-SQL language. Here are some examples of how expressions are represented:

```
1;          //This represents one scalar item
{2};      //This represents a collection of one element
{3, 4, 5} //This represents a collection of multiple elements
```

Query expressions in E-SQL

Query expressions are used in conjunction with query operators to perform a certain operation and return a result set. Query expressions in E-SQL are actually a series of clauses that are represented using one or more of the following:

- `SELECT`: This clause is used to specify or limit the number of elements that are returned when a query is executed in E-SQL.
- `FROM`: This clause is used to specify the source or collection for retrieval of the elements in a query.
- `WHERE`: This clause is used to specify a particular expression.
- `HAVING`: This clause is used to specify a filter condition for retrieval of the result set.

- GROUP BY: This clause is used to group the elements returned by a query.
- ORDER BY: This clause is used to order the elements returned in either ascending or descending order.

Here is the complete syntax of query expressions in E-SQL:

```
SELECT VALUE [ ALL | DISTINCT ] FROM expression [ ,...n ] as C [
WHERE expression ]
[ GROUP BY expression [ ,...n ] ] [ HAVING search_condition ] [
ORDER BY expression]
```

And here is an example of a typical E-SQL query with all clause types being used:

```
SELECT emp.FirstName FROM PayrollEntities.Employee emp,
PayrollEntities.Department dept Group By dept.DepartmentName Where
emp.DepartmentID = dept.DepartmentID Having emp.EmployeeID > 5
```

Identifiers, variables, parameters, and types in E-SQL

Identifiers in E-SQL are of the following two types:

- Simple identifiers
- Quoted identifiers

Simple identifiers are a sequence of alphanumeric or underscore characters. Note that an identifier should always begin with an alphabetical character.

As an example, the following are valid identifiers:

```
a12_ab
M_09cd
W0001m
```

However, the following are invalid identifiers:

```
9abcd
_xyz
0_pqr
```

Quoted identifiers are those that are enclosed within square brackets ([]). Here are some examples of quoted identifiers:

```
SELECT emp.EmployeeName AS [Employee Name] FROM Employee as emp
SELECT dept.DepartmentName AS [Department Name] FROM Department as
 dept
```

Quoted identifiers cannot contain a new line, tab, backspace, or carriage return characters.

In E-SQL, a variable is a reference to a named expression. Note that the naming conventions for variables follow the same rules for an identifier. In other words, a valid variable reference to a named expression in E-SQL should be a valid identifier too. Here is an example:

```
SELECT emp FROM Employee as emp;
```

In the preceding example, `emp` is a variable reference. Types can be of three versions:

- Primitive types like integers and strings
- Nominal types such as entity types, entity sets, and relationships
- Transient types like rows, collections, and references

The E-SQL language supports the following type categories:

- Rows
- Collections
- References

Row

A row, which is also known as a tuple, has no identity or behavior and cannot be inherited.

The following statement returns one row that contains six elements:

```
ROW (1, 'Joydip');
```

Collections

Collections represent zero or more instances of other instances.

You can use `SET ()` to retrieve unique values from a collection of values. Here is an example:

```
SET({1,1,2,2,3,3,4,4,5,5,6,6})
```

The preceding example will return the unique values from the set. Specifically, `2`, `3`, `4`, `5`, and `6`.

This is equivalent to the following statement:

```
Select Value Distinct x from {1,1,2,2,3,3,4,4,5,5,6,6} As x;
```

You can create collections using `MULTISET ()` or even using `{}` as shown in the following examples:

```
MULTISET (1, 2, 3, 4, 5, 6)
```

The following represents the same as the preceding example:

```
{1, 2, 3, 4, 5, 6}
```

Here is how you can return a collection of 10 identical rows each with six elements in them:

```
SELECT ROW(1,'Joydip') from {1,2,3,4,5,6,7,8,9,10}
```

To return a collection of all rows from the employee set, you can use the following:

```
Select emp from PayrollEntities.Employee as emp;
```

Similarly, to select all rows from the department set, you use the following:

```
Select dept from PayrollEntities.Department as dept;
```

Reference

A reference denotes a logical pointer or reference, to a particular entity. In essence, it is a foreign key to a specific entity set.

Operators are used to perform operations on one or more operands. In E-SQL, the following operators are available to construct, deconstruct, and also navigate through references:

- `KEY`
- `REF`
- `CREATEREF`
- `DEREF`

To create a reference to an instance of `Employee`, you can use `REF()` as shown here:

```
SELECT REF (emp) FROM PayrollEntities.Employee as emp
```

Once you have created a reference to an entity using `REF()`, you can also dereference the entity using `DREF()` as shown:

```
DEREF (CREATEREF(PayrollEntities.Employee,
ROW(@EmployeeID)))
```

Canonical functions in E-SQL

E-SQL supports a wide variety of canonical functions. These can broadly be classified into the following categories:

- **Mathematical**: These are used to perform calculations based on some numeric values.
- **Aggregate**: These are used to perform calculations based on a set of input values.
- **String**: These are used to perform string operations.
- **Bitwise**: These are used to perform bitwise operations.
- **Date and Time**: These are used to perform operations on date and time values. For example, `SystemDateTime` values.

Mathematical functions

Here is a list of the mathematical canonical functions available in E-SQL:

- `Floor (value)`: Returns the largest integer that is not greater than the value passed to it as argument.
- `Abs (value)`: Returns the absolute value of the value passed to it as argument.
- `Ceiling (value)`: Returns the smallest integer that is not less than the value passed to it as argument.
- `Round (value)`: Returns a rounded integer value, rounded to the nearest integer, for the value passed to it as argument.

Aggregate functions

The following is a list of the aggregate canonical functions available in E-SQL:

- `Avg (expression)`: Returns the average of the values passed.
- `Max (expression)`: Returns the maximum value of the values passed to it as argument.
- `Min (expression)`: Returns the minimum value of the values passed.
- `Count (expression)`: Returns a count of the values passed.
- `Sum (expression)`: Returns the sum of the values passed as an expression.

The following statement makes use of aggregate canonical functions to return the minimum, average, and maximum of the basic salary for employees from the `Salary` table:

```
SELECT MIN(s.Basic), AVG(s.Basic), MAX(s.Basic) FROM
PayrollEntities.Salary as s
```

String functions

This is a list of the string canonical functions available:

- `Length (string)`: Returns the length of the string passed to it as an argument.
- `Concat (string1, string2)`: Appends the second string to the first, and returns a new string.
- `IndexOf (string1, string2)`: Returns the index or position of the first string in the second.
- `Left (string1, length)`: Returns the number of characters specified by length from the left of the string instance represented by `string1`.
- `Trim (string1)`: Trims the leading and trailing spaces from the string instance passed to it as argument.
- `LTrim (string1)`: Trims the leading spaces only from the string instance.
- `RTrim (string1)`: Trims the trailing spaces only from the string instance.
- `Substring (string1, start position, length)`: Returns a substring from the string instance beginning with the start position and represented by the number of characters specified by length.
- `Reverse (string1)`: Reverses the string instance passed to it as argument.
- `Replace (string1, string2, string3)`: Replaces all occurrences of `string2` with `string3` in the instance `string1`.

Bitwise functions

The following is a list of the bitwise canonical functions available in E-SQL:

- `BitwiseAnd (value1, value2)`: Performs a bitwise `And` operation between `value1` and `value2`.
- `BitwiseOr (value1, value2)`: Performs a bitwise `Or` operation between `value1` and `value2`.
- `BitwiseNot (value)`: Performs a bitwise `Not` operation with the value passed to it as argument.
- `BitwiseXor (value1, value2)`: Performs a bitwise `XOR` operation between `value1` and `value2`.

Date and time functions

Here is a list of the available date and time canonical functions:

- `GetDate()`: Gets the current system datetime value.
- `Second (datetime)`: Returns the second portion of the current system datetime value.
- `Minute (datetime)`: Returns the minute portion of the current system datetime value.
- `Hour (datetime)`: Returns the hour portion of the current system datetime value.
- `Day (datetime)`: Returns the day portion of the current system date.
- `Month (datetime)`: Returns the month portion of the current system date.
- `Year (datetime)`: Returns the year portion of the current system date.

Data paging using E-SQL

Data paging is a concept that allows you to retrieve a specified number of records and display them in the user interface. The data is displayed one page at a time. You can use data paging to split the data rendered to the user into multiple pages for faster page downloads, an increase to user interface flexibility, and minimal load on the database server. Paging can be used when the volume of data to be displayed is substantial and you need it to be divided into pages of data records to be displayed more efficiently.

The following statement will return a result set that contains the top 10 records of the `Employee` table, ordered by employee names:

```
SELECT emp FROM PayrollEntities.Employee AS emp ORDER BY
emp.EmployeeName LIMIT 10;
```

Suppose you need to display records 11 to 20 from the `Employee` table. Here is how you can do this:

```
SELECT emp FROM PayrollEntities.Employee AS emp ORDER BY
emp.EmployeeName SKIP 10 LIMIT 10;
```

How does it work? When you say `SKIP 10`, it will skip 10 records while the `LIMIT` clause limits the retrieval to 10 records only. Therefore, you end up with records 11 to 20 from the `Employee` table.

LINQ to SQL also has `SKIP` and `TAKE`. It is important to know that this is database paging where only the relevant rows are returned versus the default paging of standard ASP.NET data controls.

Working with the ADO.NET Entity Client

The ADO.NET Entity Client is a data provider that provides a gateway to execute entity level queries using Entity Framework. You can use it to query against your conceptual model of data. Entity Client uses its own language called E-SQL, a storage independent language, to communicate with the conceptual model. You can execute the same E-SQL query against any data store. In other words, it is provider independent, and you need not make changes to your query if the underlying data store changes. Therefore, you can use the same E-SQL syntax to communicate to the conceptual model, regardless of the data store in use.

The E-SQL queries are converted to a command tree that is in turn passed to the storage-specific provider to generate native SQL statements. As an example, if you are using SQL Server as the database, the E-SQL queries that you are using will be converted to a command tree that will be passed to the ADO.NET provider for the SQL Server. This allows the ADO.NET provider to generate statements specific to SQL Server database.

The diagram that follows illustrates how the Object Services, Entity Client, and the ADO.NET data providers are related:

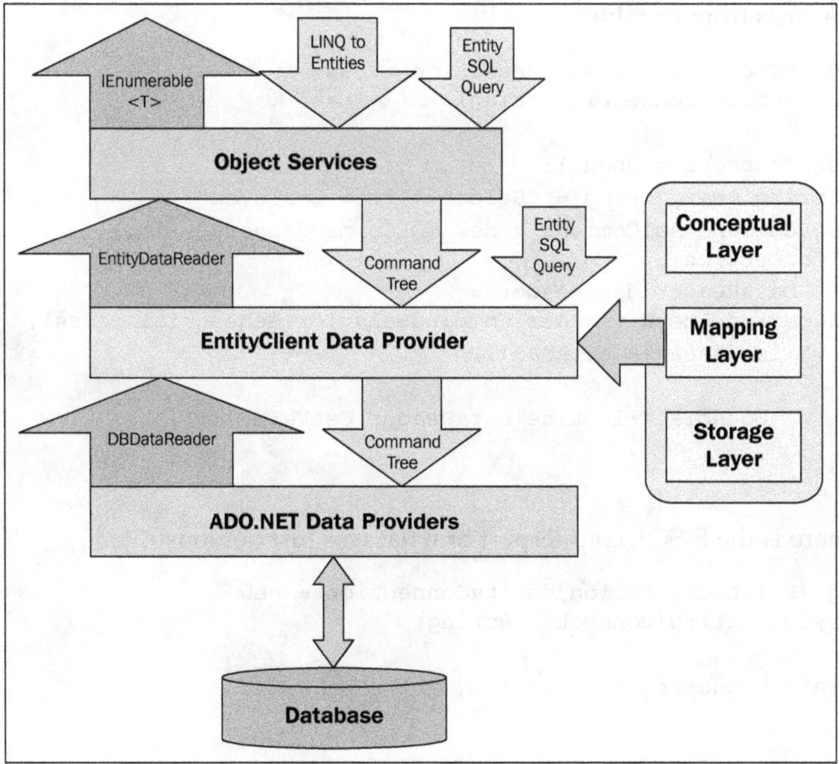

The EDM (we discussed this in *Chapter 1, Introducing the ADO.NET Entity Framework* earlier) is stored in either an `.edmx` file or using code-first approach. Prior to Entity Framework 7, there were two storage models—the EDMX file format based on XML schema or code. With Entity Framework 7, the EDMX file format would be dropped—we would have only the code-based format. Interestingly, this approach is also termed as the "Code First Only" approach.

Similar to the ADO.NET provider, the Entity Client provider follows the pattern of connection, command, or DataReader, and so forth. The class names are all prefixed with `Entity`. Therefore, you have classes, such as `EntityConnection` that represents a connection, `EntityCommand` that represents a command, `EntityDataReader` that represents a data reader, and so on.

In this section, we will take a look at how we can use the ADO.NET Entity Client to execute queries against the Entity Data Model. The `System.Data.EntityClient` namespace represents the ADO.NET Entity Client Provider. That is, a standard ADO.NET managed provider that we will use to access a database and execute queries or perform inserts, updates, and deletes. To illustrate the resemblance between Entity Client data provider and ADO.NET data provider, here are two samples:

First, this is how you use the ADO.NET data provider to connect to a database and display records from its table:

```
using (SQLConnection sqlConnection = new
SQLConnection(connectionString))
{
    sqlConnection.Open();
    String queryString = "Select * from Employee";
    SQLCommand sqlCommand = new SQLCommand(queryString,
  sqlConnection);
    SQLDataReader dataReader =
  sqlCommand.ExecuteReader(CommandBehavior.SequentialAccess);
     while (dataReader.Read())
      {
          Console.WriteLine(dataReader.GetValue(0));
      }
}
```

Second, here is the E-SQL counterpart of what was just demonstrated:

```
using (EntityConnection entityConnection = new
EntityConnection(connectionString))
{
    entityConnection.Open();
```

```
    String queryString = "Select value e from
  PayrollEntities.Employee as e";
    using (EntityCommand entityCommand = new
  EntityCommand(queryString, entityConnection))
    {
        using (DbDataReader dataReader =
  entityCommand.ExecuteReader(CommandBehavior.SequentialAccess))
         {
           while (dataReader.Read())
           {
               Console.WriteLine(dataReader.GetValue(0));
           }
         }
    }
}
```

Let's get into action

The following is a sequence of steps you can follow to work with the Entity Client:

1. Building a connection string.
2. Creating an entity connection.
3. Opening the connection.
4. Executing queries using entity command.
5. Closing the connection.

Building the connection string

You can use the `EntityConnectionStringBuilder` class to create your database connection string and use it to connect to the database. This section discusses how this is accomplished.

To build a connection to use with the Entity Client, follow these steps:

1. Create an instance of the `SqlConnectionStringBuilder` class and specify the data source, database name, database server to connect to the user ID and password:

   ```
   SqlConnectionStringBuildervar
   sqlConnectionStringBuilder =
   new SqlConnectionStringBuilder();
   sqlConnectionStringBuilder.DataSource = ".";
   sqlConnectionStringBuilder.InitialCatalog = "test";
   sqlConnectionStringBuilder.IntegratedSecurity = false;
   ```

```
sqlConnectionStringBuilder.UserID = "sa";
sqlConnectionStringBuilder.Password = "sa";
```

2. Now, create an instance of the `EntityConnectionStringBuilder` class and specify the metadata location, the provider name, and the provider connection string:

```
    EntityConnectionStringBuilder var
  entityConnectionStringBuilder =
    new EntityConnectionStringBuilder();
    entityConnectionStringBuilder.Metadata = ".";
    entityConnectionStringBuilder.Provider =
  "System.Data.SqlClient";
    entityConnectionStringBuilder.ProviderConnectionString
  = sqlConnectionStringBuilder.ToString();
    entityConnectionStringBuilder.Metadata = ".";
```

Creating an entity connection

Now that we have built our entity connection string, we will create an entity connection instance and open the connection.

You need to create the entity connection instance using the `EntityConnection` class and pass the connection string we just created to the constructor. This is how it is done:

```
EntityConnection var entityConnection =
    new
  EntityConnection(entityConnectionStringBuilder.ToString());
```

Opening the connection

To open the connection, you need to invoke the `Open` method on the entity connection instance as shown here:

```
entityConnection.Open();
```

Before we move ahead, we should test the connection to verify whether the connection was opened successfully. Here is how you can do this:

```
using (EntityConnection var entityConnection =
    new
  EntityConnection(entityConnectionStringBuilder.ToString()))
{
    entityConnection.Open();
    if(entityConnection.State == ConnectionState.Open)
    Console.WriteLine("Connection opened successfully.");
}
```

Note the use of the keyword `using`. When you execute the mentioned snippet, the message **Connection opened successfully** will be displayed. Once you have opened the connection, you can begin executing your queries using E-SQL.

Executing queries using the entity command

Let's use an example to help us understand how you can make use of E-SQL to leverage the power of EDM. Suppose you need to display the names and contact details of all the employees who are working in the HR department, this is how you can do it using T-SQL:

```
SELECT Employee.FirstName, Employee.LastName, Contact.Address,
Contact.PhoneNo FROM Employee, Contacts, Department
INNER JOIN
    Contacts ON Employee.ContactID = Contact.ContactID
INNER JOIN
    Department ON Employee.DepartmentID = Department.DepartmentID
WHERE Department.DepartmentName = "HR"
```

If you use E-SQL, the query can become much simpler:

```
SELECT FirstName, LastName, Address, PhoneNo FROM HREmployees
```

No joins! Yes, now you can do this without joins. You simply need to inherit a new entity called `HREmployees` from `Employee`, `Contacts`, and `Department` entities. Note that the fields `FirstName`, `LastName`, `Address`, and `PhoneNo` will be the properties of this new derived entity. We just changed from the database schema-specific T-SQL to a more abstract E-SQL that queries against a conceptual model of our data, rather than a logical model as in the former case.

What we require now is an entity command instance to execute the query. Here is how you can do this:

```
String sqlString = "SELECT FirstName, LastName, Address, PhoneNo
FROM HREmployees";
EntityCommand entityCommand = new EntityCommand (sqlString,
entityConnection);
```

So, what did we just do? We created an entity command instance and passed the query string and the entity connection instance to its constructor as parameters.

Now that our entity command instance is in place, we can execute the query as shown:

```
EntityDataReadervar entityDataReader = entityCommand.ExecuteReader
(CommandBehavior.SequentialAccess);
```

Refer to the preceding code snippet. We called the `ExecuteReader` method on the entity command instance to execute the query. This method will execute the query and return a result set as an entity data reader instance.

To iterate through the records, we need to call the `Read` method on the entity data reader instance as shown here:

```
while (reader.Read())
{

}
```

We will now iterate this instance and display the records as shown:

```
while (reader.Read())
 Console.Write(reader[0].ToString()+"\t"+
 reader[1].ToString());
```

Adding properties that do not have a corresponding database mapping

Note that you cannot add a property in the model unless it has a corresponding database mapping. You can, however, overcome this limitation using partial classes. Here is how you can add a new property called `PFACCNo` (that doesn't have a corresponding mapping in the database) in the `Employee` entity:

```
namespace Payroll
{
  public partial class Employee
  {
     public int PFACCNo
     {
       get;set;
     }
  }
}
```

Closing the connection

If you are done using the entity connection instance, you should close your connection by invoking the `Close` method on your entity connection instance. This is how you can do this:

```
entityConnection.Close();
```

You can also check whether the connection is open prior to closing using the `ConnectionState` enum as shown here:

```
if(entityConnection.State == ConnectionState.Open)
        entityConnection.Close();
```

And, this is the complete source code of what we just did:

```
SqlConnectionStringBuildervar sqlConnectionStringBuilder =  new
SqlConnectionStringBuilder();
sqlConnectionStringBuilder.DataSource = ".";
sqlConnectionStringBuilder.InitialCatalog = "test";
sqlConnectionStringBuilder.IntegratedSecurity = false;
sqlConnectionStringBuilder.UserID = "sa";
sqlConnectionStringBuilder.Password = "sa";

EntityConnectionStringBuildervar entityConnectionStringBuilder =
new EntityConnectionStringBuilder();
entityConnectionStringBuilder.Metadata = ".";
entityConnectionStringBuilder.Provider = "System.Data.SqlClient";
entityConnectionStringBuilder.ProviderConnectionString =
sqlConnectionStringBuilder.ToString();
entityConnectionStringBuilder.Metadata = ".";

using (EntityConnection var entityConnection =
    new EntityConnection(entityConnectionStringBuilder.ToString()))
{
   entityConnection.Open();
   String var sqlString = "SELECT FirstName, LastName, Address,
  PhoneNo FROM HREmployees";
   EntityCommand var entityCommand = new EntityCommand (sqlString,
  entityConnection);
   EntityDataReadervar entityDataReader =
  entityCommand.ExecuteReader
  (CommandBehavior.SequentialAccess);

   while (reader.Read())
    Response.Write(reader[0].ToString()+"\t"+
    reader[1].ToString());

    if(entityConnection.State == ConnectionState.Open)
        entityConnection.Close();
}
```

Other operations with E-SQL

In this section, we will take a look at how we can perform some additional operations with the E-SQL language. We will discuss the following:

- Inserting a record using E-SQL
- Inserting a record with a foreign key constraint
- Retrieving native SQL from `EntityCommand`
- Transaction management in E-SQL

Inserting a record using E-SQL

You can use E-SQL statements and easily perform CRUD operations. Let's assume that you have a stored procedure called `InsertDesignation` and you would like to use it to store a record in the designation table of your `Payroll` database. This is the code:

```
using (EntityConnection var conn = new
EntityConnection("Name=PayrollEntities"))
 {
 try
  {
    conn.Open();
    EntityCommandvar cmd = conn.CreateCommand();
    cmd.CommandText = "PayrollEntities.Employee_Insert";
    cmd.CommandType = CommandType.StoredProcedure;
    cmd.Parameters.AddWithValue("FirstName", "Joydip");
    cmd.Parameters.AddWithValue("LastName", "Kanjilal");
    cmd.Parameters.AddWithValue("Address", "Kolkata");
    cmd.Parameters.AddWithValue("Phone", "123456789");
    cmd.Parameters.AddWithValue("JoiningDate", DateTime.Now);
    cmd.Parameters.AddWithValue("LeavingDate", null);
    cmd.Parameters.AddWithValue("DepartmentID", 2);
    cmd.Parameters.AddWithValue("DesignationID", 1);
 cmd.ExecuteNonQuery();
  }
 catch (Exception ex)
  {
    Console.Write(ex.ToString());
  }
}
```

Inserting a record with a foreign key constraint

Here is an example that shows how you can insert a single row that has a foreign key constraint without doing an extra select:

```
Employeevar employee = new Employee();
employee.EmployeeID = 25;
employee.EmployeeName = "Rituraj";
employee.DepartmentMasterReference = new
System.Data.Objects.DataClasses.EntityReference<Department>();
employee.DepartmentMasterReference = new
EntityKey("PayrollEntities.Department", "DepartmentID", "3");
```

Retrieving native SQL from EntityCommand

You can retrieve native SQL from an `EntityCommand` instance using the `ToTraceString` method on the `EntityCommand` instance. Here is an example:

```
using (EntityConnection var entityConnection = new
EntityConnection
(ConnectionString))
{

Stringvar sqlString = "SELECT VALUE emp from
PayrollEntities.Employee as emp";

                EntityCommandvar entityCommand =
  entityConnection.CreateCommand();
                entityCommand.CommandText = sqlString;
                entityConnection.Open();

                // Displaying the Entity SQL text using the
  CommandText property

                Console.WriteLine(entityCommand.CommandText);

                // Display the T-SQL text using the
  ToTraceString() method.

                Console.WriteLine(entityCommand.ToTraceString());

    //Other code

    entityConnection.Close();

}
```

Transaction management in E-SQL

A transaction is a group of statements that are guaranteed to be executed in their entirety atomically. If any statements inside a transaction fail, the entire transaction is rolled back. In other words, any changes to the database are rolled back, if changes were indeed made. You can use transactions in two ways in Entity Framework. Namely, using either the `EntityTransaction` class or the `System.Transactions` namespace. `EntityTransaction` is an enhanced version of `System.Data.Common.DbTransaction` with better support for transaction commit and rollbacks. However, you can't create an instance of `EntityTransaction` as its constructor is internal.

This is an example of how you can use the `EntityTransaction` class for transaction management in Entity Framework:

```
using(EntityConnection var entityConnection = new EntityConnection
(connectionString))
{
  entityConnection.Open();
  EntityTransaction var entityTransaction = entityConnection.
  BeginTransaction(IsolationLevel.Snapshot);
  EntityCommandvar entityCommand1 =
  entityConnection.CreateCommand();
  entityCommand1.CommandText = "SELECT VALUE e FROM
  PayrollEntities.Employee AS e";
  entityCommand1.Transaction = entityTransaction;
  EntityDataReader var entityDataReader1 =
  entityCommand.ExecuteReader();
   while(entityDataReader1.Read())
   {

      //Some code
      EntityCommandvar entityCommand2 = con.CreateCommand();
      entityCommand2.CommandText =
              "SELECT Value s from PayrollEntities.Sales as s
               Where s.EmployeeID = @EmployeeID";
      entityCommand2.Transaction = entityTransaction;
      DbDataReader dataReader = entityCommand2.ExecuteReader();
      // Do some processing here
   }
  entityTransaction.Commit();
}
```

It should be noted that when you call the `BeginTransaction` method on the connection instance, it starts an explicit transaction on that instance. However, if you want to perform a number of operations on different databases within a single transaction, you can use a transaction scope. In other words, if you are using multiple connection instances belonging to different databases, then, using a transaction scope is a better choice.

You can start a transaction scope by creating an instance of the `TransactionScope` class as shown:

```
TransactionScope var transactionScope = new TransactionScope();
```

Here is an example that illustrates how you can use `TransactionScope` in your applications:

```
EntityConnection var entityConnection = new EntityConnection
(ConnectionString);
using (TransactionScope var transactionScope = new
TransactionScope())
   {
                using (PayrollEntitiesvar payrollEntities =
                new PayrollEntities(entityConnection))
                {
                    var query = payrollEntities.CreateQuery
                    <Employee>("Select value e from Employee
                     as e");
                    foreach (Employee emp in query)
                    {
                        Console.WriteLine(emp.FirstName);
                    }
                }
                using (PayrollEntitiesvar payrollEntities =
                new PayrollEntities(entityConnection))
                {
                    var query = payrollEntities.CreateQuery
                    <Department>("Select value d from
                    Department as d");
                    foreach (Department dept in query)
                    {
Console.WriteLine(dept.DepartmentName);
                    }
                }
                ts.Complete();
   }
```

Deferred, eager, and lazy loading

Eager loading refers to the process in which a query, when executed on a particular type of an entity, also loads the related entities at the same time. Lazy loading and eager loading are used for loading related entities that pertain to an entity. In the former case, the related entities are not loaded automatically along with its parent entity unless they are requested. In the latter case, the related entities are loaded automatically along with the parent entity.

To achieve eager loading in Entity Framework, you need to make use of the `Include` method.

Here is an example:

```
using (var context = new SecurityContext())
{
    // Load all user types and the related users
    var data = context.UserTypes
                            .Include(u => u.Users)
                            .ToList();
     // Load one user type and its related users
    var data = context.UserTypes
                          .Where(u => u.UserType == "ADUser")
                          .Include(b => b.Users)
                          .FirstOrDefault();
}
```

The following code snippet illustrates how eager loading can be achieved at multiple levels:

```
using (var context = new SecurityContext())
{
    // Load user types, all the related users and all related user
  login history
    var data = context.UserTypes
                         .Include(u => u.UserTypes.Select(x =>
  x.UserLoginHistory))
                         .ToList();
}
```

Lazy loading on the contrary is a process in which an entity or a collection of entities are loaded automatically only from the database the first time when a property of the entity or entities are accessed. Lazy loading enables an entity to be loaded late—it's loaded on demand actually. To achieve lazy loading of entities in Entity Framework, virtual properties in the POCO entity classes are used.

```
public class UserType
{
    public int UserTypeId { get; set; }
    public virtual ICollection<User> Users { get; set; }
}
```

To turn off lazy loading for entities, you can set the `LazyLoadingEnabled` property to `false` in your data context.

```
public class SecurityContext : DbContext
{
    public SecurityContext()
    {
        this.Configuration.LazyLoadingEnabled = false;
    }
}
```

Note that even if lazy loading is disabled in your data context, you can still explicitly lazy load entities. To do this, you will need to explicitly invoke the `Load` method on the entity. Here is an example code that illustrates this:

```
using (var context = new SecurityContext())
{
    var data = context.UserTypes.Find(2);

    // Load the user related to a given user type
    context.Entry(data).Reference(p => p.User).Load();

   // Load the user related to a given user type using a string
    context.Entry(data).Reference("User").Load();
}
```

Summary

In this chapter, we explored E-SQL and how it can be used with the Entity Client provider to perform CRUD operations in our applications. We discussed the differences between E-SQL and T-SQL and the differences between E-SQL and LINQ. We also discussed when one should choose E-SQL instead of LINQ to query data in applications.

In the next chapter, we will take a look at Object Services and discuss how they can be used to perform CRUD operations against the Entity Data Model.

6
Working with LINQ to Entities

Language Integrated Query (**LINQ**) is a query translation pipeline that has been introduced as part of the C# 3.0 language. It is an extension to the C# language and provides a simplified framework to access relational data in a strongly typed and object-oriented way. You can even use LINQ to query data from other data sources, such as XML, objects, and collections. Before LINQ, we used PL-SQL and T-SQL to query data from databases. However, none of them is type safe and does not have compile time checks to verify whether the statements are correct at compile time.

In this chapter, we will discuss **LINQ to Entities**. You will learn how to use LINQ on top of Entity Framework and how LINQ can be used to query data against the EDM. We will start our discussion with a quick look at what LINQ is and examine some of its features.

In this chapter, you will learn about the following:

- Introducing LINQ
- Benefits and features of LINQ
- Components of the LINQ architecture
- Understanding LINQ to Entities
- Operators in LINQ
- Expressions in LINQ
- Querying data from the `Security` database using LINQ to Entities

Introducing LINQ

LINQ is a query execution pipeline used in the managed environment of .NET Framework. In essence, LINQ is Microsoft's object relational mapper between your business objects and the underlying data sources, and provides a simplified framework for accessing relational data in an object-oriented fashion.

LINQ can be used to map your business objects and the underlying data sources. These data sources can be databases, objects, collections of objects, or even XML document files. Note that both C# (from version 3.0 on) and VB.NET (from version 9 on) have support for LINQ.

LINQ is a part of the new versions of the C# and VB.NET compilers, and it comes with a powerful set of operators to ease the task of querying different data sources, such as SQL Server, XML, and so on. LINQ comprises a standard set of operators to facilitate query operations. We will learn more about LINQ query operators later in this chapter.

Why LINQ?

We often require querying data and display them in the presentation layer of our applications. Before LINQ, we used PL-SQL and T-SQL queries to query data from data sources. The problem with such queries is that there are no compile-time checks. With LINQ, you now can do a compile-time check and use your type-safe queries to query data not only from databases, but also from XML data sources, objects, and collections of objects. Also, LINQ offers several additional methods, such as `Any`, `First`, and `Last` to name a few, which aren't available in traditional SQL (or need vendor-specific syntax). Now, why should I switch to LINQ? It should be noted that LINQ is very useful for querying local collections and XML DOMs. LINQ was introduced to help developers work with databases without needing to use T-SQL and SQL. LINQ was introduced as common query syntax to let it work with storage types, such as XML datasets, objects (collections and arrays), and SQL database tables.

The main problem LINQ solves is that it works to remove the impedance mismatch with the relational data store. Note that LINQ also offers several additional methods, such as `Any`, `First`, and `Last` to name a few, which aren't available in traditional SQL to facilitate querying data.

LINQ is a useful new feature available as a part of C# 3.0 and higher. It allows you to integrate queries directly into your programs. It is an extension to the C# language and provides a simplified framework for accessing relational data in a strongly typed and object-oriented manner.

Here is how you can search for an employee from our `Employee` table using LINQ:

```
var result =
    from emp in Employee
    where emp.FirstName == "Sabita"
    select c.EmployeeID;
```

The preceding query will return an array of the employee IDs for employees whose `FirstName` starts with `Sabita`.

Note that there are two different syntaxes of LINQ. One using query syntax and the other one using extension (or dot) syntax. Apart from being type safe and having the ability to check queries at compile time, you can easily debug your LINQ queries comfortably, which is a very important feature indeed.

Understanding the LINQ architecture

A query language is one that is used to query data in our applications. In LINQ, we have compile-time checks and type safety. Your queries will be verified for accuracy (if the database hasn't changed) during the compile time itself!

In this section, we will discuss the basic components of the architecture of LINQ. We will now familiarize ourselves with LINQ fundamentals, the components involved in its architecture, and so on. The following image illustrates the LINQ architecture:

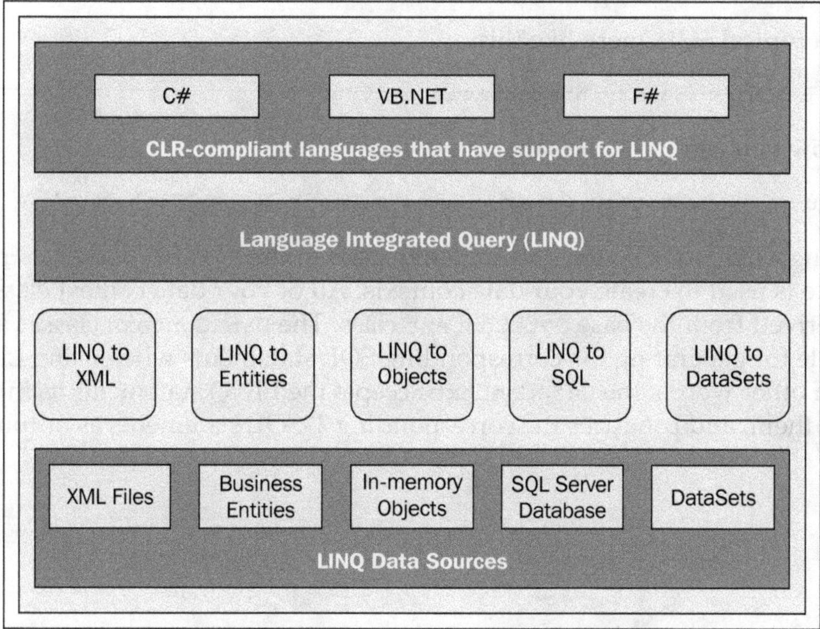

The following sections discuss the different flavors of LINQ in brief.

LINQ to XML

LINQ to XML maps your LINQ queries or LINQ statements to the corresponding XML data sources. It allows you to use the LINQ standard query operators to retrieve XML data. LINQ to XML is commonly known as **XLINQ**. You can also use LINQ to query your in-memory collections and business entities, objects that contain data related to a particular entity, seamlessly.

LINQ to SQL

Similar to XLINQ, you also have **Dynamic LINQ (DLINQ)**, which is an implementation of LINQ that allows you to query your databases. LINQ to SQL, or DLINQ as it is called, is actually a very simple basic ORM tool. It is not a complete ORM tool because it lacks some of the features that an ORM has. For example, it does not support state management and data generations.

DLINQ provides a runtime framework that translates LINQ queries into SQL. Once these SQL statement(s) are executed, the results are then translated back into the objects defined in the object model. This enables your application to manipulate these objects as needed. As you change the objects in-memory, DLINQ tracks these changes. This helps you to optionally submit these changes back to the database to perform CRUD operations.

Think of a typical SQL query like this:

```
SELECT * from Salary Where Basic > 5000
```

Here is how you can write the same query using LINQ:

```
var query = from s in Salary where s.Basic > 5000 select s;
```

When using LINQ to SQL, the `DataContext` class in the `System.Data.Linq` namespace is used to create your data contexts. All of your data context classes will be derived from the base `DataContext` class. The `DataContext` classes are responsible for generating the corresponding SQL statements when using LINQ to SQL. In other words, the `DataContext` accepts the LINQ statements as input, processes them, and produces the corresponding T-SQL statements as output.

The following code snippet illustrates how a new database can be created using the `DataContext` class:

```
static string GetConnectionString()
        {
            System.Data.SqlClient.
SqlConnectionStringBuilderSqlConnectionStringBu
ildervar builder =
                        new
  System.Data.SqlClient.SqlConnectionStringBuilder();
            builder["Data Source"] = "JoydipPC";
            builder["integrated Security"] = true;
            builder["Initial Catalog"] = "PacktDB";
            return builder.ConnectionString;
        }

static void Main(string[] args)
        {
            DataContextDataContextvar context = new
            DataContext(GetConnectionString());
            context.CreateDatabase();
        }
```

The `DataContext` class creates a connection to the database, converts objects to SQL statements, and performs CRUD operations against the database. To use LINQ in your programs, you must add a reference to `System.Core.dll` and specify the `System.Linq` namespace in the using statement.

LINQ to Objects

LINQ to Objects is another flavor of LINQ that is used to query in-memory objects or collections of objects. Note that LINQ to Objects works with `System.Collections.IEnumerable<T>` or `T:System.Collections.Generic` in-memory objects or collections of objects. Here is an example of a typical LINQ to Objects query that displays the numbers 1 to 9:

```
var myCollection = new[] { 1, 2, 3, 4, 5, 6, 7, 8, 9 };
var data = from d in myCollection
            select d;
foreach (var i in data)
{
Console.WriteLine(i);
      }
```

Let's look at another example that illustrates how you can use LINQ to query a collection of objects. Consider an `Employee` class with three properties as follows:

```
class Employee
    {
        public string FirstName { get; set; }
        public string LastName { get; set; }
        public string Address { get; set; }
    }
```

Now, you can use LINQ to Objects to query instances of `Employee` as follows:

```
var employees = new List<Employee> { new Employee
        { FirstName = "Joydip", LastName = "Kanjilal",Address
         = "Bangalore" },
        new Employee { FirstName = "Douglas", LastName =
        "Paterson",Address =  "Birmingham"},
        new Employee { FirstName = "Sabita", LastName =
        "Kanjilal", Address = "Kolkata" }
        };
        var query =
            from employee in employees
            orderby employee.FirstName
            select employee;
```

In the preceding code snippet, a list of employee objects is created, and then LINQ to Objects is used to iterate the collection.

LINQ to Entities

LINQ, as we already know, defines a set of operators, such as query operators and projection operations, that enables you to query data, traverse data, and express the query and projection operations declaratively in any programming language that targets the Microsoft .NET Framework.

LINQ to Entities enables you to query your business objects from within the language in a strongly typed manner. You can use it to query business objects or collections of business objects from the conceptual data model such as the EDM. LINQ to Entities uses Object Services to query data from the EDM. Object Services can be used to query data from almost any data store with less code. Apart from enabling you to perform CRUD operations, the Object Services Layer provides many additional services such as change tracking, lazy loading, and support for querying data using Entity SQL and LINQ to Entities. Note that the Object Services Layer internally uses an `ObjectQuery` object for query processing. We will take a detailed look at Object Services in the next chapter.

> Note that LINQ to Objects is a set of extension methods that work on `IEnumerable<T>` and can be used to execute queries on an arbitrary sequence of objects. In essence, LINQ to Objects refers to the usage of LINQ queries with any `IEnumerable` or an `IEnumerable` collection, but without the usage of any LINQ provider like LINQ to XML or LINQ to SQL. On the contrary, LINQ to Entities is a data provider in LINQ that contains a set of extension methods that work on `IQuerable<T>`. Note that because the `IQueryable<T>` interface extends `IEnumerable<T>`, anything that is possible with `IEnumerable<T>` is also possible with `IQueryable<T>`. The `IEnumerable<T>` interface has a method called `GetEnumerator()` that returns `Enumerator<T>`. You use LINQ to Entities to query data against the EDM.

Querying data using LINQ to Entities

Here is an example of a typical LINQ to Entities query that returns all department names from the `Department` table of the `Payroll` database:

```
PayrollModel.PayrollEntitiesvar ctx = new PayrollModel.
PayrollEntities();

        var query = from dept in ctx.Departments
                    select dept;

        foreach (var department in query)
            Console.WriteLine(department.DepartmentName);
```

LINQ to Entities and Entity Framework

Where does LINQ to Entities fit in exactly? You can use LINQ to Entities to query the EDM to retrieve entities or collections of entities. In essence, LINQ to Entities provides you strongly typed access to data that is exposed by the Entity Data Model. In other words, LINQ to Entities enables you to write your queries against a conceptual model of data. It also enables you to create and execute strongly typed and composable queries against the EDM to retrieve entities or collections of entities.

LINQ to Entities uses the Object Services infrastructure to query data from the conceptual model. The `ObjectContext` and `ObjectQuery` classes are two of the most important classes that you use when working with LINQ to Entities. The `ObjectContext` class is used to compose an `ObjectQuery` instance. The generic `ObjectQuery` class represents an entity or a collection of typed entity instances. It should be noted that LINQ to Entities queries are internally translated to canonical query trees. They are then converted internally to corresponding SQL queries in a form expected by your underlying database.

This is how LINQ to Entities and Entity Framework are related to each other:

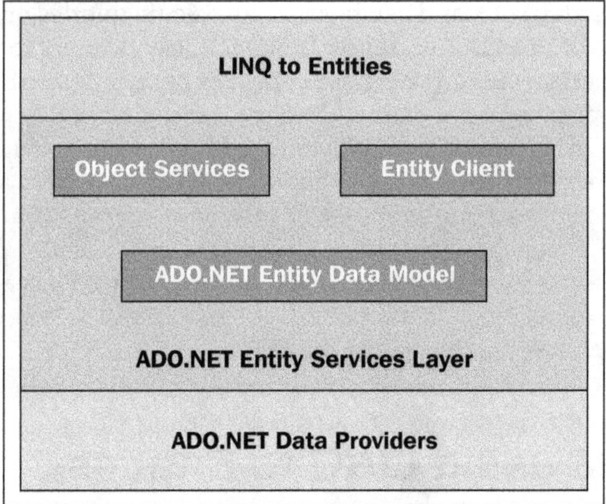

Differences between LINQ to Entities and LINQ to SQL

LINQ to Entities is a super set of LINQ to SQL. The primary use of LINQ to Entities is in defining a domain model for the application and using it for persisting data in the underlying data store that the application uses. LINQ to SQL, on the other hand, is ideal for two-tiered, three-tiered, or even n-tiered applications.

It should be noted that Microsoft initially had plans to provide support for multiple databases in LINQ to SQL. However, Microsoft has lost interest in the development of LINQ to SQL. Microsoft is more interested in the development of Entity Framework primarily because it has numerous powerful features such as entity splitting, support for table per class, and table per type inheritance models, and it can also support multiple databases.

Two of the major areas where LINQ to Entities is superior to LINQ to SQL are entity inheritance and entity composition. Using LINQ to Entities, you can create new entities by inheriting existing ones and even create entities that are composed of properties of one or more entities.

Both LINQ to SQL and LINQ to Entities support default inheritance models. That is, you can use both of them to inherit new entities from existing ones.

So, which one should you choose and when should you choose it? Generally, Entity Framework and LINQ to Entities is a good choice over LINQ to SQL (formerly, DLINQ), if you want your application's code to be loosely coupled and isolated from the changes that may occur in the relational or logical schema of data. It is also a good choice if you want to inherit or compose entities. These features are otherwise not provided by default with LINQ to SQL.

Parallel LINQ

Parallel LINQ is a concurrency execution engine from Microsoft that can be used to execute LINQ queries in parallel by leveraging the multicore processors. It is a part of the managed concurrency library called **Parallel Extensions Library**. The Parallel Extensions library is comprised of the following:

- **Task Parallel Library** (TPL)
- **Parallel LINQ** (PLINQ)

In their MSDN article, *Running Queries On Multi-Core Processors*, Joe Duffy and Ed Essey state:

> *"PLINQ is a query execution engine that accepts any LINQ-to-Objects or LINQ-to-XML query and automatically utilizes multiple processors or cores for execution when they are available."*

The reference is available at: `http://msdn.microsoft.com/en-us/magazine/cc163329.aspx`.

The following code snippet illustrates how PLINQ can be used:

```
Int32[] data = new Int32[100];
   for (intintvar index = 0; index < 100; data[index] =
   index + 1, index++);
   var result = from x in data.AsParallel() select x;
   result.ForAll(p => Console.WriteLine(p));
```

Operators in LINQ

Operators are those that operate on operands to perform a certain task. Powered by a rich set of query operators and expressions, you can use LINQ with absolutely any data, such as relational databases and XML files. Moreover, LINQ is type safe and extensible.

It's worth noting that in some LINQ implementations, not every operator will be available.

LINQ offers a collection of powerful operators that make the task of querying data much easier. We will explore how we can work with LINQ operators in the sections that follow.

Most standard query operators operate on a sequence where the latter is an object of type `IEnumerable<T>` or the `IQueryable<T>` interfaces. The standard query operators can be divided into two groups. One group works on objects of type `IEnumerable<T>`, and the other group works with objects of type `IQueryable<T>`.

Aggregation

You can use the aggregation operator `Sum` in a LINQ to Entities query as shown here:

```
using (PayrollEntitiesvarentities = new PayrollEntities())
        {
            var query = from s in entities.Salaries
                        where entities.Salaries.Sum(sal => s.Basic
                        + sal.Allowances) >= 15000
                        select s;
            foreach (var salary in query)
            {
                Console.Write(salary.Employee.EmployeeName);
            }
        }
```

The mentioned query returns the names of employees whose total salary exceeds `15000`.

Similarly, you can use the `Count` operator to display the total number of records retrieved from the mentioned query as shown in the following code snippet:

```
using (PayrollEntitiesvarentities = new PayrollEntities())
        {
            var query = (from s in entities.Salaries
                        where entities.Salaries.Sum(sal => s.Basic
                        + s.Allowances) >= 15000
                        select s).Count();

            Console.Write("Total no of records: " +
              query.ToString());
        }
```

Projections

The following query illustrates how you can create a projection of a new entity that contains the gross salary of employees, which includes the total of the allowances and basic:

```
using (PayrollEntitiesvarentities = new PayrollEntities())
        {
            var query = from s in entities.Salaries
                        where entities.Salary.Sum(sal => s.Basic +
s.Allowances) >= 150000
                        select new {Gross = s.Allowances + s.Basic};

            foreach (var v in query)
                Console.Write(v.Gross);
        }
```

Ordering

You can also order the result set in an ascending or descending order. Here is a code snippet that illustrates how you can do this:

```
using (PayrollEntitiesvar entities = new PayrollEntities())
        {
            var query = from s in entities.Salaries
                        where entities.Salaries.Sum(sal => s.Basic
                        + s.Allowances) >= 150000
                        select new { Gross = s.Allowances +
                        s.Basic };

            foreach (var v in query.OrderByDescending(x=>x.Gross))
                Response.Write("<BR>" + v.Gross);
        }
```

This is how you can use the `orderby` operator in your LINQ to Entities query to order the result set in ascending order of employee names:

```
using (PayrollEntitiesvar entities = new PayrollEntities())
        {
            ObjectQuery<Employee> employees = entities.Employees;
            IQueryable<Employee> sortedEmployees =
                from emp in employees
             orderby emp.EmployeeName
                select emp;
```

```
            foreach (var emp in sortedEmployees)
                Console.Write(emp.EmployeeName);

        }
```

Quantifiers

A quantifier operation returns a `Boolean` value indicative of whether or not one or more elements in a sequence satisfies a particular condition. Here is the list of the quantifier operations that can be performed by the standard query operators:

- `All`
- `Any`
- `Contains`

You can use any of the quantifiers such as `All`, `Any`, or `Contains` to search for a sequence. As an example, the following query returns true or false, depending on whether all employees who reside in Hyderabad joined the organization in January:

```
var query = (from emp in entities.Employees
    where emp.EmployeeAddress == "Hyderabad"
    select emp).All(e => e.JoiningDate.Month == 1);
```

Similarly, you can change the preceding query to return either a true or a false value, depending on whether any employee in the organization joined in January and resides in the UK:

```
var query = (from emp in entities.Employees
    where emp.EmployeeAddress == "UK"
    select emp).Any(e => e.JoiningDate.Month == 1);
```

Restriction

You can restrict the results of a LINQ to Entities query based on a certain condition. Doing this requires the `where` operator. Here is an example that illustrates how you can use the `where` operator to restrict the results in your result set to the condition that you have specified in your query:

```
var employees =
                from emp in entities.Employees
                where emp.EmployeeAddress == "UK"
                select emp;
```

When you execute this query, only the names of employees residing in the UK are listed.

Conversion

You can use the conversion operators, such as `ToList` or `ToArray` on your LINQ to Entities query, to convert the result set to a collection of `List` or `Array` type. Here is an example that illustrates how you can use the `ToList` operator:

```
var results = (from s in payrollEntities.Salaries
                  select s.Employee).ToList();

              foreach (var emp in results)
              {
Console.Write(emp.EmployeeName);
               }
```

Similarly, you can use the `ToArray` operator to covert the same result set to a collection of type `Array` as shown in the following code snippet:

```
using (PayrollEntitiesvar payrollEntities = new PayrollEntities())
        {
              ObjectQuery<Salary> salary = payrollEntities.Salaries;
              Array result = (from s in salary
                                  select s.Employee).ToArray();

              foreach (Employee emp in result)
                  Console.Write(emp.EmployeeName);
        }
```

Element

You can use the `First` or the `Last` operator to retrieve the first or last object in a sequence as follows:

```
using (PayrollEntitiesvarentities = new PayrollEntities())
        {
              var query = (from emp in entities.Employees
                               where emp.EmployeeAddress == "UK"
                               select emp).First();

              Console.Write(query.EmployeeName);
        }
```

Set

This is an example that uses the `Distinct` operator to display the employee names stored in the `Salary` table:

```
var results = (from s in payrollEntities.Salaries
            select s.Employee).Distinct();

            foreach (var emp in results)
             {                 Console.Write(emp.EmployeeName);
             }
```

Querying data using LINQ

Let's take a look at how we can use LINQ to query data in our applications. The following code snippet illustrates how you can use LINQ to display the contents of an array:

```
String[] employees = {"Joydip", "Douglas", "Jini", "Piku", "Amal",
                      "Rama", "Indronil"};
var employeeNames = from employee in employees select employee;
foreach (var empName in employeeNames)
    Response.Write(empName);
```

Now, let's discuss how to use LINQ to query a generic list. Consider the following `GenericEmployeeList` list:

```
public List<String> GenericEmployeeList = new List<String>()
{
  "Joydip", "Douglas", "Jini", "Piku",
  "Rama", "Amal", "Indronil"
};
```

You can use LINQ to query this list as shown in the following code snippet:

```
IEnumerable<String> employees = from emp in GenericEmployeeList
   select emp;
  foreach (string employee in employees)
  {
    Response.Write(employee);
  }
```

You can use conditions with your LINQ query as well. The following example shows how:

```
IEnumerable<String> employees = from emp in GenericEmployeeList
where
emp.Length > 4 select emp;
  foreach (var employee in employees)
  {
    Console.Write(employee);
  }
```

In this code snippet, we use LINQ to display the employee names more than four characters in length. The preceding query displays the following output:

```
Joydip
Douglas
Indronil
```

Here is another example of how you can use conditional queries with LINQ. To display the names of employees whose names start with the letter `"J"`, you can use the following:

```
IEnumerable<String> employees = from emp in GenericEmployeeList
where
    emp.StartsWith("J")
    select emp;
foreach (String employee in employees)
{
  Console.Write(employee);
}
```

This code snippet will result in the following employee names being displayed:

```
Joydip
Jini
```

As you can see from the preceding output, only those employees whose names start with the letter `"J"` are displayed.

Consider the `Employee` class as follows:

```
public class Employee
{
    public string EmpCode { get; set;}
    public string EmpName { get; set;}
    public string DeptCode { get; set;}
    public DateTime JoiningDate { get; set;}
    public decimal Salary { get; set;}
}
```

The following code snippet illustrates how you can use LINQ to DataSet to retrieve the details of specific employees from a `DataTable` instance, which contains a collection of employees:

```
DataTablevar empDataTable = new DataTable();
empDataTable.Columns.Add("EmpCode", typeof(String));
empDataTable.Columns.Add("EmpName", typeof(String));
empDataTable.Columns.Add("DeptCode", typeof(String));
empDataTable.Columns.Add("Salary", typeof(Decimal));
empDataTable.Rows.Add("E0001", "Joydip", "D0001",23000);
empDataTable.Rows.Add("E0002", "Douglas", "D0002", 45000);
empDataTable.Rows.Add("E0003", "Sabita", "D0001", 12000);
empDataTable.Rows.Add("E0004", "Piku", "D0003", 13000);
empDataTable.Rows.Add("E0005", "Rama", "D0003", 27500);
empDataTable.Rows.Add("E0006", "Amal", "D0002", 19500);

var empRecords = from row in empDataTable.AsEnumerable()
  where row.Field<decimal>("Salary") > 15000
       select row;

foreach (var emp in empRecords)
Console.Write(emp["EmpCode"].ToString() + "\t" +
emp["EmpName"].ToString() + "\t" + emp["Salary"].ToString());
```

We will now demonstrate how to use LINQ to query data from a generic list. This is the code that illustrates how to do this:

```
List<Employee>var empList = new List<Employee>()
{
         new Employee
         {
              EmpCode = "E0001", EmpName = "Joydip", DeptCode =
                        "D0001", Salary = 23000
         },
         new Employee
         {
             EmpCode = "E0002", EmpName = "Douglas", DeptCode =
                       "D0003", Salary = 45000
         },
         new Employee
         {
             EmpCode = "E0003", EmpName = "Sabita", DeptCode =
             "D0002",
                       Salary = 15000
         }
```

```
};

var empRecords = from row in empList.AsEnumerable()
  where row.Salary > 15000
       select row;

foreach (var emp in empRecords)
    Console.Write(emp.EmpCode.ToString() + "\t" +
      emp.EmpName.ToString() + "\t" + emp.Salary.ToString());
```

Required namespaces

You should include the `System.Linq` namespace if you want to use LINQ for SQL, LINQ to XML, or LINQ to Objects. For using lambda expressions, you should include the `System.Linq.Expressions` namespace.

Expressions in LINQ to Entities

An expression in LINQ is a piece of code that can be evaluated to one of the following:

- Single value
- Object
- Method

Expressions will contain one of the following:

- A literal
- An operator
- A method call

The results of LINQ to Entities queries are returned as one of the following:

- EDM compatible CLR types
- Collection of one or more entity instances
- `IQueryable` instances
- `IGrouping` instances
- Anonymous types

To use expressions in LINQ to Entities, you need to include the `System.Linq.Expressions` namespace in your programs.

This is an example that illustrates how an expression can be used:

```
IQueryable<string> employeeContact = from emp in employees
where emp.City = "Hyderabad" select emp.EmpName;
```

In the preceding example, the employee is an instance of the `Employee` class. It is a business object that relates to the entity called `Employee`. The mentioned query will return the names of all employees who live in Hyderabad.

Constant expressions

Constant expressions are used to evaluate constant values. These expressions are evaluated to constant command-tree expressions directly. Here is an example that illustrates how constant expressions are evaluated:

```
var salaryInfos =
                    from s in payrollContext.Salaries
                    where s.Basic >= (5000 + 1000)
                    select s.EmployeeID;

                foreach (var empID in salaryInfos)
                {
                    Console.WriteLine(empID);
    }
```

The preceding query lists the IDs of employees having `Basic` greater than or equal to `6000`. Note that the value `1000` in the mentioned query represents a constant.

Comparison expressions

A comparison expression is used to check whether a constant, a property, or a result from a method call is equal to, not equal to, greater than, or less than another value. Refer to the following code snippet that illustrates how such expressions can be used:

```
using (PayrollEntitiesvar payrollContext = new PayrollEntities())
          {
            var salaryInfos =
                   from s in payrollContext.Salaries
                   where s.Basic <= 15000
                   select s.EmployeeID;

                foreach (var empID in salaryInfos)
                {
```

```
                    Console.WriteLine(empID);
                }

            }
```

The mentioned query will list the employee IDs of employees whose `Basic` is less than or equal to `15000`.

The following code snippet illustrates how you can use comparison expressions to display the names of the employees who work in the `HR` department:

```
PayrollEntitiesvar payrollEntities = new
PayrollModel.PayrollEntities();
        var result = from emp in payrollEntities.Employee where
  emp.DepartmentMaster.DepartmentName == "HR" select emp;

        foreach (Employee e in result)
        {
            Concole.Write(e.EmployeeName);
        }
```

The following example shows how you can display the names of all employees who have joined the organization on or after a specified date:

```
using (PayrollEntities var payrollContext = new PayrollEntities())
            {

                DateTimevar joiningDate =
                 new DateTime(2004, 1, 1);
                 ObjectQuery<Employee> employee =
                 payrollEntities.Employee;
                 IQueryable<string> employeeInfo =
                     from emp in Employee
                     where emp.JoiningDate >= joiningDate
                     select emp.EmpName;

                 foreach (String empName in employeeInfo)
                 {
                     Console.WriteLine(empID);
                 }
            }
```

The preceding query will list the names of all employees who have joined the organization on or after January 1, 2004.

Initialization expressions

Initialization expressions are used to initialize a new instance. The following code snippet illustrates how you can use initialization expressions to compose and initialize a new instance:

```
using (PayrollEntities var payrollContext = new PayrollEntities())
    {

        DateTimevar joiningDate =
        new DateTime(2004, 1, 1);

        ObjectQuery<Employee> employee =
        payrollContext.Employee;

        var employeeInfo =
        from emp in Employees
        where emp.JoiningDate >= joiningDate
        select new {emp.EmpName, emp.JoiningDate};

        foreach (var e in employeeInfo)
        {
         Console.WriteLine("Name:
          "+e.EmpName+"\t"+"Joining Date:
           "+e.JoiningDate);
      }
    }
```

When you execute the preceding query, the names and joining dates of the employees who have joined the organization on or after January 1, 2004 will be listed.

> A query in LINQ is a generic query. Namely, it is of type `ObjectQuery<T>`, a class that implements the `IQueryable` and `IEnumerable<T>` interfaces. When the query is executed, that is, when you enumerate or iterate through the collection a generic `ObjectResult`, an object of type `ObjectResult<T>` is returned. Actually, `ObjectQuery` represents the query prior to its execution. `ObjectResult`, on the other hand, represents the same after the query has been executed.

Null comparisons

Consider a column called `Tax` in the `Employee` table. The value for this column will be `null` for employees having no tax or will display the taxable amount to be deducted otherwise. This is a T-SQL statement that illustrates how you perform null comparisons:

```
SELECT EmpName from Employee where Tax is null
```

The preceding query lists the names of all employees who don't fall into the tax bracket. In other words, their salary is not taxable.

The same can be done in LINQ as shown here:

```
var result = from emp in payrollContext.Employee where emp.Tax ==
null select emp.EmpName;
```

Navigation properties

Navigation properties enable you to navigate from one end of an entity to another. In essence, you can use them to locate entities at the end of an association.

Consider the following custom entity class called `EmployeeContact`:

```
public class EmployeeContact
{
    private String name;
    private String address;

    public string Name
    {

      get;set;
    }
    public string Address
    {
       get;set;
    }
}
```

We will now see how to use navigation properties to compose a collection of instances of this class using LINQ to Entities. Here is the code:

```
PayrollEntitiesvar payrollEntities = new
PayrollModel.PayrollEntities();
        IQueryable<EmployeeContact> query =
        payrollEntities.Employee
        .Where(emp => emp.JoiningDate >= new DateTime(2004,01,01))
        .Select(emp => new EmployeeContact { Name =
        emp.EmployeeName, Address = emp.EmployeeAddress });
```

Note that these extension methods are just a different syntax for the mentioned LINQ syntax. What did we do? We created an instance of our DbContext called `PayrollEntities`, and then we used a query to retrieve the names and addresses of those employees who have joined the organization on or after January 1, 2004. We composed instances of the `EmployeeContact` entity with the results retrieved.

We can also use the `Load` method to load-related entities.

Now that our `IQueryable` instance contains a collection of `EmployeeContact` instances, we can iterate through the collection of `EmployeeContact` instances and display the values as shown:

```
foreach (EmployeeContact empContact in query)
{
    Console.Write(empContact.Name+" "+empContact.Address);
}
```

Immediate and deferred query execution

Once a LINQ query is created and executed, it is converted into a command tree. This is a representation of the query that is compatible with Entity Framework. Note that the LINQ to Entities queries are executed at the time the results are iterated. Such an execution is also referred to as **deferred execution**. The query is executed each time you iterate over the query variable inside a loop. On the contrary, immediate execution occurs when the queries return a single value computed or otherwise. Examples of such queries are when `Min`, `Max`, `Count`, and `Average` are used to compute results. You can also force immediate execution of a query by invoking the `ToList` or `ToArray` methods on a query or query instance.

Here are two methods. The first illustrates deferred execution, and the second one illustrates immediate execution:

```
public static void DeferredExecution()
  {
     int[] intArray = new int[] { 1, 2, 3, 4, 5};
     int index = 0;
     var query = from i in intArray select ++index;
     Console.WriteLine("Illustrating Immediate
     Execution\n");
     foreach (var number in query)
        Console.WriteLine("The value of number is: {0}. The
        value of index is: {1}", number, index);
  }

public static void ImmediateExecution()
  {
     int[] intArray = new int[] { 1, 2, 3, 4, 5 };
     int index = 0;
     var query = (from i in intArray select
     ++index).ToList();

     Console.WriteLine("\n\nIllustrating Deferred
     Execution\n");

     foreach (var number in query)
       Console.WriteLine("The value of number is: {0}. The
       value of index is: {1}", number, index);
  }
```

The first example is actually deferred execution and the second is immediate. When you call `ToList()` on an `IQueryable`, it immediately executes it. The first example is deferred as it is not executed until the iteration starts in the loop. In the second example, by the time the for loop starts, the query is already executed. It is executed when you called `ToList()`.

The following code will invoke both these methods one by one as shown in the following code snippet:

```
ImmediateExecution();
DeferredExecution();
Console.WriteLine("\nPress any key...");
Console.Read();
```

When you execute the program, the output looks like the following screenshot:

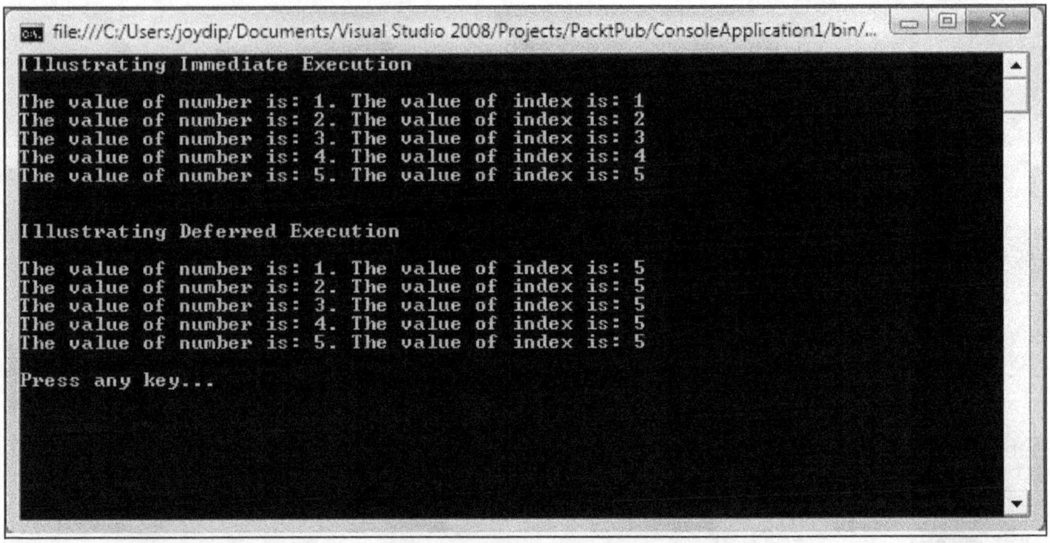

```
file:///C:/Users/joydip/Documents/Visual Studio 2008/Projects/PacktPub/ConsoleApplication1/bin/...
Illustrating Immediate Execution

The value of number is: 1. The value of index is: 1
The value of number is: 2. The value of index is: 2
The value of number is: 3. The value of index is: 3
The value of number is: 4. The value of index is: 4
The value of number is: 5. The value of index is: 5


Illustrating Deferred Execution

The value of number is: 1. The value of index is: 5
The value of number is: 2. The value of index is: 5
The value of number is: 3. The value of index is: 5
The value of number is: 4. The value of index is: 5
The value of number is: 5. The value of index is: 5

Press any key...
```

When calling without the `ToList()` elements of the resulting `IEnumerable` are evaluated on the fly, right inside the `foreach` loop, hence the execution is immediate. Therefore, the index will be incremented gradually during the `foreach` loop, as the elements are iterated. If, for example, you were to break out of that loop after the first element, the other four will not even be evaluated and the index will remain 1. When calling with `ToList()`, however, the `ToList` method forces the LINQ query to be executed first, before the `foreach` loop, caching the results in the returned list. Therefore, the index will be bumped up to `5` before the `foreach` loop. Then, when `foreach` is called, it will simply loop through the list, but the index is no longer touched. It is already `5`.

Retrieving entity data from the Security database

In this section, we will explore how we can retrieve entity data from the `Security` database using LINQ to Entities.

The following code snippet illustrates how you can query the list of user IDs from the database table `User` using LINQ to Entities:

```
using (SecurityDBEntitiesvar context = new SecurityDBEntities())
            {
                ObjectContext objectContext =
                ((IObjectContextAdapter)context).ObjectContext;
```

```
            ObjectSet<User> query =
            objectContext.CreateObjectSet<User>("Users");

            foreach (User result in query)
                Console.Write("User ID: "+result.UserID);

        }
```

Refer to the following code snippet. Note that the `ObjectSet` class implements the `IObjectSet` interface. Now, in order to convert `DbSet` to `ObjectContext`, we make use of the `IObjectConverterAdapter` interface and cast the `DbSet` instance to the `ObjectContext` instance called `objectContext`. Now, we can pass the `objectContext` instance as an `ObjectQuery` type and query data. It should be noted that the `ObjectContext` class contains a set of properties of type `ObjectQuery` that represent queries on specific entity sets.

The following code snippet shows how you can retrieve the `UserAuthenticationTypeID` value for the `UserAuthenticationType` windows:

```
using (SecurityDBEntitiesvar context = new SecurityDBEntities())
        {
            ObjectContext objectContext =
            ((IObjectContextAdapter)context).ObjectContext;
            ObjectSet<UserAuthenticationType> query =
            objectContext.CreateObjectSet
            <UserAuthenticationType>("User
            AuthenticationTypes");

            var data = from x in query where
            x.UserAuthenticationTypeDescription == "Windows"
            select x.UserAuthenticationTypeID;
        }
```

The `CreateObjectSet<T>` method returns `ObjectSet<T>` that contains a collection of generic objects, with the ability to manipulate the objects in this collection. The following code snippet illustrates how a generic repository class can be implemented that supports `.edmx` files as well as DbContext:

```
public abstract class GenericEntityFrameworkRepository<TClass>
   where TClass : class, new()
{
    private readonly ObjectSet<TClass> objectSet;

    protected GenericEntityFrameworkRepository(IObjectContextAdapter
    context)
    {
```

```
            objectSet = context.ObjectContext.CreateObjectSet<TClass>();

        }

        protected GenericEntityFrameworkRepository(ObjectContext context)
        {
            objectSet = context.CreateObjectSet<TClass>();
        }

        public ObjectSet<TClass> GetObjectSet()
        {
            return objectSet;
        }
    }
```

Summary

In this chapter, we discussed LINQ to Entities and learned how it can be used to query data against the EDM. We looked at the standard query operators and expressions in LINQ and how they can be used. We also discussed two of the most important features in LINQ, namely, immediate and deferred query execution and compiled queries.

In the next chapter, we will explore the Object Services layer in Entity Framework and discuss how it can be used in our applications. We will also see how we can use LINQ with Object Services to query data in our applications.

7
Working with the Object Services Layer

We explored multiple features of Entity Framework in the last few chapters. We had a look at the Object Service Layer and the consolidated programming model it presents in the form of strongly-typed objects. With this, you can represent entities as object instances of data classes mapping to the entity types in the model. The Object Service Layer can keep track of changes made to the objects in-memory and update the database accordingly. The results of the execution of a query in the EDM are available as objects—this enables you to have the option to choose either from EntityClient or Object Services in your application.

In this chapter, we will explore Object Services and how they can be used to perform CRUD operations against the Entity Data Model. Object Services provide services such as identity resolution, change tracking, object persistency, and also update processing. The Object Services Layer internally uses an `ObjectQuery` object for query processing. To use Object Services, you should include the `System.Data.Objects` and `System.Data.Objects.DataClasses` namespaces.

In this chapter, we will discuss the following:

- An introduction to Object Services
- Understanding the code-first, model-first, and database-first approaches to domain design
- Using Entity Framework 7
- Using Object Services to perform CRUD operations
- Handling data concurrency conflicts using `ObjectContext`
- Inheritance in the EDM
- State management, identity management, and relationship management

- Reading objects from the `Security` database
- Inserting objects into the `Security` database
- Editing objects in the `Security` database
- Deleting objects in the `Security` database

What are Object Services?

Object Services enables you to work with entities such as in-memory objects. In-memory objects are those that reside in the memory of your system—you can persist them to a persistent storage device if you need to. The Object Services Layer strives to eliminate the impedance mismatch that exists between the relational and the programming models. You can use Object Services for change tracking, data binding objects to data controls, inheritance, lazy loading, relationship navigation, and handling concurrency conflicts. Object Services support both LINQ and Entity SQL queries. The classes of the Object Services Layer are contained in the `System.Data.Objects` and `System.Data.Objects.DataClasses` namespaces. The `ObjectContext` class is the core of the Object Services Layer. The Object Services Layer processes the LINQ to Entities and `ObjectQuery` queries and then materializes the query results as objects. It also keeps track of the state information of the objects, the relationships between the objects, and the metadata using the `ObjectContext` class.

The Object Services Layer fits in between the Entity Client Provider and the Query layer.

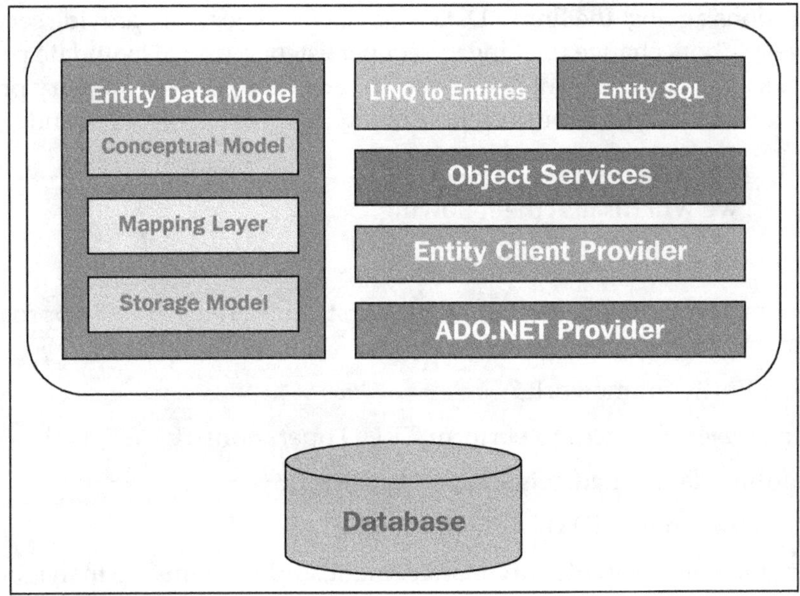

The ObjectContext class encapsulates the following:

- An EntityConnection instance
- A MetadataWorkspace instance
- An instance of ObjectStateManager

While the EntityConnection instance is responsible for connecting to the database, the instance of MetadataWorkspace contains the metadata information that describes the EDM. The ObjectContext class also encapsulates an ObjectStateManager instance that enables you to track an object's state while a CRUD operation is performed.

The ObjectContext class is the gateway to the EDM. You use it to connect to the model and perform CRUD operations. You can use it to read data using the CreateQuery method, add entities using the AddObject method, delete entities using the DeleteObject method, persist the changes to the database using the Save method, and attach or detach entities to and from the ObjectContext class using the Attach and Detach methods respectively. When objects are attached to the object context, their state is tracked and managed by the object context. On the contrary, objects that have been detached from the object context are no longer tracked by the object context and such objects can be cleaned up at runtime.

You use the SubmitChanges method of the data context to submit the changes to the entities in memory back to the database.

SubmitChanges works with LINQ to SQL and belongs to the DataContext class, while SaveChanges is used on EF and is a method of the ObjectContext class. The former starts a transaction and rolls back if an exception has occurred.

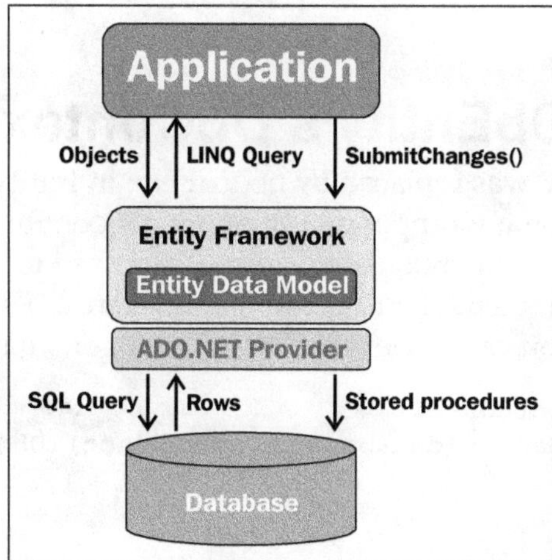

You should use the EntityClient when you would like to use dynamic queries or raw, unmapped SQL. This would provide you with a way to use the traditional ADO.NET style of interacting with your databases to perform CRUD operations. Use LINQ to Entities when you would like to use strongly-typed queries. You should use Object Services when you would like to explore the powerful features of the Object Services Layer. This might include tracking and identity resolution, efficient ways to managing transactions, object serialization, and queries that are not checked at compile time.

Features at a glance

Here are some of the striking features of Object Services at a quick glance:

- Querying data as objects
- Materializing objects and managing objects
- Support for change tracking and identity resolution
- Data merging
- Object serialization and data binding
- Transaction management
- Support for entity persistence
- Querying data with LINQ or Entity SQL
- Support for state management
- Support for entity inheritance
- Support for deferred execution
- Future queries

The SecurityDbEntity's DbContext class

Note that `ObjectContext` was replaced by `DbContext` in Entity Framework 4.1. `DbContext` is an adapter or a wrapper on top of `ObjectContext`. To retrieve the `ObjectContext` instance from `DbContext`, you would need to cast the `DbContext` instance to an `IObjectContextAdapter` interface reference. The following code snippet illustrates how you can retrieve the `ObjectContext` instance from `DbContext`:

```
ObjectContext objectContext =
((IObjectContextAdapter)databaseContextObject).ObjectContext;
```

The following code listing shows what the `SecurityDBEntiti` class's data context class looks like:

```
public partial class SecurityDBEntities : DbContext
    {
        public SecurityDBEntities()
            : base("name=SecurityDBEntities")
        {

        }

        protected override void OnModelCreating(DbModelBuilder
        modelBuilder)
        {
            throw new UnintentionalCodeFirstException();
        }

        public DbSet<Control> Controls { get; set; }

        public DbSet<ControlType> ControlTypes { get; set; }

        public DbSet<Role> Roles { get; set; }

        public DbSet<User> Users { get; set; }

        public DbSet<UserAuthentication> UserAuthentications
        { get; set; }

        public DbSet<UserAuthenticationType>
        UserAuthenticationTypes { get; set; }

        public DbSet<UserLoginHistory> UserLoginHistories
        { get; set; }

        public DbSet<UserRole> UserRoles { get; set; }
    }
```

`ObjectContext` is only needed if you would like to implement a model-first and database-first approach. On the contrary, if you are using Entity Framework 4.1 and above, you should use `DbContext`.

> Note that while the ADO.NET POCO Entity Generator is based on the `ObjectContext` class' API, the ADO.NET DbContext Generator is based on the `DbContext` class' API.

Querying data as in-memory objects

Object Services are used to work with your entities as in-memory objects, or a collection of in-memory objects. The Object Services Layer internally uses an `ObjectQuery` object for query processing and supports querying data using both Entity SQL and LINQ. The `ObjectQuery` class implements the `IQueryable<T>` and `IEnumerable<T>` generic interfaces.

Queries are created using the `ObjectQuery` class that internally contains a list of query builder methods. Upon execution, the `ObjectQuery` instance returns the result set in terms of an instance of `ObjectResult`.

Note that the query you executed using `ObjectQuery` is executed late. That is, it is executed only after you enumerate the `ObjectResult` instance. This deferred execution is a great feature of the Object Services Layer.

The basic reason for using Object Services is that you can program against objects, such as storing and retrieving objects or collections of objects, to and from any data store while writing much less code.

Using Entity Framework 7

Entity Framework 7 is more lightweight and better in performance compared to its earlier counterparts. With Entity Framework 7, all models will be represented through code—the EDMX approach will be removed and there is only a single code-based approach. This approach is also known as the *code-first only* approach. Code-based modeling is less repetitive and simple to use, test, manage, and maintain.

With Entity Framework 7, you have excellent support for no-SQL databases and in-memory data for unit testing.

The following code snippet illustrates how you can write a unit test method for when you are using Entity Framework 7:

```
[TestMethod]
public void AddEmployeeTest(Employee emp)
{
var options = new DbContextOptions()
.UseInMemoryStore();
using (var db = new PayrollContext(options))
{
```

```
//Code to add an employee instance to the data store
//Assert the results
}
}
```

Entity Framework 7 now supports the following providers:

- SQL Server
- SQLite
- Azure Table Storage
- Redis
- In-memory (for unit testing)

Performing CRUD operations on objects

In this section, we will discuss how you can use Object Services to add, modify, and delete an object within `ObjectContext`.

Adding an object to the `ObjectContext` class requires the use of the `AddObject` method. It accepts the entity set name and entity instance as parameters and adds the object passed to it to the `ObjectContext` class. Once you have added an object to the `ObjectContext` class, you can call `SaveChanges` to persist the changes to the database.

Here is an example that shows how you can add an object to the `ObjectContext` class and then call the `SaveChanges` method to persist the changes to the database:

```
SecurityDBEntities dbContext = new SecurityDBEntities();

            using (ObjectContext objectContext =
            ((IObjectContextAdapter)dbContext).ObjectContext)
            {
                UserLoginHistoryvar userLoginHistory = new
                UserLoginHistory();

                userLoginHistory.UserID = 1;
                userLoginHistory.UserLoginDate = DateTime.Now;

                objectContext.AddObject("UserLoginHistory",
                userLoginHistory);
                objectContext.SaveChanges();
            }
```

In the preceding code example, a new record is added in the `UserLoginHistory` table. Note that you need to call the `SaveChanges` method of the `ObjectContext` class to apply the changes.

Here is an example that shows how you can use `ObjectContext` and LINQ to update a record in the database:

```
using (ObjectContext ctx =
((IObjectContextAdapter)dbContext).ObjectContext)
            {
                var query = (from u in
                ctx.CreateQuery<UserLoginHistory>
                ("UserLoginHistory")
                             select u).Where(u => u.UserID == 8);
                foreach (var userLoginHistory in query)
                {
                    userLoginHistory.UserLoginDate = DateTime.Now;
                }
                ctx.SaveChanges();
            }
```

To delete the record you just inserted, use the `DeleteObject` method of the `ObjectContext` class as shown in the following code snippet:

```
using (ObjectContext ctx =
((IObjectContextAdapter)dbContext).ObjectContext)
            {
                var userLoginHistory = (from u in
                ctx.CreateQuery<UserLoginHistory>
                ("UserLoginHistory")
                             select u).Where(u => u.UserID ==
                             8).FirstOrDefault();

                ctx.DeleteObject(userLoginHistory);
                ctx.SaveChanges();
            }
```

Attaching and detaching objects to and from ObjectContext

You can use the `Attach` or `Detach` methods of the `ObjectContext` class to attach or detach objects. It should be noted that `Attach` will attach the entire object graph. The method cannot determine which objects are new and which already exist in `ObjectContext`. Note that when you execute a query on `ObjectContext`, the objects that are returned as a result of the query are attached in `ObjectContext`.

You can attach an object to `ObjectContext` by calling any of the following methods on `ObjectContext`:

- `Attach`
- `AddObject`
- `AttachTo`
- `ApplyPropertyChanges`

But what does `Attach` and `Detach` mean here? You use `Attach` to attach an object to the context. You should use `Attach` when the entity already exists in the database and you want the context to know about it without performing a query to locate the entity. When you attach an entity to `ObjectContext` using the `Attach` method, it sets `EntityState` of the object being attached to the `Unchanged` state. In other words, these objects switch to a unmodified state in `ObjectContext`.

On the contrary, if the entity in question is new and is not present in the context, and you also want to insert data into your database, then you should use `Add`. Here is how you can use the `Attach` method in the `ObjectContext` class to attach an object:

```
ctx.Attach(userLoginHistory);
```

Now, the `User` object and `UserLoginHistory` object have a relationship between them. If you were to attach the `User` object to the `UserLoginHistory` object, you would use the following code:

```
context.Attach(detachedUser);
detachedUser.UserLoginHistory.Add(userLoginHistory);
```

You can also use the `ObjectContext` class to attach objects, even objects that were detached from `ObjectContext` earlier. When you no longer need an object to be referenced in your `ObjectContext` class, you can detach it. Note that detached objects are de-referenced. In other words, they are not referenced by `ObjectContext` anymore. So, you can detach objects when they are no longer needed to facilitate garbage collection. You can detach objects from the `ObjectContext` class by calling the `Detach` method as shown:

```
ctx.Detach(ctx.UserLoginHistory.First());
```

You can also attach a detached instance. Here is how you can attach a detached user object:

```
context.Attach(detachedUser);
```

The `AttachTo` method is used to attach an object, or an object graph, into the object context in an unchanged state. You can use this method to attach entity objects, or graphs of entity objects, if the object being added is null, a single object, or an object that is a part of the object graph. Here is how this method can be used in code:

```
context.AttachTo("User",userObject);
```

When you execute a query inside an object context, the objects that are returned by the query are all attached to the object context in use.

Serializing and deserializing entity instances

Serialization is defined as the process of converting an object into a stream of bytes (as a memory stream) so that it can be persisted in the memory or to a permanent storage device such as a database or a file. You can serialize or deserialize an entity instance using `ObjectContext`. To do this, you need to call the `Serialize` or the `Deserialize` method of the `BinaryFormatter` class as shown in the following code snippets:

```
public static void Serialize(sString fileName, oObject obj)
  {
      BinaryFormatter var binaryFormatter = new
      BinaryFormatter();
      FileStreamvar fileStream = new
      FileStream(fileName,FileMode.Create);
         try
         {
             binaryFormatter.Serialize(fileStream, obj);
         }

         catch (SerializationException ex)
         {
             throw new ApplicationException("The object graph
             could not be serialized", ex);
         }
         finally
         {
             fileStream.Close();
         }
      }
```

The `Serialize` method just shown accepts a file name and the object to be serialized as parameters, then serializes it using a `BinaryFormatter` instance, and then stores the serialized instance of the file.

Here is the `DeSerialize` method that accepts the name of the file where the serialized instance is stored and returns the deserialized instance back:

```
public static Object DeSerialize(String fileName)
{
    BinaryFormatter var binaryFormatter = new
    BinaryFormatter();

    FileStreamvar fileStream = new FileStream(fileName,
    FileMode.Open);


    try
    {
        fileStream.Seek(0, SeekOrigin.Begin);
        return binaryFormatter.Deserialize(fileStream);
    }

    catch (SerializationException ex)
    {
        throw new ApplicationException("Serialization
        Exception: " + ex.Message);
    }

    finally
    {
        fileStream.Close();
    }
}
```

Let's assume that the serialize and deserialize methods have been moved to a `Utilities` class. The following code shows how you can use the `Serialize` and `DeSerialize` methods we defined earlier:

```
void Serialize()
    {
        SecurityDBEntitiesvar dbContext = new
        SecurityDBEntities();

        using (ObjectContext objectContext =
        ((IObjectContextAdapter)dbContext).ObjectContext)
```

```
            {
                UserLoginHistory userLoginHistory = null;
                ObjectQuery<UserLoginHistory> query = null;
                query =
                objectContext.CreateQuery<UserLoginHistory>
                (@"SELECT VALUE u
                FROM UserLoginHistory AS u");
                userLoginHistory = query.Where(ulh => ulh.UserID
                == 1).First();
                Utilities.Serialize("C:\\Test\\Test.txt",
                userLoginHistory);
            }
        }
```

Note that the `Utilities` class contains the `Serialize` and the `DeSerialize` methods defined earlier. The preceding code serializes the instance of the first `userLoginHistory` of the `UserLoginHistory` table and stores the serialized instance in the `Test.txt` file. Now, to deserialize the instance and get back the original instance, you need to call the `DeSerialize` method as shown:

```
void DeSerialize()
        {
            UserLoginHistory userLoginHistory =
            (UserLoginHistory)Utilities.DeSerialize
            ("C:\\Test\\Test.txt");
            Response.Write("User ID: " +
            userLoginHistory.UserID.ToString());
            Response.Write("<BR>User Login ID: " +
            userLoginHistory.UserLoginID.ToString());
            Response.Write("<BR>User Login Date: " +
            userLoginHistory.UserLoginDate.ToString());
        }
```

Change tracking and identity resolution using ObjectContext

Change tracking in Entity Framework is a feature that enables you to detect and resolve conflicts that arise out of concurrent data updates on a particular entity. Such scenarios are commonly known as **concurrency conflicts**.

Two modes used to handle data concurrencies in a multiuser environment are:

- Optimistic
- Pessimistic

In the optimistic mode, the record is read but not locked. You need to check whether a record to be saved has already been modified. In essence, you need to track the changes in the data before you perform any changes.

In the pessimistic mode, the record being modified is locked from other users until the lock on the record is released. Therefore, pessimistic concurrency is not a good choice, especially when you have a large number of users accessing the application at the same point in time. For further details, please refer to `http://www.asp.net/mvc/tutorials/getting-started-with-ef-using-mvc/handling-concurrency-with-the-entity-framework-in-an-asp-net-mvc-application`.

By default, Entity Framework follows the optimistic concurrency model. When the Object Services Layer saves the changes in an object to the database due to a call to its `SaveChanges` method, any checks for concurrency are bypassed. In other words, it does not check whether there are any concurrency conflicts in the database.

You can, however, set the `ConcurrencyMode` attribute of an entity property in the Conceptual Layer to enable the Object Services Layer to check for concurrency violations when it tries to save changes to the data back to the database. Here is how you can set the `ConcurrencyMode` attribute of an entity property:

```
<Property Name="FirstName" Type="String" Nullable="false"
MaxLength="50" Unicode="false"  ConcurrencyMode="Fixed"/>
```

> If the `ConcurrencyMode` attribute is set for an entity in the EDM, the Object Services Layer will always check for changes in the database before it saves the data in the database. When any conflict occurs, an `OptimisticConcurrencyException` exception will be thrown.

Understanding the code-first, model-first, and database-first approaches to domain design

There are three approaches to developing data-driven applications using Entity Framework. These are:

- **Code-first**: In this approach, you would create your POCO classes first and then generate the database using these POCO classes
- **Model-first**: In this approach, you would create your model first using the ADO.NET Entity Data Model Designer and then generate your database from this model

- **Database-first**: In this approach, you would create your database first and then generate your model using the ADO.NET Entity Data Model Designer from this database

Using the code-first approach

In this approach, you would create your POCO classes first and then generate the database using these classes. Let's create a POCO class as shown:

```
public class Customer
    {
        public int CustomerID { get; set; }
        public string FirstName { get; set; }
        public string LastName { get; set; }
    }
```

The context class should be derived from `DbContext` class as shown here:

```
public class CustomerContext : DbContext
    {
        public CustomerContext() : base()
        {

        }
        public DbSet<Customer> Customers { get; set; }
    }
```

To insert data using the context class you have just created, write this code:

```
using (CustomerContextvar ctx = new CustomerContext())
        {
            var customer = new Customer()
            { CustomerID = 1, FirstName = "Joydip", LastName
             = "Kanjilal"};
            ctx.Customers.Add(customer);
            ctx.SaveChanges();
        }
```

When executed, a new database would automatically be created with a `Customers` table inside it and the above record would be inserted into the database table.

To explicitly set a property to be a primary key of a particular entity, you can use the HasKey method as shown in the following code example:

```
ctx.Entity<Vehicle>().HasKey(t => t.VehicleId);
```

If you would like to define a composite key, here is how you would specify it using the HasKey method:

```
ctx.Entity<Department>().HasKey(t => new {
t.DepartmentID, t.Name });
```

Using the model-first approach

In the model-first approach, you would create entities, their relationships, and inheritance hierarchies using the EDM Designer and then generate the database based on the model created.

You would need to specify **Empty model** when prompted in the **Entity Data Model Wizard** dialog as you would be creating a model first, which would be used to generate the database:

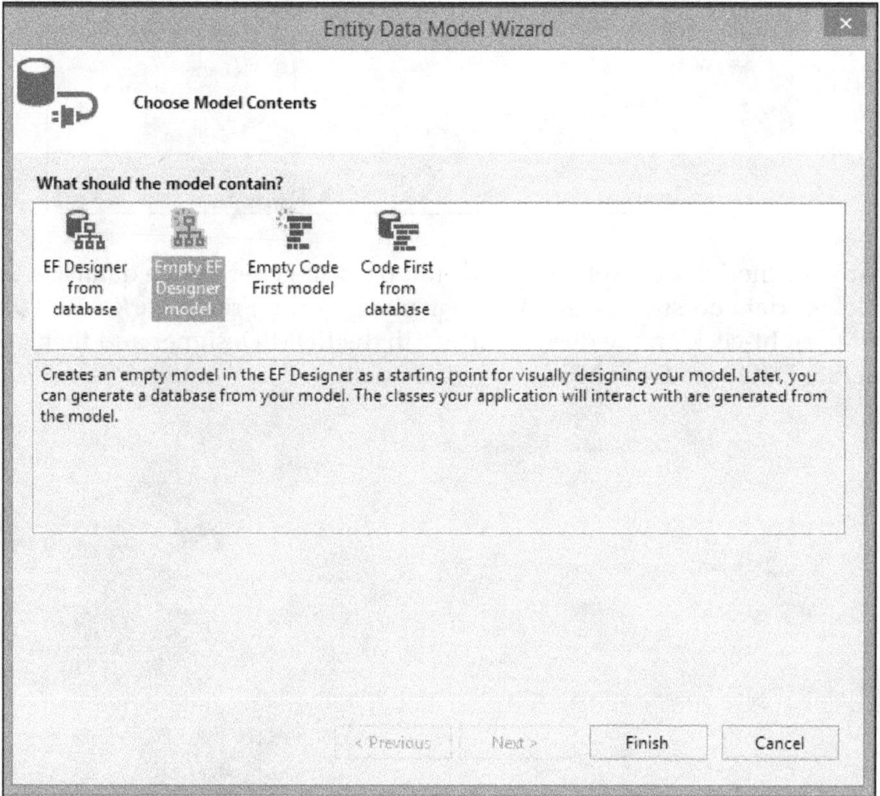

You would typically use the EDM Design to generate your object model. Here's how a typical model would look like in the designer view:

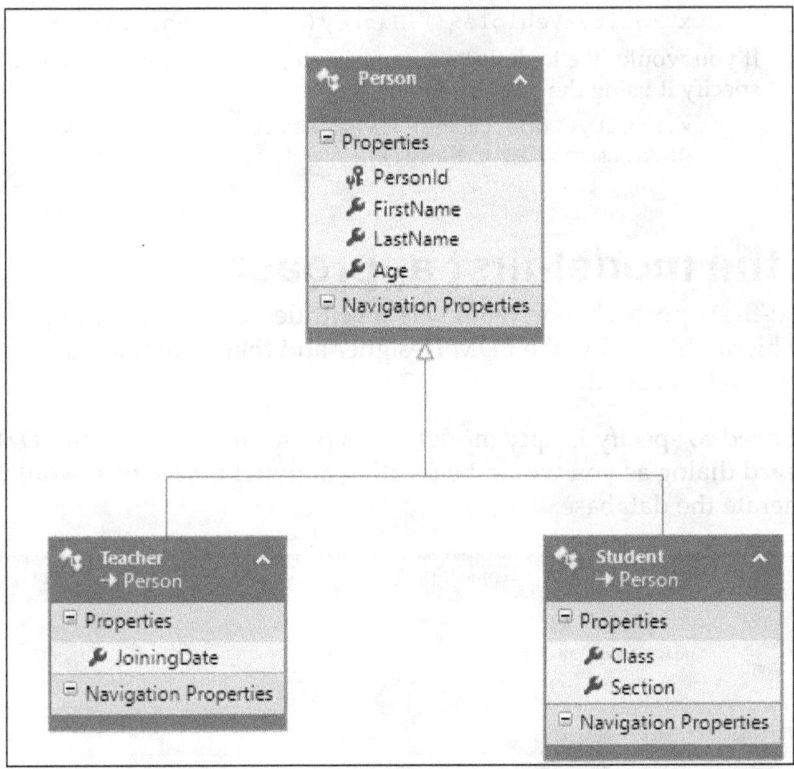

Now that your model is complete, you would need to generate the database using this model for data persistence and retrieval using Entity Framework API. To do this, you need to right-click on the design surface in the EDM Designer and then click on the **Generate Database from Model...** option as shown in the next screenshot:

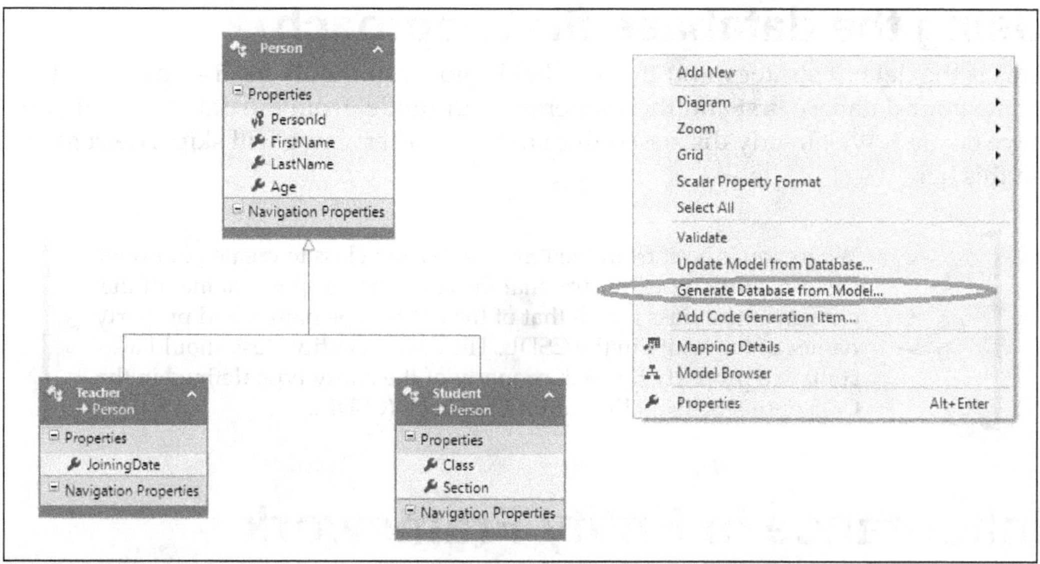

Since the database doesn't exist, you will be prompted to create a new one. Click **Yes** and the new database will be generated from your model:

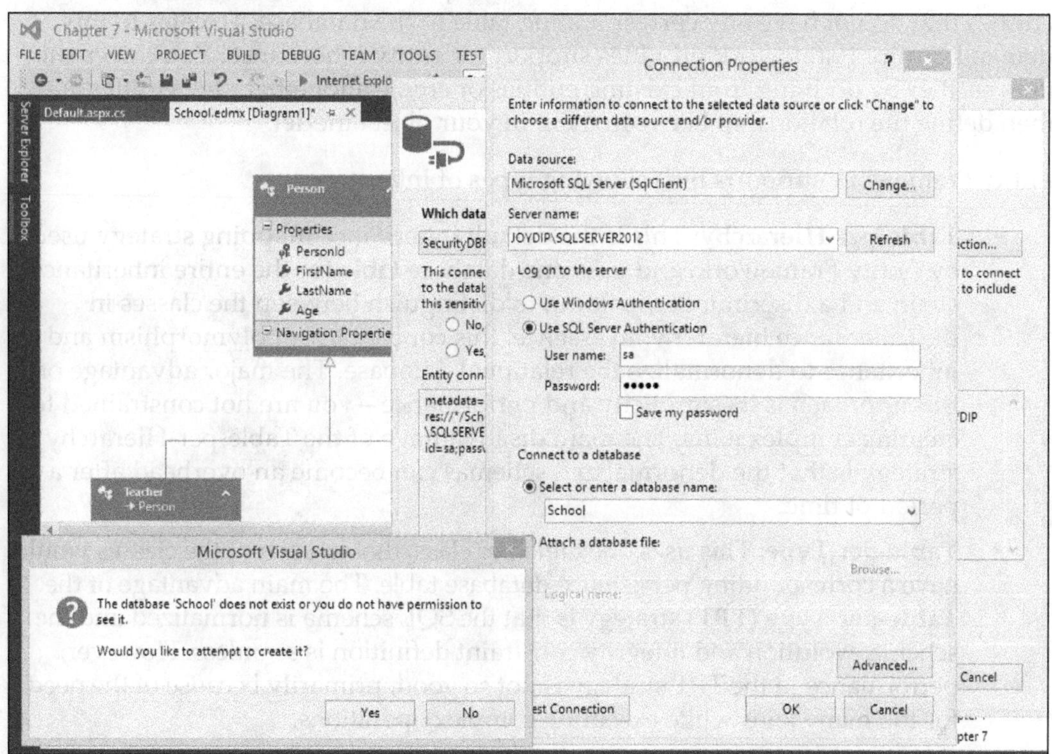

Using the database-first approach

This is the default strategy and the one that is most commonly used—you'll need to create your database first and then generate your model from the database that you have created. We already discussed this strategy earlier so we will skip a discussion on this here.

When you inherit from the `EntityObject` class to create your own custom entity types, ensure that the class and property names of the custom entity class match that of the entity type names and property names of the entity in the CSDL. The custom entity class should also contain a property for each property of the entity type defined in the Conceptual Schema Definition Language (CSDL).

Inheritance in Entity Framework

Inheritance is a property of object-oriented programming that enables you to extend new classes from existing ones and provide additional functionality to them. There are scenarios when the number of entities in the database does not match exactly with the number of the entities we need in the object model. We may need some entities that do not have any corresponding table in the database. To cater to this demand, Entity Framework provides support for entity inheritance. You can create new entities by deriving from existing entities or create altogether new entities and then define the relationship between them in your object model.

Entity Framework supports the following types of inheritance:

- **Table-per-Hierarchy**: This is the default inheritance mapping strategy used by Entity Framework, and uses one database table for the entire inheritance chain and a discriminator column to distinguish between the classes in the inheritance hierarchy. In essence, this concept uses polymorphism and inheritance to denormalize the relational database. The major advantage of this approach is its simplicity and performance—you are not constrained to creating complex joins. The main disadvantage of the Table-per-Hierarchy strategy is that the denormalized schemas can become an overhead after a period of time.
- **Table-per-Type**: This uses one table per class, that is, each of the classes would have a corresponding persistence database table. The main advantage of the **Table-per-Type (TPT)** strategy is that the SQL schema is normalized and the schema evolution and integrity constraint definition is seamless. However, performance in the TPT strategy is not so good, primarily because of the need for too many joins while executing complex operations.

- **Table-per-Concrete Type**: This uses one table for each non-abstract or concrete class, but not for the abstract class. You can use **Table-per-Concrete Type** (**TPC**) if polymorphic associations are not needed. If changes to the base class in the hierarchy are unlikely, TPC is a good choice.

Table-per-Hierarchy

To implement **Table per Hierarchy** (**TPH**), or Single Table Inheritance, simply inherit a new class from your existing entity class and add the properties you need. In this example, we will use the code-first approach.

We will first implement the object model with the code-first approach. Here are the POCO classes in our model:

```
public abstract class Vehicle
    {
        public int VehicleId { get; set; }
        public string Model { get; set; }
        public DateTime Year { get; set; }
    }
    public class Car : Vehicle
    {
        public Int32 ushort Wheels { get; set; }
        public string Color { get; set; }
    }
    public class Bike : Vehicle
    {
        public Int32 ushort Wheels { get; set; }
        public string Color { get; set; }
    }
```

The `VehicleContext` class given next is our data context that extends the `DbContext` class and contains the `Vehicles` property:

```
public class VehicleContext : DbContext
    {
        public DbSet<Vehicle> Vehicles { get; set; }
    }
```

You can now use the following code to add a new car:

```
using (var ctx = new VehicleContext())
            {
                Carvar car = new Car() {  Color="Red", Model =
                "Indica", VehicleId = 759, Wheels = 4, Year = 2004
```

```
            };
            ctx.Vehicles.Add(car);
            ctx.SaveChanges();
        }
```

To add a new bike, you can use the following code:

```
using (VehicleContextvar ctx = new VehicleContext())
        {
            var bike = new Bike() { Color = "Red", Model =
            "Indica", VehicleId = 759, Wheels = 2, Year = 2004
             };
            ctx.Vehicles.Add(bike);
            ctx.SaveChanges();
        }
```

Table-per-Type

In this kind of inheritance, every type or entity is represented as a table in the database. So, all types are mapped to individual tables. The derived type has an associated `BaseType` class from which it is derived. It is not, however, associated to any EntitySet in the EDM. In other words, in the TPT inheritance model, you define inheritance relationships in the EDM and store the data pertaining to each of these entities using their corresponding tables in the database. Let's implement TPT inheritance using the code-first approach.

If we follow the code-first strategy, Entity Framework would first create a table for the base type and then create individual tables for each of the sub types in the hierarchy. We would need to override the `OnModelCreating` method of `DbContext` and write the following code:

```
protected override void OnModelCreating(DbModelBuilder
modelBuilder)
        {
            modelBuilder.Entity<Car>().ToTable("Cars");
            modelBuilder.Entity<Bike>().ToTable("Bikes");
            base.OnModelCreating(modelBuilder);
        }
```

Table-per-Concrete Type

In the TPC inheritance model, each table in our database represents the entity in its entirety. In essence, the individual tables contain the complete information of the entity. In TPC, we use one table for each non-abstract class.

The following `VehicleMappingContext` class can be used to map the `Car` and `Bike` classes to the `Vehicle` abstract class and perform CRUD operations:

```
public class VehicleMappingContext : DbContext
    {
        public DbSet<Vehicle> Vehicles { get; set; }

        protected override void OnModelCreating(DbModelBuilder
        modelBuilder)
        {
            modelBuilder.Entity<Car>().Map(m =>
            {
                m.MapInheritedProperties();
                m.ToTable("Cars");
            });

            modelBuilder.Entity<Bike>().Map(m =>
            {
                m.MapInheritedProperties();
                m.ToTable("Bikes");
            });
        }
    }
```

The `EntityMappingConfiguration` class is used for inheritance mapping when using the code-first strategy. Here is what the class looks like:

```
namespace
System.Data.Entity.ModelConfiguration.Configuration.
Mapping
{
    public class EntityMappingConfiguration<TEntityType>
  where TEntityType : class
    {
        public ValueConditionConfiguration
        Requires(string discriminator);
        public void ToTable(string tableName);
        public void MapInheritedProperties();
    }
}
```

Implementing complex types in the EDM

A complex type can contain zero or more properties. To create a complex type, right-click on the design view mode of your EDM and create a new entity. Then, specify the properties you require. Here is how the complex type **Address** looks in the designer view:

And here is how the complex type `Address` is represented in the EDM:

```
<ComplexType Name="Address">
  <Property Name="Street" Type="String" />
  <Property Name="City" Type="String" />
  <Property Name="PinCode" Type="String" />
  <Property Name="Country" Type="String" />
  <Property Name="Phone" Type="String" />
</ComplexType>
```

An entity, such as `Employee`, can then refer to this complex type in our EDM as shown:

```
<EntityType Name="Employee">
          <Key>
            <PropertyRef Name="EmployeeID" />
          </Key>
          <Property Name="EmployeeID" Type="Int32"
           Nullable="false" />
          <Property Name="FirstName" Type="String"
           Nullable="false" MaxLength="50" Unicode="false" />
          <Property Name="LastName" Type="String" Nullable="false"
           MaxLength="50" Unicode="false" />
```

```
            <Property Name="Address" Type="PayrollModel.Address"
             Nullable="false" MaxLength="50" Unicode="false" />
            <Property Name="Phone" Type="String" Nullable="false"
             MaxLength="50" Unicode="false" />
            <Property Name="JoiningDate" Type="DateTime"
             Nullable="false" />
            <Property Name="LeavingDate" Type="DateTime" />
</EntityType>
```

> To implement an abstract entity in the EDM, we need to create an entity type in our EDM and set its `Abstract` flag to `true`. Then, the code generator will automatically generate an abstract class that corresponds to this abstract type. Although the designer view requires that an abstract type should be mapped to a table, there is no such restriction imposed by the runtime, provided you are working with the generated CSDL, Mapping Specification Language (MSL), and Store Schema Definition Language (SSDL) files.

State management, identity management, and relationship management

Change tracking or tracking the modifications to objects in Entity Framework is handled by a component called `ObjectStateManager`. The context delegates change tracking management calls to this component at runtime. The state manager is responsible for adding, deleting, and attaching entities to and from the context. It also holds the in-memory collection of objects, does the necessary identity checks, and keeps track of relationships of entities. Note that `ObjectStateManager` is exposed as a property called `ObjectStateManager` of `ObjectContext`.

Here's how the `ObjectStateManager` instance of the `SecurityDBEntities` class can be accessed:

```
using (SecurityDBEntitiesvar ctx = new SecurityDBEntities())
    {
         var objStateManager = ctx.ObjectStateManager;
    }
```

In relational databases, relationships, or associations between the database tables are defined through the use of foreign keys. A foreign key is just another column in a database table that is a primary key in another database table. Refer to the image:

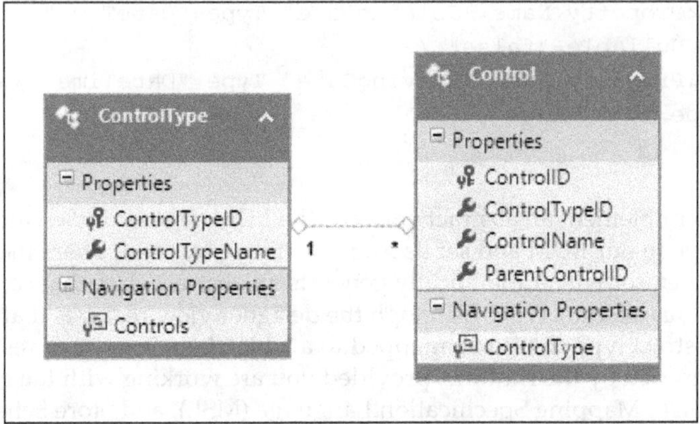

Entity Framework defines relationships among entities using associations. These relationships are defined in the CSDL using an association element. These associations have two ends—one that describes the entity type and the other that defines the multiplicity of the type, that is, one-to-one, one-to-many, and so on. Note that these relationships are governed by the referential integrity constraints as defined in the database tables from which the EDM has been created in the designer. The following code snippet shows the CSDL schema of the `Security` database and how the associations have been defined there:

```
<Association Name="FK_Control_ControlType">
   <End Role="ControlType" Type="Self.ControlType"
    Multiplicity="1" />
   <End Role="Control" Type="Self.Control" Multiplicity="*"
    />
   <ReferentialConstraint>
     <Principal Role="ControlType">
       <PropertyRef Name="ControlTypeID" />
     </Principal>
     <Dependent Role="Control">
       <PropertyRef Name="ControlTypeID" />
     </Dependent>
   </ReferentialConstraint>
 </Association>
 <Association Name="FK_UserRole_Role">
   <End Role="Role" Type="Self.Role" Multiplicity="1" />
   <End Role="UserRole" Type="Self.UserRole"
    Multiplicity="*" />
```

```
        <ReferentialConstraint>
          <Principal Role="Role">
            <PropertyRef Name="RoleID" />
          </Principal>
          <Dependent Role="UserRole">
            <PropertyRef Name="RoleID" />
          </Dependent>
        </ReferentialConstraint>
      </Association>
      <Association Name="FK_UserAuthentication_User">
        <End Role="User" Type="Self.User" Multiplicity="1" />
        <End Role="UserAuthentication"
         Type="Self.UserAuthentication" Multiplicity="*" />
        <ReferentialConstraint>
          <Principal Role="User">
            <PropertyRef Name="UserID" />
          </Principal>
          <Dependent Role="UserAuthentication">
            <PropertyRef Name="UserID" />
          </Dependent>
        </ReferentialConstraint>
      </Association>
```

The association between `Control` and `ControlType` is defined as shown in the following code snippet:

```
public partial class ControlType
    {
        public ControlType()
        {
            this.Controls = new HashSet<Control>();
        }

        public int ControlTypeID { get; set; }
        public string ControlTypeName { get; set; }
        public virtual ICollection<Control> Controls { get; set; }
    }
```

To let the `SecurityDBContext` class know the relationship between the `ControlType` and `Control` entities, you can use the following code:

```
((IObjectContextAdapter)context).ObjectContext.
         ObjectStateManager.
          ChangeRelationshipState(controlType, control, c
          => c.ControlType, EntityState.Added);
```

However, before you add a relationship, you must delete any preexisting relationship:

```
((IObjectContextAdapter) context).ObjectContext.
            ObjectStateManager.
            ChangeRelationshipState(controlType, control, c
            => c.ControlType, EntityState.Deleted);
```

Reading objects from the Security database

There are three ways in which you can load related entities using Entity Framework. These are—eager loading, lazy loading, and explicit loading. In eager loading, a query on a particular type of an entity loads the related entities also as part of the query execution. The following code snippet illustrates how you can implement eager loading:

```
using (SecurityDBEntities context = new SecurityDBEntities())
{
     // Load all controls and control types
    var data = context.Controls
                          .Include(b => b.ControlTypes)
                          .ToList();
}
```

You can load entities lazily even if lazy loading is disabled by making an explicit call. This is known as **explicit loading** and is illustrated in the following code snippet:

```
using (SecurityDBEntities context = new SecurityDBEntities())
{
    var data = context.Controls.Find(2);
}
```

Lazy loading is a feature that enables you to load data only at the time when it is requested. When lazy loading is turned on, an entity or collection of entities is loaded from the database at the first time a property referring to the entity or collection of entities is accessed. The following code snippet illustrates how you can load the objects from the `Security` data context using lazy loading. Lazy loading (also known as deferred loading) loads objects late—they are loaded only when they are requested.

```
using (SecurityDBEntities context = new SecurityDBEntities())
            {
                Control controlObj = new Control
                {
```

```
            ControlID = 1, ControlName = "ComboBox",
            ControlTypeID = 1, ParentControlID = 1
        };
        context.Controls.Add(controlObj);
        //You can now access the Control and ControlType
        //objects on the newly
        // added object without having to load the
        //references explicitly
        Console.WriteLine("Control ID {0}:",
        controlObj.ControlID);
        Console.WriteLine("Control Type ID {0}:",
        controlObj.ControlTypeID);
    }
```

> You can turn off lazy loading for all entities by turning the `LazyLoadingEnabled` property to `false` as shown in the following code snippet:
>
> ```
> public class SecurityDBEntities : DbContext
> {
>     public SecurityDBEntities()
>     {
>         this.Configuration.LazyLoadingEnabled =
> false;
>     }
> }
> ```

Inserting objects from the Security database

The following code shows how you can create your custom data context by deriving from the `SecurityDBEntities` class:

```
public class CustomDBContext : SecurityDBEntities
    {
        public DbSet<Role> Roles { get; set; }
    }
```

You can now use the custom data context to add new roles to the database:

```
using (var context = new CustomDBContext())
            {
                Rolevar role = new Role {  RoleID = 1,
                RoleDescription = "Sample" };
                context.Roles.Add(role);
                context.SaveChanges();
            }
```

Editing objects from the Security database

Using the custom data context we created in the earlier section, you can edit a role description using the following code:

```
using (var context = new CustomDBContext())
            {
                var role = context.Roles.Where(r => r.RoleID ==
                2).FirstOrDefault();
                if (role != null)
                {
                    role.RoleDescription = "Updated Role
                    Description";
                    context.SaveChanges();
                }
            }
```

Deleting objects from the Security database

The following code snippet illustrates how you can delete a particular role using its ID:

```
using (var context = new CustomDBContext())
            {
                var result = from r in context.Roles where
                r.RoleID == 2 select r;
                if (result.Count() > 0)
                {
                    Role role = result.First();
```

```
                    context.Roles.Remove(role);
                    context.SaveChanges();
                }
            }
```

To delete bulk records, you can use a `foreach` loop as shown in the following code snippet:

```
using (var context = new CustomDBContext())
            {
                var result = from r in context.Roles where
                r.RoleID == 2 select r;

                if (result.Count() > 0)
                {
                    foreach(Role role in result)
                    {
                        context.Roles.Remove(role);

                    }
                  context.SaveChanges();
                }
            }
```

Summary

Object Service Layer in Entity Framework keeps track of the changes made to the object and updates the database accordingly. In this chapter, we discussed Object Services and saw how it can be used to perform CRUD operations against the EDM. We discussed how we can serialize and deserialize an entity instance. We implemented a sample application that demonstrated how we can detect and resolve concurrency conflicts. We also discussed how we can extend, or inherit, new entities from existing ones and use them in our applications.

In the next chapter of this book, we will take a look at WCF Data Services and learn how we can use them with Entity Framework in our applications.

8
Working with WCF Data Services

ADO.NET Data Services, formerly known as **Project Astoria**, comprises a collection of patterns and libraries that can be used to expose an application's data as a service. This service can then be consumed by client applications using HTTP calls. You can use ADO.NET Data Services to isolate the Data Access Layer, and it exposes data via WCF services to discover, manipulate, and retrieve data in a corporate network. You can also use ADO.NET Data Services to expose data that is retrieved using the Entity Data Model as a service and then access this service using WCF service calls over the HTTP protocol.

WCF Data Services replaces ADO.NET Data Services with more added features. WCF Data Services (formerly known as ADO.NET Data Services) enables you to build RESTful services that leverage the **Open Data Protocol** (**OData**) to expose and consume data over the web or intranet.

In this chapter, we will examine the following points:

- Understanding REST and RESTful WCF Services
- Understanding OData Protocol
- An overview of WCF Data Services
- Creating a WCF Data Service
- Working with Protobuf Services
- Guidelines and best practices

Introducing WCF Data Services

Primarily designed in order to separate the presentation layer and data in a REST-based model, WCF Data Services are used to expose data as a service so it can be accessed via HTTP requests. You can use the standard HTTP verbs `MERGE`, `GET`, `POST`, `PUT`, and `DELETE` and perform CRUD operations against the service. WCF Data Services expose the database schema in terms of XML metadata. It uses Atom and JSON data formats for data transfers over the HTTP protocol.

WCF Data Services isolate the Data Access Layer and expose data via WCF Services. We do not need to have the presentation layer as a consumer of Data Services. We could also have another service as occurs in SOA scenarios.

You can use WCF Data Services to expose data through Web Services in terms of EDM abstractions such as EDM objects. These objects can then be accessed by any application in much the same way such as a Web Service is accessed.

How do WCF Data Services and Web Services differ?

The primary difference is that Web Services is based on SOAP and WCF Data Services is based on a REST-model. While the former defines messages and exposes them, the latter defines resources and exposes them through URIs. Moreover, unlike using WSDL to define the endpoint of a service as in a Web Service, the REST-based model of WCF Data Services uses the query string and the URL string to define the endpoint's URI. We will take a look at what the REST-based model is in the section that follows.

What is Representational State Transfer (REST)?

WCF Data Services uses HTTP as its transport protocol and is based on a REST-model. In a REST-based model, the application's state and functionality is divided into resources. These are in turn addressable using URIs over HTTP. REST provides a stateless, client-server, and a cacheable model for data access. SOAP-based web service communication, which uses all web service protocols, is much heavier than REST-based WCF Data Services.

Representation State Transfer (commonly known as **REST**) is an architectural paradigm that is based on the stateless HTTP protocol and is used to design applications that can inter-communicate. In REST, resources are used to represent state and functionality and note that a resource is the most important concept in a REST-style architecture.

The RESTful Web Services map the HTTP methods to the corresponding CRUD operations. The following is the list of operations supported in a typical REST-style architecture:

- **HTTP method**: CRUD action
- **GET**: Retrieve a resource
- **POST**: Create a new resource
- **PUT**: Update an existing resource
- **DELETE**: Delete an existing resource
- **HEAD**: Retrieves metadata information on a resource

RESTful services provide much better performance and scalability and the payload is much less compared to SOAP-based services. Moreover, you can cache REST reads but you can't cache SOAP-based reads. You can use many different data formats with REST-based services while you are constrained to use only XML when working with SOAP-based (SOAP supports only XML) services.

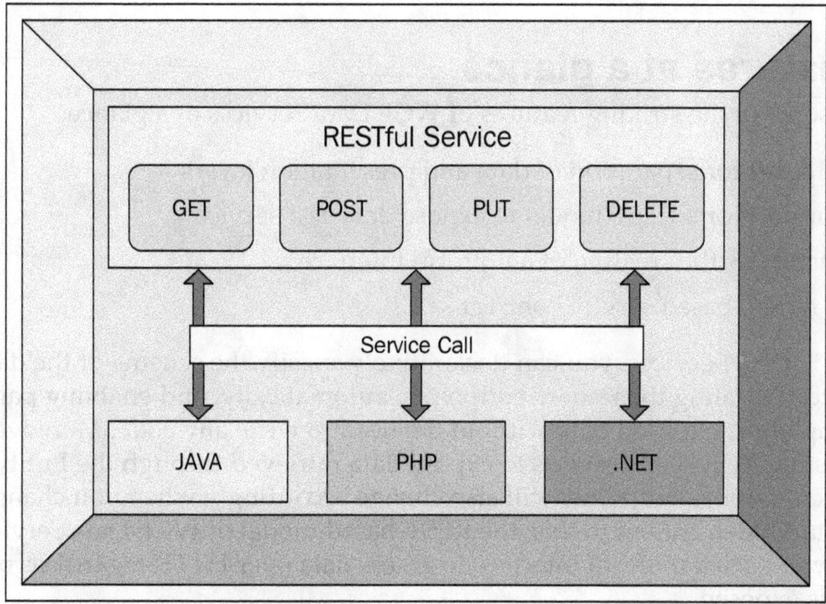

The basic features of a REST-based architecture are:

- Resources are used to divide an application's state and its functionality
- Resources share a uniform interface and are uniquely addressable

The major benefits of a REST-based approach are as follows:

- Improved performance and response time
- Improved scalability and interoperability
- Reduced KLOC at the client side
- Works on top of the HTTP protocol

Why use WCF Data Services?

The primary goal of WCF Data Services is to create a REST-based model to expose data services. REST is an architecture that is used in distributed hypermedia systems to transmit domain-specific data over the HTTP protocol. WCF Data Services provides support for optimistic concurrency to detect data concurrency conflicts. It uses eTags, which are HTTP response headers in string format, to detect changes. These e-Tags, which are supported by HTTP 1.1, are used to denote the version or state of a resource. To find out more on how concurrency is handled by WCF Data Services, you can refer to the following website: `http://msdn.microsoft.com/en-us/library/cc668770.aspx`.

The features at a glance

Here are some of the striking features of WCF Data Services at a glance:

- Support for separation of data and presentation layers
- Support for a REST model to expose data as a service
- Facilitates the creation of a uniform interface
- A model-based service contract

Using WCF Data Services, you can declaratively specify the schema of the data. This includes creating the remote endpoints, automatically, and enabling paging and sorting of the exposed data without the need to write any code. Moreover, if you are using WCF Data Services to expose data retrieved through the Entity Data Model, these remote endpoints will also change accordingly when you change your Entity Data Model. Added to this, the REST-based model of WCF Data Services provides you with a uniform interface to access data over HTTP regardless of the data that is exposed.

You can define the service operations and interceptors you are using, which allow you to then define a method on the server that is identifiable using URIs. Next, you can call that method using the URI specified. You can use the interceptors to plug your custom validation logic into the request/response pipeline. The best part of WCF Data Services is that it uses HTTP entry points. In doing so, any HTTP client application can connect to it and perform CRUD operations.

Exposing data as a service using WCF Data Services

You have two options to expose data as a service using WCF Data Services:

- Use a relational database as the data source
- Use a data source other than a relational database

If you are using a relational database as the data source, you can use LINQ to SQL or Entity Framework to expose the data. On the other hand, you can use collections of objects as a data source too. In either case, you need to create a WCF Data Service using the designer. In the next section, we will discuss how we can create an ADO. NET Data Service.

Why do we need REST?

In a typical client-server communication over a network, a server is connected to one or more clients using some protocols, that is, HTTP or TCP, and so on.

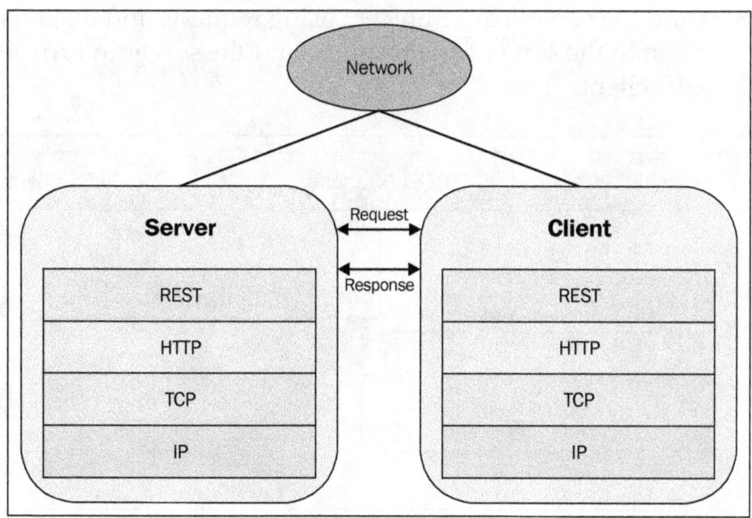

What is REST? Why is it becoming so popular over time? Is REST an alternative to Web Services? How can I make use of the .NET Framework to implement RESTful Services? We will answer these questions as we progress through the sections in this chapter.

REST is an architectural style for designing distributed applications that can intercommunicate. Note that REST is not a technology or a set of standards. Rather, it is a set of constraints that can be used to define a new style of architecture. Essentially, it is a client-server architectural style where the connections are stateless.

> The REST architecture style can be applied to other protocols as well. The word "stateless" applies to HTTP/HTTPS protocols. The REST architectural style is popular in the HTTP world and gives better results when used in combination with the HTTP protocol.

REST is not a standard; rather, it is an architectural alternative to RPC and Web Services. In the REST architectural style, you can communicate among systems using the HTTP protocol (if HTTP is the protocol in use). Actually, the **World Wide Web (WWW)** can be viewed as a REST-based architecture. A RESTful architecture is based on a cacheable and stateless communication protocol.

REST is an architectural style that divides an application's state and functionality into resources. These resources are in turn addressable using URIs over HTTP. These resources have a common interface and are uniquely addressable. A REST-based model is stateless, client-server based, and cacheable.

As discussed, in a REST-based model, resources are used to represent state and functionality. Resources are identified through logical URLs. In a typical REST-based model, the client and the server communicate using requests and responses. The client sends a request to the server for a resource and the server in turn sends the response back to the client.

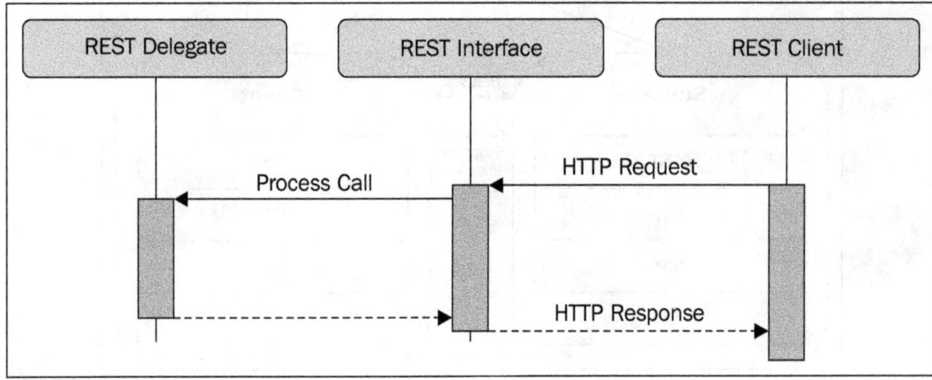

The main design goals of the REST architectural style include:

- Independent deployment of the components
- Reduced latency
- High security of service interactions
- Scalability
- High performance

The basic difference between SOAP and REST is that while the former emphasizes on verbs, the latter emphasizes on resources. In REST, you define resources and then use a uniform interface to operate on them using HTTP verbs. It should also be noted that REST is simpler to deal with, since it heavily leverages the HTTP transport mechanism for formatting, caching, routing, and operations performed on the given resources. On the contrary, with SOAP, there usually aren't such conventions. A SOAP-based service can easily be exposed via TCP/IP, UDP, SMTP, or any other transport protocol, and so it doesn't have to be dependent on the HTTP protocol.

In a REST-based model, a request comprises an endpoint URL, a developer ID, parameters, and the desired action. The endpoint URL is used to represent the complete address. The developer ID is a key that uniquely identifies each request's origin. The desired action is used to denote the action to be performed.

The REST architecture makes use of some common HTTP methods for CRUD operations. These are as follows:

- `GET`: This is used to request a specific representation of a resource.
- `HEAD`: This is used to retrieve the resource headers only.
- `PUT`: This is used to update a resource.
- `DELETE`: This is used to delete the specified resource.
- `POST`: This is used to submit data that is to be processed by the identified resource. Ideally, `POST` should be used only to create resources, while `PUT` is used only to update them.

Resources in REST-based architecture

The resource concept is one of the most important ones in REST. A few examples of public implementations of REST include the following:

- Google Fusion Tables
- Sones GraphDB—a graph-oriented database written in C#
- Nuxeo—an open source document manager

A resource is identified using a URI. In the REST style of architecture, communication between a server and a client takes place using requests and responses. The client (also known as the consumer) requests a resource from the server. The server then sends the response back to the client.

In the REST architectural paradigm, resources are used to represent the state and functionality of the resources, and they are identified by using logical URIs so that they can be universally addressable. The REST architecture is essentially based on HTTP—a stateless protocol. Resources can however be cached as and when needed. Note that since HTTP provides a cache mechanism, REST implemented on top of HTTP protocol provides the features and benefits of HTTP. Also, you can set cache expiration policies for the cached data.

Any REST request comprises the following components:

- **An endpoint URL**: This denotes the complete address of the script.
- **DeveloperCaller ID**: This is a key that is sent with each request. This is used to identify the origin of the request. Note that the `developerCaller` ID is not required for all REST Services.
- **Parameters**: This denotes the parameters of the request. This is optional.
- **Desired action**: This denotes the action for the particular request. Actions are based on HTTP verbs.

The REST architectural constraints

The REST architectural paradigm defines the following constraints to the architecture:

The client-server model

A RESTful implementation is based on a client-server model. The servers and the clients are clearly isolated. This implies that the servers and clients can be modified independent of each other. The server is not at all concerned with the user interface. Similarly, the user interface is not concerned how data is persisted.

Stateless

The REST architecture is based on the stateless HTTP protocol. In a RESTful architecture, the server responses can be cached by the clients. Any request from the client to the server should have enough information so that the request can be understood and serviced, but no client context would be stored on the server. This type of design ensures that the servers are more visible for performance monitoring and are scalable.

Cacheable

In a typical REST architecture, the clients should be able to cache data. To manage cache better, the architecture allows you to set whether or not a response can be cached. This feature improves scalability and performance.

Code on demand

The servers in a REST architecture can (if needed) extend or customize the functionality of a particular client. Known as "code on demand," this feature allows the servers in a REST architecture implementation to transfer logic to the clients if such a need arises.

The uniform interface

The REST architectural style defines a uniform interface between the clients and the servers, hence allowing only a limited set of operations defined using the standard HTTP verbs such as `GET`, `PUT`, `POST`, and `DELETE`.

Resource management

Resources are identified using unique URIs. Note that resource representations can exist in any combination of any digital format (HTML, XML, JSON, RSS, and so on).

> It should be noted here that the actual resource usually has only one representation on the server. It is the client that specifies in which representation it accepts the resources, that is, how they should be formatted.

REST is an architectural paradigm that is used to model how data is represented, accessed, and modified on the web. REST uses the stateless HTTP protocol and the standard HTTP operations (`GET`, `PUT`, `POST`, and `DELETE`) to perform CRUD operations. REST allows you to do all that you can do with SOAP and XML-RPC. Added to that, you can use firewalls for security and also use caching for enhanced performance.

REST attributes

Let's now take a closer look at the WCF REST attributes one by one and their purpose. Incidentally, all these attributes are available in the `System.ServiceModel.Web.dll` library. In this section, we will discuss the attributes that we will frequently make use of while working with RESTful services.

WebServiceHost

Using the `WebServiceHost` attribute simplifies hosting web-based services. It is derived from the `ServiceHost` class, overrides the `OnOpening` method, and automatically adds the `WebHttpBehavior` class to the endpoint. The following code snippet illustrates how the `WebServiceHost` attribute is used:

```
WebServiceHost var host = new WebServiceHost(typeof(ClassName),
  baseAddress);
WebHttpBindingvar binding = new WebHttpBinding();
host.AddServiceEndpoint(typeof(ISomeContract),
  binding, "WebServiceHost");
host.Open();
```

WebHttpBinding

The `WebHttpBinding` attribute produces an appropriate HTTP-based transport channel. The security here is handled by the `WebHttpSecurity` class. Services can be exposed using the `WebHttpBinding` binding, by using either the `WebGet` or `WebInvoke` attributes.

WebHttpBehavior

The `WebHttpBehavior` attribute customizes the HTTP-based dispatching logic, and it overrides operation selection, serialization, and invocation.

WebOperationContext

The `WebOperationContext` attribute is used to access HTTP specifics within methods. You can retrieve the current context using the `WebOperationContext.Current` property. It provides properties for the incoming/outgoing request/response context.

The following code snippet illustrates how to get the HTTP status code:

```
HttpStatusCode status = WebOperationContext.
  Current.IncomingResponse.StatusCode;
```

WebMessageFormat

This attribute is used to control the message format in your services.

You can control the format of your messages using the `RequestFormat` and `ResponseFormat` properties. Here is an example:

```
[OperationContract]
[WebGet(ResponseFormat = WebMessageFormat.Json, BodyStyle =
  WebMessageBodyStyle.WrappedRequest)]
public Employee GetData()
{
  return new Employee
  {
    Firstname = "Joydip",
    Lastname = "Kanjilal",
    Email = "joydipkanjilal@yahoo.com";
  };
}
```

The WebGet attribute

The `WebGet` attribute exposes operations using the `GET` verb. In other words, the `WebGet` attribute is used to map the incoming HTTP `GET` requests. How this attribute is defined in the `System.ServiceModel.Web` namespace is shown in the following code snippet:

```
[AttributeUsageAttribute(AttributeTargets.Method)]
public sealed class WebGetAttribute : Attribute,
  IOperationBehavior
```

An example that illustrates how you can use the `WebGet` attribute is shown as follows:

```
[OperationContract]
  [WebGet(UriTemplate="/employee/{id}")]
  public Employee GetEmployee(int id)
  {
    Employee empObj = null;
    // Get employee object from the database
    return empObj;
  }
```

The WebInvoke attribute

The `WebInvoke` attribute exposes services that use other HTTP verbs such as `POST`, `PUT`, and `DELETE`. In other words, the `WebInvoke` attribute is used for all other HTTP verbs, other than `GET` requests. The following code snippet shows how this attribute is defined in the `System.ServiceModel.Web` namespace:

```
[AttributeUsageAttribute(AttributeTargets.Method)]
public sealed class WebInvokeAttribute : Attribute,
  IOperationBehavior
```

Here is an example that illustrates the use of the `WebInvoke` attribute:

```
[OperationContract]
  [WebInvoke(Method = "DELETE", UriTemplate = "/employee/{id}")]
  public void DeleteEmployee(int id)
  {
    // Code to delete an employee record in the database
  }
```

UriTemplate

The `UriTemplate` class belongs to `System.UriTemplate` and implements URI template syntax that enables you to specify variables in the URI space. `UriTemplate` is a class that represents a URI template. `UriTemplate` is a URI string that contains variables enclosed by braces (`{, }`). Note that the `UriTemplate` property is specified on the `WebGet` and `WebInvoke` attributes we used earlier to identify an employee resource.

The following code snippet illustrates how `UriTemplate` is used:

```
[WebGet(UriTemplate =
  "RetrieveUserDetails/{userCode}/{projectCode}")]
public string RetrieveUserDetails(string userCode,
  string projectCode)
  {

  }
```

REST-based Web Services

A RESTful Web Service (or the RESTful Web API) is a service that comprises a collection of resources. These resources include a base URI that is used to access the Web Service, a MIME type (that is, JSON, XML, and so on) and a set of defined operations (that is, `POST`, `GET`, `PUT`, or `DELETE`). A RESTful Service is platform and language neutral. However, unlike a Web Service, there isn't any official standard set for RESTful Services. The basic advantages of using REST are transport neutrality and the ability to use advanced `WS-*` protocols. REST is interoperable, simple to use, and has a uniform interface.

RESTful Web Services are services that are based on the REST architectural paradigm. Essentially, these (also known as a RESTful Web API) are Web Services that comprise a collection of resources. These include:

- A base URI used to access the Web Service
- A MIME type that defines the format of the data that the Web Service supports, that is, JSON, XML, and so on
- A set of operations that the Web Service supports using the HTTP methods that include `POST`, `GET`, `PUT`, or `DELETE`

Similar to Web Services, a REST service is platform and language independent, based on HTTP, and can be used even with firewalls. Note that unlike Web Services that are based on the SOAP protocol, there is no official standard for RESTful Services. REST is simply an architectural style that doesn't have any standards set.

The following code snippet illustrates an example of a SOAP request:

```
<?xml version = "1.0"?>
<soap:Envelope>
xmlns:soap="http://www.w3.org/2001/12/soap-envelope"
soap:encodingStyle="http://www.w3.org/2001/12/soap-encoding">
  <soap:body emp="http://localhost/payroll">
    <emp:GetEmployeeDetails>
       <emp:EmployeeID>1</emp:EmployeeID>
    </emp:GetEmployeeDetails>
  </soap:Body>
</soap:Envelope>
```

The following URL shows how the same can be represented using REST:

```
http://localhost/payroll/EmployeeDetails/1
```

Software architecture refers to the overall structure of a system and the interrelationships of entities and components that make up the system. There are various architectural styles such as object-oriented architecture, service-oriented architecture, cloud-oriented architecture, and resource-oriented architecture.

Service-oriented architecture (**SOA**) and **resource-oriented architecture** (**ROA**) are architectural design patterns that provide the concepts and the necessary development tools and technologies to implement distributed application architectures. Distributed architectures comprise services that can be used by the clients over a network using well-defined interfaces. These components that are used by the clients are called resources in ROA and services in SOA.

What is the OData Protocol?

With the rise in the availability of data, it is extremely important that we keep our data in a structured format as much as possible. Whether we choose to work on a mainframe, a mini, a server farm or a PC, a standardized API to deal with the data in a structured format is needed. If the data is relational, SQL provides a set of operations to query and also update it. However, not all data is relational. Further, not all relational data is exposed for use in processing SQL statements or on a wider perspective over the world-wide Internet.

OData is an open protocol for sharing data and exposing data as a web-friendly data feed. It provides you with a uniform way of representing structured data in Atom and JSON formats and a uniform URL for navigation, sorting, filtering, and paging data retrieved from a Data Service.

The official website for OData states:

> *"The Open Data Protocol (OData) is a Web protocol for querying and updating data that provides a way to unlock your data and free it from silos that exist in applications today. OData does this by applying and building upon Web technologies such as HTTP, Atom Publishing Protocol (AtomPub) and JSON to provide access to information from a variety of applications, services, and stores."*

The reference is available at `http://www.odata.org/`.

OData is a web protocol that is used to query and update data. It is a REST-based protocol that you can use for CRUD operations on your data against resources exposed as data services. The OData is a new standard that follows the REST architectural style whose goal is to enable applications to expose data as a service through an intranet or the web. It relies on HTTP, **Atom Publishing Protocol** (**AtomPub**) and JSON. It is the web-based equivalent of ODBC, OLEDB, ADO.NET, and JDBC.

OData v4 is an OASIS standard and is available for many platforms including iOS and Android, and OData payloads are based on the Atom and AtomPub formats. Note that the **Organization for the Advancement of Structured Information Standards (OASIS)** is a non-profit international consortium that promotes development, adoption, and convergence of e-business and Web Service standards. REST doesn't provide details on what the URLs and the request/response formats should look like. It also doesn't provide information on the operations and resources that a service provides support for. OData provides a rich query language and standardizes the request/response formats in JSON and AtomXml. The rich query language that OData provides enables service consumers to query your service for exactly the information that is needed.

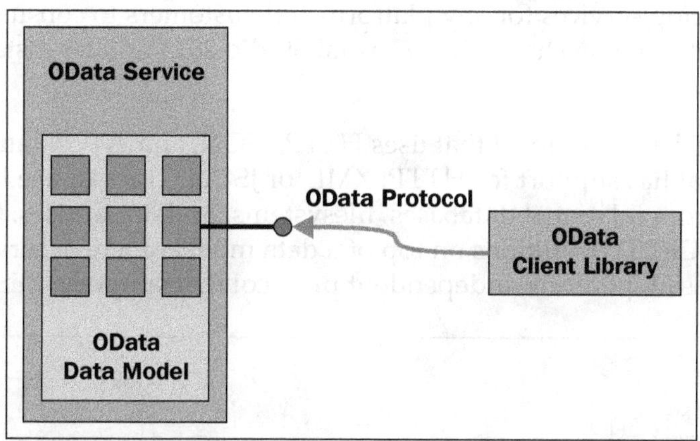

OData service returns data in the AtomXml format, though it also supports the JSON format. If you use OData, you can avoid code duplication and maintenance issues when working with data—you can write your service once and let your service consumer dictate how the data needs to be retrieved. In essence, in using OData, you write your service once and have many different clients consume the data in the format they need to seamlessly.

In OData, data is provided through URIs and common HTTP verbs such as `GET`, `PUT`, `POST`, and `DELETE`:

- `GET`: Get a collection of entries (as a feed document) or a single entry (as an entry document)
- `PUT`: Update an existing entry with an entry document
- `POST`: Create a new entry from an entry document
- `DELETE`: Remove an entry

OData is a smart application and is implemented by IBM's WebSphere, SQL Server Azure, Microsoft SharePoint, and Microsoft's "Dallas" information marketplace, to be the protocol of choice for the Open Government Data Initiative. It is supported by .NET 4.0 via the WCF Data Services framework. Note that WCF Data Services (previously known as WCF Data Services) is the implementation of OData in .NET applications.

It is such a versatile technology that it can also be consumed by Excel's PowerPivot, plain vanilla JavaScript and Microsoft's own Visual Studio development tool. The specifications of the OData are published under the license of **Microsoft Open Specification Promise** (**OSP**), which allows third parties (including open source projects) to develop services for any platform and customers to consume them. To work with OData, you should have Visual Studio 2013 or later installed on your system.

OData is a REST-based protocol that uses HTTP, JSON, and ATOM and supports any platform that has support for HTTP, XML, or JSON. You can use it to expose data retrieved from relational databases, filesystems, or data services. OData enables you to perform CRUD operations on top of a data model or a data service. In essence, it is an HTTP-based, platform-independent protocol that supports REST.

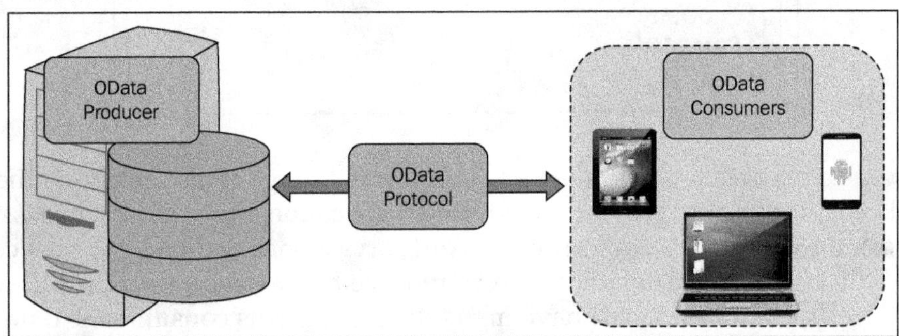

In OData, data is provided through the use of URIs and common HTTP verbs such as `GET`, `PUT`, `POST`, `MERGE`, and `DELETE`. Note that WCF Data Services is the implementation of OData in .NET applications.

The official website of OData exposes data as an OData Service. Here is the service URL: `http://services.odata.org/V3/(S(zldatqoyyeulias4w1qhvpqp))/OData/OData.svc/`.

When you open the page in a browser, this is how the XML markup looks:

```
<service xml:base="http://services.odata.org/Website/odata.svc/">
<workspace>
<atom:title>Default</atom:title>
```

```
<collection href="ODataConsumers">
<atom:title>ODataConsumers</atom:title>
</collection>
<collection href="ODataProducerApplications">
<atom:title>ODataProducerApplications</atom:title>
</collection>
<collection href="ODataProducerLiveServices">
<atom:title>ODataProducerLiveServices</atom:title>
</collection>
</workspace>
</service>
```

A collection of entity sets or feeds is referred to as **workspace**.

Working with WCF Data Services and Entity Framework

In this section, we will discuss how we can create a WCF Data Service using Entity Framework and the `AdventureWorks` database. To add a WCF Data Service application to an existing web application, follow these steps:

1. Create an ASP.NET application:

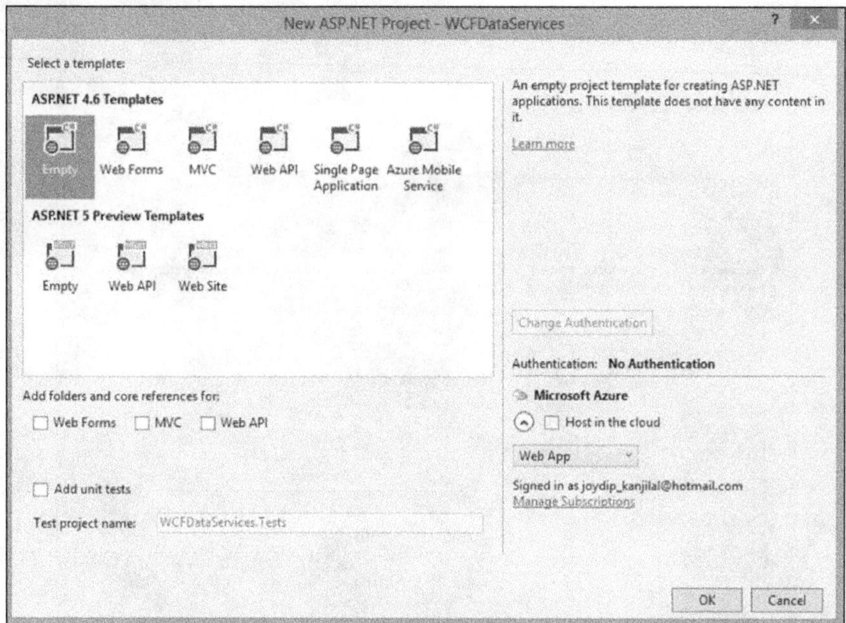

2. Create a new Entity Data Model and name it `AdventureWorks`:

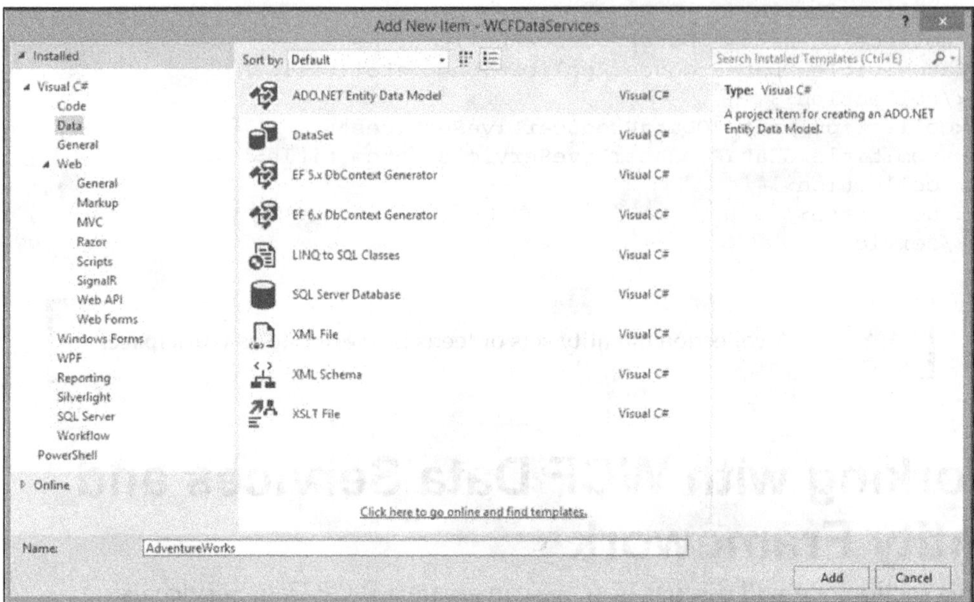

3. Select **Code First from database**:

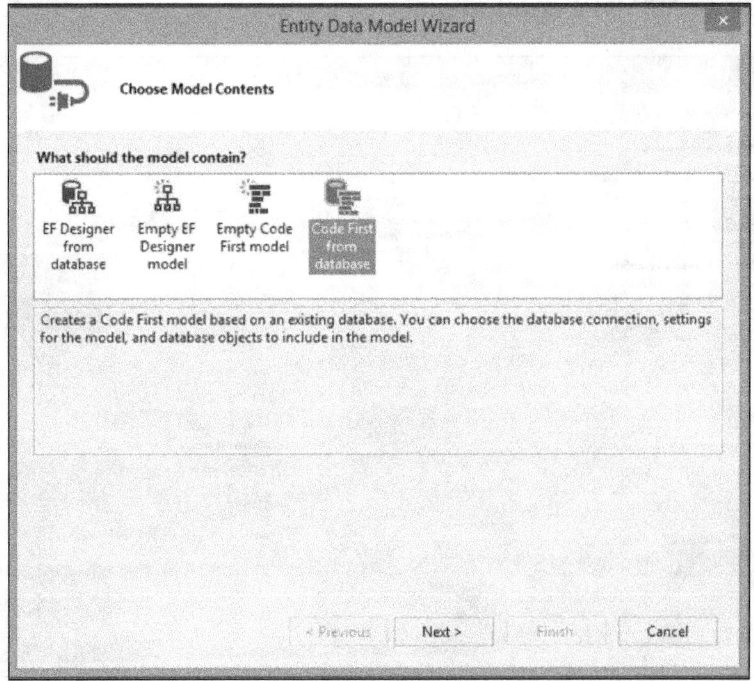

4. In the **Entity Data Model Wizard** dialog, specify the data connection properties and click **Next**:

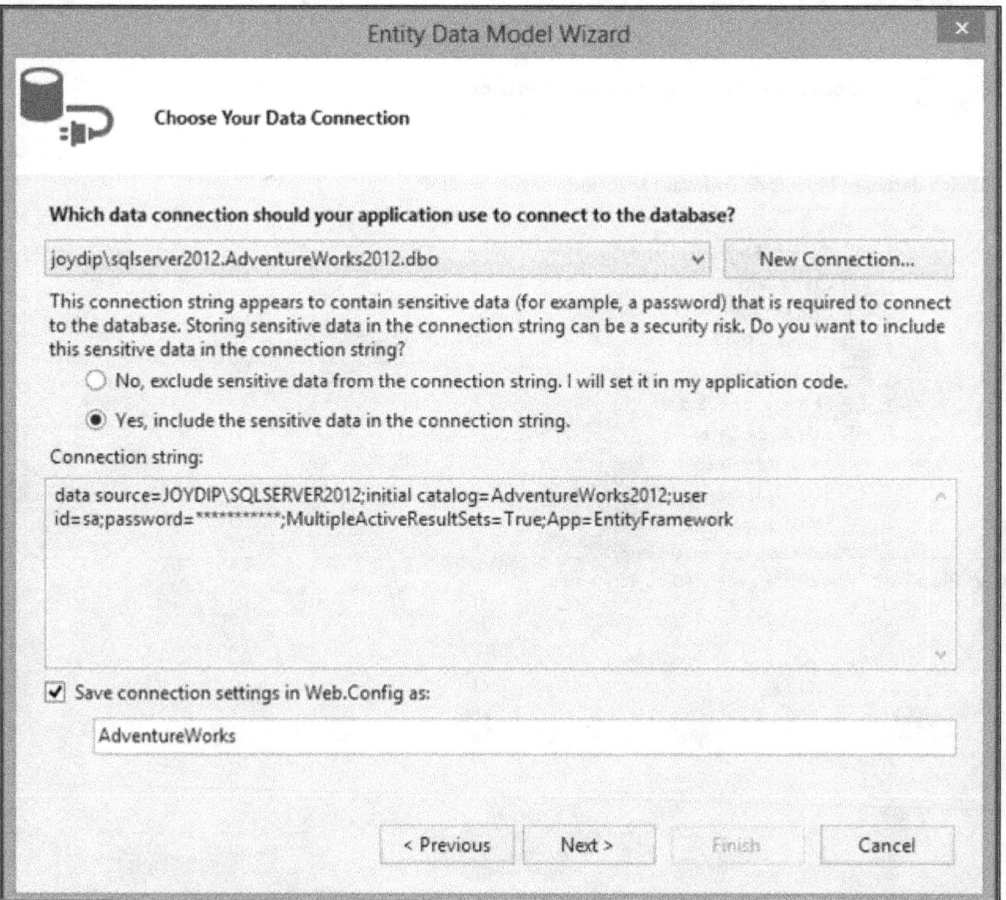

5. Next, choose the database objects you want to be part of the Entity Data Model:

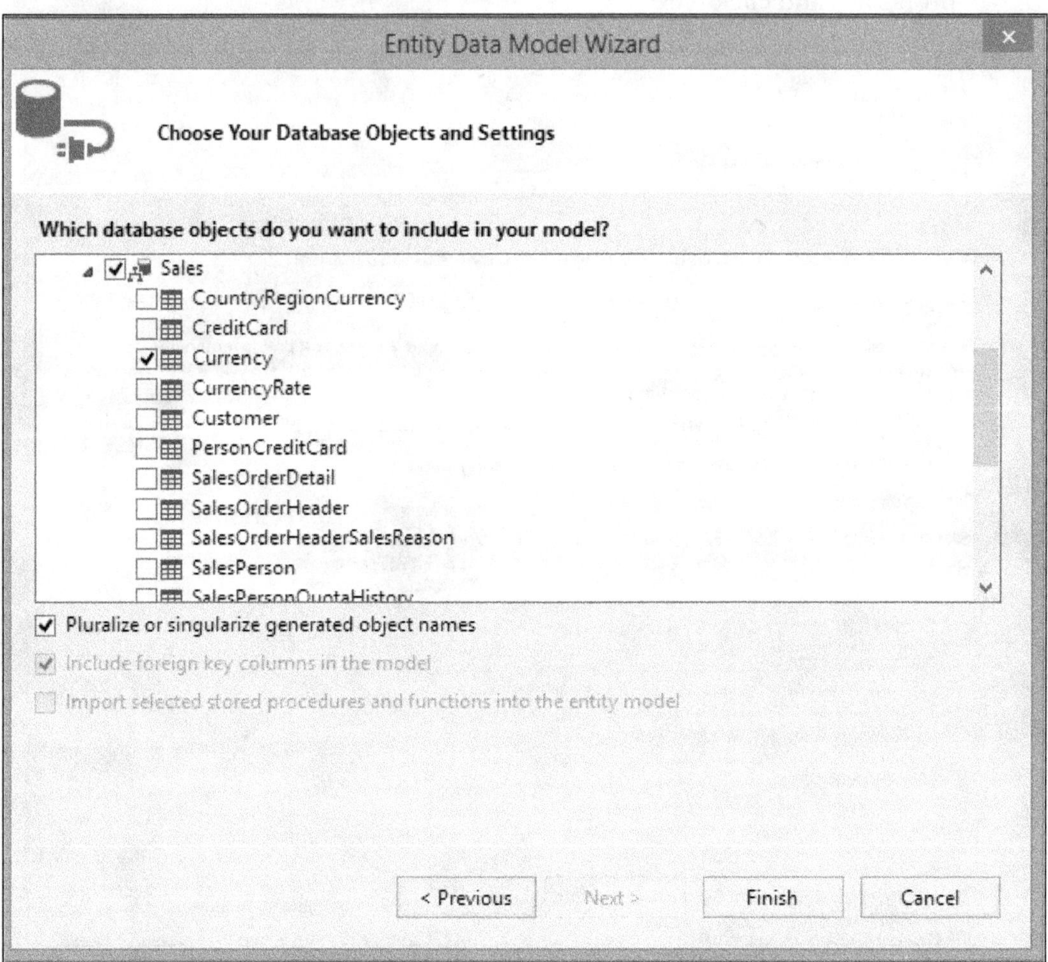

6. Now, right-click on the project in the solution explorer window and select **Add New Item**.

7. Select WCF Data Service from the list of the templates displayed, specify a name, and click **OK**.

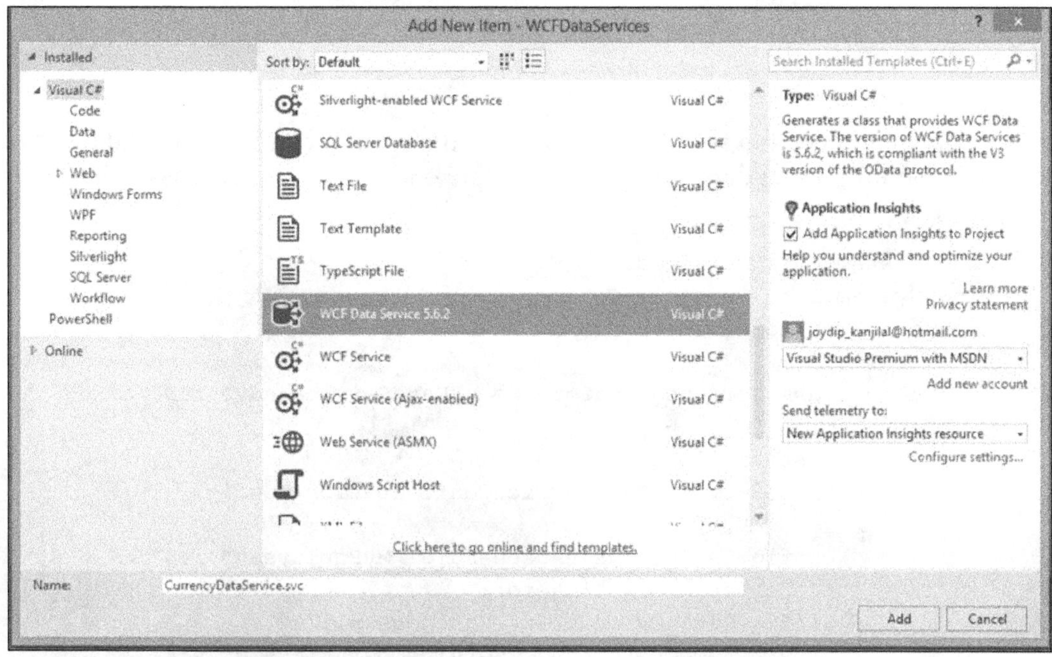

And, you are done! At first glance, the WCF Data Service class looks like this:

```
using System.Data.Services;
using System.Data.Services.Common;
namespace WCFDataServices
{
    public class CurrencyDataService : DataService< /* TODO: put
    your data source class name here */ >
    {
        // This method is called only once to initialize service-
        wide policies.
        public static void
        InitializeService(DataServiceConfiguration config)
        {
            // TODO: set rules to indicate which entity sets and
            service operations are visible, updatable, etc.
            // Examples:
            // config.SetEntitySetAccessRule("MyEntityset",
            EntitySetRights.AllRead);
            // config.SetServiceOperationAccessRule
```

```
                ("MyServiceOperation", ServiceOperationRights.All);
                config.DataServiceBehavior.MaxProtocolVersion =
                DataServiceProtocolVersion.V3;
            }
        }
    }
```

You will typically need to specify the data context class and configure the data service behavior. The updated version of the `CurrencyDataService` class will look like this:

```
using System.Data.Services;
using System.Data.Services.Common;
namespace WCFDataServices
{
    public class CurrencyDataService : DataService<AdventureWorks>
    {
        public static void
        InitializeService(DataServiceConfiguration config)
         {
            config.SetEntitySetAccessRule("MyEntityset",
            EntitySetRights.AllRead);
            config.SetServiceOperationAccessRule
            ("MyServiceOperation", ServiceOperationRights.All);
            config.DataServiceBehavior.MaxProtocolVersion =
            DataServiceProtocolVersion.V3;
         }
    }
}
```

Working with OData Services using WCF and ASP.NET MVC Framework

In this section, we will discuss how we can create an OData Service and consume it from an ASP.NET MVC application. To get started using OData in .NET applications, you need to first create a WCF Data Service. You can create and use an Entity Data Model using the ADO.NET Entity Framework template in Visual Studio.

Here are the steps to create an OData Service:

1. Create an Entity Data Model or a source of data using LINQ to SQL. You can also use a custom data model, but it should implement the `IUpdateable` and `IQueryable` interfaces.

2. Expose the data model as a WCF Data Service.
3. Host the WCF Data Service.
4. Consume the WCF Data Service in a client application.

To create a WCF Data Service, click on **Project | Add New Item** and then select WCF Data Service from the list of the templates displayed. Note that you will need to add these references to your project:

- `System`
- `System.Core`
- `System.ServiceModel`
- `System.ServiceModel.Web`
- `System.Data.Services`

This is how your data context class will look:

```
public class CustomerDataContext : DbContext
{
public CustomerDataContext()
: base("CustomerEntitiesConnectionString")
{
}
public CustomerDataContext(string connectionString)
: base(connectionString)
{
}
public DbSet Customers { get; set; }
}
```

The next step would be to create a WCF Data Service and specify permissions as appropriate:

```
public class CustomersDataService : DataService
{
public static void InitializeService(DataServiceConfiguration
config)
{
config.SetEntitySetAccessRule("Customers",
EntitySetRights.AllRead);
config.DataServiceBehavior.MaxProtocolVersion =
DataServiceProtocolVersion.V2;
}
}
```

To host the WCF Data Service, you can use the following code:

```
using System;
using System.Collections.Generic;
using System.Data.Services;
using System.Linq;
namespace CustomerODataServiceHost
{
class Program
{
static void Main(string[] args)
{
string WCFServiceAddress = "http://localhost:1012";
Uri[] uriArray = { new Uri(WCFServiceAddress) };
Type serviceType = typeof(CustomerDataService);

using (var host = new DataServiceHost(serviceType, uriArray)) {
host.Open();
Console.WriteLine("Service Started...Press any key to stop
service");
Console.ReadLine();
}
}
}
```

Now that your data context and data service have been created and configured, we will examine how we can consume the service. After the WCF Data Service has been created, you need to add a service reference to the service in your ASP.NET MVC project if you need to access the OData Service from your ASP.NET MVC application. Once done, you can use the OData Client library (this is added as soon as you add a reference to the service) and the service proxy to query data in your controller:

```
public ActionResult Index()
{
var serviceURI = new Uri("http://customer//view");
var context = new CustomerServiceReference.CustomerDataService(servic
eURI);
var query = from c in context.Customers
where c.Name == "Peter"
select c;
var result = query.ToList();
return View(result);
}
```

Working with Protobuf WCF Services

Protocol Buffers (**Protobuf**) is a serialization format developed by Google that is fast and easy to use. Frequently referred to as "Protobuf," the technology consists of a language- and platform-neutral, extensible, binary format for fast data exchange that relies on an interface description language, which is compiled to native code. In this section, we will explore Protobuf and how we can work with Protobuf and **Windows Communication Foundation** (**WCF**), which is Microsoft's unified programming model for building service-oriented apps.

Protobuf-net is much faster than the other binary serializers available, and is much faster than BinaryFormatter when it comes to serialization, with a much reduced payload too.

To work with Protobuf, you need to have the following installed on your system:

- Visual Studio 2013 or higher
- Protocol Buffers for .NET (Protobuf-net)

You can freely download a copy of Protocol Buffers for .NET from `https://code.google.com/p/protobuf-net/`.

Before we delve deep into implementing Protobuf WCF services in .NET, let's take a quick tour of the basics of Protobuf services: what are they and how they are used.

Protocol Buffers

The idea behind Protocol Buffers is to provide a platform-and language-independent format for exchanging serialized, structured data. Protocol Buffers are lighter and faster to handle than XML or JSON. The other major advantages of Protocol Buffers are:

- Reduced size of the data packets
- Platform independence
- Extensibility

Creating Protobuf-net objects

Note that all Protobuf-net classes are stored in files that have `.proto` extensions. You can store one or more proto classes in a `.proto` file. Here is an example that illustrates what a typical Protobuf-net class looks like:

```
package Packt;
message User
{
 required int32  UserID = 1;
 required string UserName = 2;
 required string UserEmail = 3;
 required string Password = 4;
 optional string Address = 5;
}
```

Note that `required` in the preceding message implies that it is a mandatory property. So, `UserID`, `UserName`, `UserEmail`, and `Password` are mandatory properties. The `Address` property is an optional property and is prefixed with the optional keyword. Note that a message in Protobuf implies a class. If you have a class that contains a list of objects, you need to use the `repeated` keyword when defining your Protobuf classes. Here is an example:

```
package Packt;
message Customer {
  required string CustomerCode = 1;
  required string FirstName = 2;
  required string LastName = 3;
  repeated Contact ContactList = 4;
}
```

As you can see, the `Customer` message contains a list of objects of the type `Contact`. The `Contact` message is defined as follows:

```
package Packt;
message Contact
{
  required string ContactCode = 1;
  required string Address1 = 2;
  required string Address2 = 3;
  required string Address3 = 4;
  required string Phone = 5;
  required string Email = 6;
}
```

One important thing to note when creating Protobuf-net classes is that each of the properties of the class should be explicitly numbered, that is, each of them should have a proper ordering.

Integrating Protobuf.NET with Visual Studio

Protocol Buffers is a binary serialization format that can be used to serialize objects that are much smaller in size and are portable across various platforms. To integrate Protobuf.NET with Visual Studio, you can copy the `ProtoBuf.zip` file from the protobuf-net installation directory to the Visual Studio installation directory and then execute the command `devenv /installvstemplates` to apply the new item templates. In doing so, you can create Protobuf classes from within your Visual Studio IDE.

You can also install protobuf-net using the NuGet Package Manager. To install protobuf-net, execute the following command in the Package Manager console:

```
Install-Package protobuf-net
```

Implementing the WCF Service

We will now implement a sample application that makes use of Protobuf WCF services. To do this, follow these steps:

1. Open the Visual Studio IDE.
2. Click on **File** | **New** | **Project**.
3. Select **WCF Service Application** from among the list of the project types.
4. Save the WCF Service application project with a name of your choice.
5. Create data contract classes for this service.
6. Create a service contract and a service implementation class for this service.
7. Repeat steps 3 and 4 to create another WCF Service application with the same implementation.

In this example, we will authenticate a user based on the supplied credentials. We will have one operation contract called `AuthenticateUser` that accepts an instance of the `AuthenticateUserRequest` class and returns an instance of `AuthenticateUserResponse`:

```
[ServiceContract,ProtoBuf.ProtoContract]
public interface ISecurity
{
    [OperationContract]
```

```
        AuthenticateUserResponse
        AuthenticateUser(AuthenticateUserRequest userRequestObj);
    }
```

The complete implementation of the `AuthenticateUser` operation contract is given here:

```
public AuthenticateUserResponse
AuthenticateUser(AuthenticateUserRequest userRequestObj)
{
    AuthenticateUserResponse responseObj = new
    AuthenticateUserResponse();

    if ((userRequestObj.UserID == 1) &&
    (userRequestObj.Password == "Pwd"))
    {
        responseObj.StatusCode = 1;
        responseObj.StatusMessage = "Success";
        responseObj.IsAuthenticated = true;
    }
    else
    {
        responseObj.StatusCode = 2;
        responseObj.StatusMessage = "Not authenticated";
        responseObj.IsAuthenticated = false;
    }

    return responseObj;
}
```

Specifying binding information

To consume the WCF Protobuf-net service, you need to specify `protoEndpointBehavior` as shown:

```
<client>
  <endpoint
        address=""
        binding="wsHttpBinding"
        contract="Packt.Services.ISecurity"
        behaviorConfiguration="protoEndpointBehavior">
    <identity>
      <dns value="localhost"/>
    </identity>
  </endpoint>
```

```
    </client>
    <extensions>
      <behaviorExtensions>
        <add name="protobuf"
         type="ProtoBuf.ServiceModel.ProtoBehaviorExtension,
         protobuf-net, Version=2.0.0.480, Culture=neutral,
         PublicKeyToken=257b51d87d2e4d67"/>
      </behaviorExtensions>
    </extensions>
```

Summary

REST is now all set to be the architectural paradigm of choice for designing and implementing scalable services. It is an architectural paradigm that is based on the stateless HTTP protocol and is used to design applications that can inter-communicate. In REST, resources are used to represent state and functionality and these resources are in turn represented using user-friendly URLs. The RESTful Web Services expose resources through URIs and use the HTTP methods to perform CRUD operations. The REST architectural paradigm not only opens up a lot of possibilities, but also challenges. The OData protocol allows you to query data over the HTTP protocol and then get the results back in Atom, JSON, or XML formats.

Google's Protocol Buffers is a binary serialization format used for data exchanges. Protocol Buffer is fast becoming the technology of choice as a popular serialization format in REST-based WCF services as it is a way of encoding structured data in an extensible format.

In this chapter, we discussed RESTful WCF Services, OData and how we can work with RESTful Services, OData, and Entity Framework. We also discussed how we can work with Protobuf and WCF Services.

```
    </client>
    <extensions>
      <behaviorExtensions>
        <add name="protobuf"
          type="ProtoBuf.ServiceModel.ProtoBehaviorExtension,
          protobuf-net, Version=2.0.0.480, Culture=neutral,
          PublicKeyToken=257b51d87d2e4d67"/>
      </behaviorExtensions>
    </extensions>
```

Summary

REST is now all set to be the architectural paradigm of choice for designing and implementing scalable services. It is an architectural paradigm that is based on the stateless HTTP protocol and is used to design applications that can inter-communicate. In REST, resources are used to represent state and functionality, and these resources are in turn represented using user-friendly URIs. The RESTful Web Services expose resources through URIs and use the HTTP methods to perform CRUD operations. The REST architectural paradigm not only opens up a lot of possibilities but also challenges. The OData protocol allows you to query data over the HTTP protocol and then get the results back in Atom, JSON, or XML formats.

Google's Protocol Buffers is a binary serialization format used for data exchanges. Protocol Buffer is fast becoming the technology of choice as a popular serialization format in REST-based WCF services as it is a way of encoding structured data in an extensible format.

In this chapter, we discussed RESTful WCF services, OData and how we can work with RESTful services, OData, and Entity Framework. We also discussed how we can work with Protobuf and WCF services.

Advanced Concepts

In this chapter we will cover a few advanced concepts. These include: REST and REST-based service frameworks and OData. We would also explore the HTTP methods and the request and response codes. Lastly, we will take a look at the new features in Entity Framework 7.

REST and REST-based service frameworks

Representation State Transfer (commonly known as **REST**) is an architectural paradigm that is based on the stateless HTTP protocol and is used for designing applications that can intercommunicate. In REST, resources are used to represent state and functionality, and these resources are in turn represented using user-friendly URLs. Note that the REST architecture style can be applied to other protocols as well. The word "stateless" implies the HTTP/HTTPS protocols. The REST architectural style is popular in the HTTP world and gives better results when used in combination with the HTTP protocol.

The key goals of REST include the following:

- Scalability
- Compatibility with other technology and platforms
- Generality of interfaces
- Discoverability; that is, interconnectivity between resources
- Components that can be deployed independently of one another
- Reduced latency
- Better security
- Extensibility

A RESTful Web API is a web API that conforms to the REST principles. The main principles of REST include:

- Identification of resources
- Stateless communication
- Manipulation of resources through representations
- Self-descriptive messages

In this section, we will examine the popular REST-based service frameworks.

Here is the list of the popular REST-based service frameworks or APIs:

- Ruby on Rails
- Restlet
- Django
- Flickr
- Google
- Yahoo

Ruby on Rails

Ruby on Rails is an optimized open source web application framework that runs on top of the Ruby programming language. Ruby on Rails follows the basic software engineering patterns and principles. The Rails Web API is a framework that facilitates the creation of web applications based on the **Model-View-Controller** (**MVC**) framework. The view layer is composed of "templates," and most of these templates are HTML-based with embedded Ruby code. The model layer represents the domain model, the business logic classes, and the data access classes. The controller layer handles incoming HTTP requests. Note that the Rails controller can generate XML, JSON, PDFs, and also mobile-specific views. You can get more information on this framework from `http://api.rubyonrails.org/`.

Restlet

Restlet provides support for an extensive list of extensions that include the following:

- Spring
- WADL
- XML
- JSON
- JAX-RS API

The benefits of Restlet include the following:

- Support for a fully symmetric client and server API
- Support for connector protocols other than HTTP
- Support for complete URI routing control through the Restlet API
- Fast and scalable
- Powerful filtering support
- Support for a consistent client and server API

You can explore more on this API from `http://restlet.org/discover/features`.

Django REST

The Django REST framework provides a powerful and flexible API, using which you can build Web APIs seamlessly. This API provides an extensive documentation and excellent community support. You can know more about this framework from `http://django-rest-framework.org/`.

The Flickr REST API

The Flickr REST API is simple and easy to use. Flickr also has some JSON APIs that you might make use of for invoking the API through JavaScript. You can get more information about this from `http://www.flickr.com/services/api/request.rest.html`.

The Google API

The **Custom Search JSON/Atom API** from Google enables developers to write applications that can leverage this API and retrieve and display custom search in the applications. This API allows you to use RESTful calls for web search and get the results in JSON or Atom format. You can know more on this API from `https://developers.google.com/custom-search/json-api/v1/overview`.

Note that Google provides a much wider range of API services than APIs, such as Google Maps, AdWords, Translate, Google Analytics, and so on.

Yahoo Social REST APIs

The Yahoo Social REST APIs provide a collection of URI resources that can provide access to the following:

- Users' profiles
- Status messages
- Status updates

These URIs are actually grouped into APIs, depending on the information that they return. For more information, you can refer to `http://developer.yahoo.com/social/rest_api_guide/web-services-intro.html`.

Exploring OData

The **Open Data Protocol (OData)** is a protocol that is built on web standards, such as HTTP, Atom, and JSON, and standardizes how data is exposed and consumed. It is a data access protocol that provides a uniform way of performing CRUD operations on the data. It is used to expose and access information from different data sources; that is, relational databases, filesystems, content management systems, and so on.

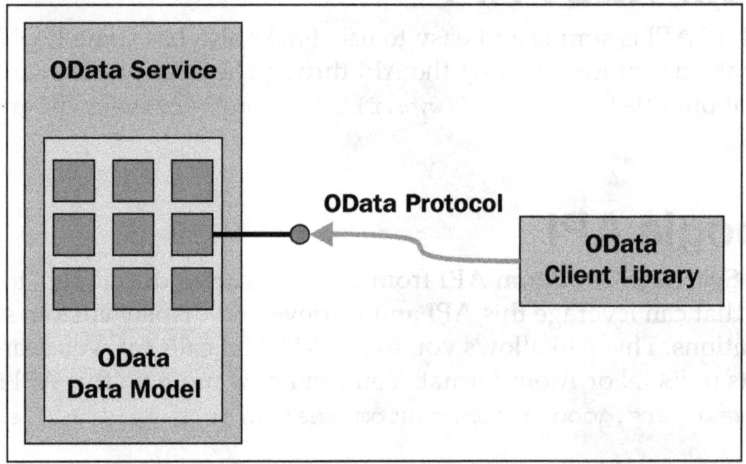

OData is a standardized protocol that builds on top of core protocols, such as HTTP and architecture paradigms, such as REST. Like RSS, Atom is a way to expose feeds. Note that AtomPub makes use of HTTP verbs such as `GET`, `POST`, `PUT`, and `DELETE`, to facilitate the publishing of data. OData v4 is now an OASIS standard. It is an open protocol that enables the creation and consumption of queryable and interoperable RESTful APIs.

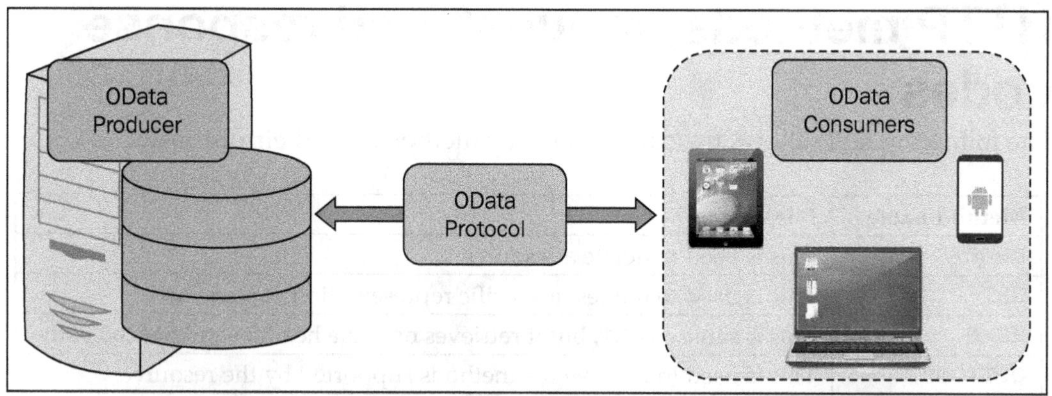

OData is a REST-based protocol that uses HTTP, JSON, and ATOM, and supports any platform that has support for HTTP, XML, or JSON. You can use it to expose data retrieved from relational databases, filesystems, or data services. OData enables you to perform CRUD operations on top of a data model or a data service. In essence, it is an HTTP-based, platform-independent protocol that supports REST. In OData, data is provided through the usage URIs and common HTTP verbs, such as `GET`, `PUT`, `POST`, `MERGE`, and `DELETE`. Note that WCF Data Services (previously known as ADO. NET Data Services) is the implementation of OData Protocol in .NET applications.

The official website of OData Protocol exposes data as an OData Service. The service URL is `http://services.odata.org/website/odata.svc`.

When you open the page in a browser, this is what the XML markup looks like:

```
<service xml:base="http://services.odata.org/Website/odata.svc/">
<workspace>
<atom:title>Default</atom:title>
<collection href="ODataConsumers">
<atom:title>ODataConsumers</atom:title>
</collection>
<collection href="ODataProducerApplications">
<atom:title>ODataProducerApplications</atom:title>
</collection>
<collection href="ODataProducerLiveServices">
<atom:title>ODataProducerLiveServices</atom:title>
</collection>
</workspace>
</service>
```

HTTP methods, request, and response codes

The following table shows the common HTTP methods and their purposes:

Method name	Purpose
DELETE	This is used to delete a resource
GET	This is used to request a specific representation of a resource
HEAD	This is same as GET, but it retrieves only the headers and not the body
OPTIONS	This is used to retrieve the methods supported by the resource
POST	This is used to post or submit data to be processed by the resource
PUT	This is used to create or update data using a particular representation of a resource

The following table shows the HTTP status codes and their purposes:

Status code	Description
100	Informational
200	Successful
201	Created
202	Accepted
300	Redirection
304	Not modified
400	Client error
402	Payment required
404	Not found
405	Method not allowed
500	Server error
501	Not implemented

The following table shows the HTTP redirection status codes:

Status code	Description
300	Multiple choices
301	Moved permanently
302	Found (temporary redirection)

The following table shows the HTTP error status codes:

Status code	Description
400	Bad request
401	Unauthorized
403	Forbidden
404	Resource not found
405	Method not allowed
408	Request timeout
409	Conflict
413	Request entity too large
415	Unsupported media type

The following table shows the HTTP server error status codes:

Status code	Description
500	Internal server error
501	Not implemented
503	Service unavailable
505	HTTP version not supported

The following table lists some resource methods and how they can be implemented using the HTTP protocol:

Method name	Description	HTTP operation
`createResource`	This creates a new resource	`PUT`
`getResourceRepresentation`	This is used to retrieve the representation of a particular resource	`GET`
`deleteResource`	This deletes a resource	`DELETE`
`modifyResource`	This modifies a resource	`POST`
`getMetaInformation`	This retrieves metadata of a resource	`HEAD`

Abbreviations

- **HTTP**: HyperText Transfer Protocol
- **ROA**: Resource Oriented Architectures
- **SOA**: Service Oriented Architectures
- **SOAP**: Simple Object Access Protocol
- **REST**: Representational State Transfer
- **RPC**: Remote Procedure Call
- **URL**: Uniform Resource Locator
- **W3C**: World Wide Web Consortium
- **WSDL**: Web Service Description Language
- **XML-RPC**: XML Remote Procedure Call

New features in Entity Framework 7

Entity Framework 7, a major redesign of the ORM, is the latest version of Entity Framework with the vision of "New Platforms, New Data Stores."

Some of the striking features of this release include support for the following:

- **Non-relational data stores and in-memory data**: You can now use Entity Framework with NoSQL databases as well.

  Entity Framework 7 now provides support for the following data providers:

  - SQL Server
  - SQLite
  - Azure Table Storage
  - Redis
  - In Memory (for unit testing)

- **Windows Phone and Windows Store applications, Linux, and Macintosh systems**: Entity Framework 7 now provides support for Windows Phone, Windows Store, ASP.NET 5, and desktop applications.
- **Unit testing**: Entity Framework 7 now provides support for unit testing your applications against in-memory or memory-resident databases.

You can refer to this Channel 9 video to know more on Entity Framework 7: `https://channel9.msdn.com/Events/Build/2015/2-693`.

Suggested reading

- `http://www.infoworld.com/article/2924201/microsoft-net/best-practices-to-improve-entity-framework-performance.html`
- `http://www.infoworld.com/article/2883125/c-sharp/new-features-in-c-6.html`
- `http://www.infoworld.com/article/2934465/microsoft-net/best-practices-in-optimizing-linq-performance.html`
- Stephen Walther has a nice article on using Entity Framework 7 with ASP.NET 5 and AngularJS. Here's the link: `http://stephenwalther.com/archive/2015/01/17/asp-net-5-and-angularjs-part-4-using-entity-framework-7`

Index

A

ADO.NET Data Services 201
ADO.NET Entity Client
connection, opening 134-137
connection string, building 133, 134
entity connection string, building 134
queries, executing with entity command 135, 136
working with 131-133
ADO.NET Entity Data Model 2
ADO.NET Entity Data Model Designer
used, for creating EDM 35-41
ADO.NET Entity Framework
benefits 21
components 11
features 21
system requisites 22
versus ORM tools 7
ADO.NET Entity Framework 6
enhancements 22-28
aggregate canonical functions, E-SQL 128, 129
associations 63
association sets 63
Atom Publishing Protocol (AtomPub) 214
auto-compiled queries 29

B

bitwise canonical functions, E-SQL 129

C

canonical functions, E-SQL
about 128
aggregate 128, 129
bitwise 128, 129
date and time 128-130
mathematical 128
string 128, 129
code-first approach
about 90, 183
using 184, 185
collection 126
complex joins
avoiding, Entity SQL used 19
complex types
implementing, in EDM 192, 193
components, ADO.NET Entity Framework
Entity client 17
Entity Data Model (EDM) 12-15
Entity SQL 18
LINQ to Entities 17
Object Model (O-Space) 16, 17
Object Services Layer 20
components, REST request
desired action 208
DeveloperCaller ID 208
endpoint URL 208
parameters 208
Conceptual Model Layer 12
Conceptual Schema Definition Language (CSDL) 72
concurrency conflicts 182
containment 64
create function
mapping, to entities 111
CRUD operations
about 31
performing, on objects 177, 178
Custom Search JSON/Atom API 233

D

data
querying, as in-memory objects 176
querying, LINQ to Entities used 151
querying, LINQ used 158-161
Data Access Objects (DAO) 7
database
creating, model-first development used 90-104
database-first approach
about 91, 184
using 188
data binding 44
data-centric applications 3-5
data model 3
data paging, E-SQL 130
DataSource controls
about 31, 44
EntityDataSource 46
LinqDataSource 46
ObjectDataSource 44
SiteMapDataSource 45
SqlDataSource 45
XMLDataSource 45
date and time canonical functions, E-SQL 130
DbContext class, SecurityDbEntity 174, 175
DbContext Fluent Generator
URL, for downloading 85
deferred execution 166
deferred loading 23
delete function
mapping, to entities 111
derived entity types
creating 61-63
Django REST
about 233
URL 233
domain-driven design (DDD) 90
domain modeling 7
domain modeling approaches, Entity Framework
code-first approach 90
database-first approach 91
model-first approach 90
Dynamic LINQ (DLINQ) 148

E

eager loading
about 142
example 142
EdmGen
used, for creating EDM 41-43
EdmGen.exe command-line tool
options 42
enhancements, ADO.NET Entity Framework 6
about 22
other enhancements 27
spatial data types support 27
support, for better n-tier support 24
support, for built-in functions 25
support, for code-first, model-first, and database-first approaches 24
support, for custom code first conventions 28
support, for lazy loading 23
support, for model-defined functions 25
support, for persistence ignorance 22
support, for POCO change tracking 23
support, for stored procedures and functions in code first 28
support, for T4 code generation 23
support, for UDF support 25
task-based asynchronous operation 28
entities
about 56
create function, mapping to 111
delete function, mapping to 111
properties 56
update function, mapping to 111
entity classes 11, 85, 86
Entity client 17
EntityCommand
native SQL, retrieving from 139
entity containers 65-67
entity data
retrieving, from Security database 168, 169
Entity Data Model (EDM)
about 6, 12, 56
complex types, implementing in 192, 193
create function, mapping to entities 111
creating 34

creating, ADO.NET Entity Data Model Designer used 35-41
creating, EdmGen used 41-43
delete function, mapping to entities 111
entity sets, deleting in 57-61
layers 13, 14
representation 15
stored procedures, mapping to functions 108-111
update function, mapping to entities 111
used, for executing stored procedures 113, 114
EntityDataSource control
about 46
reference link 46
Entity Framework
about 1
and LINQ to Entities 151
online resources 239
used, for implementing application 46-53
working with 217-222
Entity Framework 6
performance improvements 28, 29
Entity Framework 6.x 3
Entity Framework 7
new features 30, 238
providers 177
using 176
Entity Framework, and other ORM tools
comparative analysis 7-9
entity instances
deserializing 180-182
serializing 180-182
EntityKey 57
Entity Model browser, Security EDM 70, 71
Entity-Relationship model 56
entity sets
deleting, in EDM 57-61
entity types
extending 61-63
E-SQL
about 117-119
additional operations 138
canonical functions 128
data paging 130
expressions 124
features 120
identifiers 125
need for 119
operators 121
transaction management 140, 141
types 126
used, for avoiding complex joins 19
used, for inserting record 138
variables 126
explicit loading 196
expressions, E-SQL
about 124
query 124
expressions, LINQ to Entities
about 161
comparison expressions 162, 163
constant expressions 162
deferred query execution 166-168
immediate query execution 166-168
initialization expressions 164
navigation properties 165, 166
null comparisons 165

F

factory classes 7
Flickr REST API
about 233
URL 233
Fluent NHibernate 7
foreign key constraint
record, inserting with 139
functions
stored procedures, mapping to 108-111

G

geography data type 27
geometry data type 27
Google API
about 233
URL 233

H

HTTP error status codes 237
HTTP methods
DELETE 236

GET 236
HEAD 236
OPTIONS 236
POST 236
PUT 236
HTTP methods for CRUD operations, REST architecture
DELETE 207
GET 207
HEAD 207
POST 207
PUT 207
HTTP protocol
resource methods 237
HTTP redirection status codes 237
HTTP server error status codes 237
HTTP status codes
purposes 236

I

identifiers, E-SQL
quoted 125
simple 125
identity management 193-196
inheritance, EDM
Table-per-Concrete Class (TPC) 62
Table-per-Hierarchy Model (TPH) 62
Table-per-Type Model (TPT) 62
inheritance, Entity Framework
about 188
Table per Concrete Type (TPC) 189-191
Table per Hierarchy (TPH) 188-190
Table per Type (TPT) 188, 190
in-memory objects
about 172
data, querying as 176

J

join table 68

K

Kilo Lines of Code (KLOC) 21

L

layers, Entity Data Model (EDM)
Conceptual layer 14
C-S Mapping Layer 14
Logical layer 14
layers, Security EDM
CSDL schema 72-79
MSL schema 81, 84
SSDL schema 79
lazy loading
about 23, 142
example 142
URL 23
LINQ
about 10, 145, 146
forms 10
need for 146
operators 153
used, for querying data 158-161
LINQ architecture 147
LinqDataSource control 46
LINQ to DataSet 10
LINQ to Entities
about 10, 17, 119, 145, 150
and Entity Framework 151
expressions 161, 162
used, for querying data 151
versus LINQ to SQL 152, 153
LINQ to Objects 149, 150
LINQ to SQL
about 5, 10, 11, 148, 149
versus LINQ to Entities 152, 153
LINQ to XML 10, 148
Logical Model Layer 12

M

Mapping Details window, Security EDM 68-70
Mapping Layer 12
mathematical canonical functions, E-SQL 128
Microsoft Open Specification Promise (OSP) 216
model-driven approach 25

model-first approach
about 90, 183
using 185-187
model-first development
used, for creating database 90-104
Model-View-Controller (MVC) 232
multiplicity 65

N

native SQL
retrieving, from EntityCommand 139
new features, Entity Framework 7 30
NHibernate 7
no entity set
stored procedures, mapping with 113

O

ObjectContext class
EntityConnection instance, encapsulating 173
MetadataWorkspace instance, encapsulating 173
objects, attaching to 178-180
objects, detaching from 178-180
ObjectStateManager instance, encapsulating 173
used, for modifying identity resolution 182
used, for modifying tracking 182
ObjectDataSource control 44
Object Model (O-Space) 16, 17
Object Query object 21
Object Relational Mapping (ORM) 1, 4
objects
attaching, to ObjectContext class 178-180
CRUD operations, performing on 177, 178
deleting, from Security database 198
detaching, from ObjectContext class 178-180
editing, from Security database 198
inserting, from Security database 197
reading, from Security database 196, 197
Object Services
about 172
features 174
Object Services Layer 20
OData Service
creating 222, 223
Open Data Protocol (OData)
about 201, 214
exploring 234, 235
HTTP verbs 215
URL 214
operations, REST-style architecture
DELETE method 203
GET method 203
HEAD method 203
HTTP method 203
POST method 203
PUT method 203
operators, E-SQL
about 121
arithmetic 121
case 121
comparison 121, 122
logical 121, 122
operator precedence 124
reference 121, 122
set 121, 123
type 121, 123
operators, LINQ
about 153
aggregation 154
conversion 157
element 157
ordering 155
projections 155
quantifiers 156
restriction 156
set 158
Organization for the Advancement of Structured Information Standards (OASIS) 215
ORM tools
versus ADO.NET Entity Framework 7

P

Parallel Extensions Library
about 153
Parallel LINQ (PLINQ) 153
Task Parallel Library (TPL) 153
URL 153

Parallel LINQ 153
performance improvements, Entity Framework 6 28, 29
persistence ignorance 22
Plain Old CLR Objects (POCO) 22
Project Astoria 201
Protobuf.NET
integrating, with Visual Studio 227
Protobuf-net objects
creating 226
Protobuf WCF services
implementing 227
working with 225
Protocol Buffers (Protobuf)
about 225
advantages 225
URL 225

Q

query expressions, E-SQL
FROM 124
GROUP BY 125
HAVING 124
ORDER BY 125
SELECT 124
WHERE 124
quoted identifiers 125

R

record
inserting, E-SQL used 138
inserting, with foreign key constraint 139
reference 127
relational store 3
relationship 63
relationship management 193-196
Remote Data Objects (RDO) 7
resource-oriented architecture (ROA) 214
resources, REST-based architecture 207
REST
about 203, 231
goals 231
need for 206
REST architectural constraints
about 208
cacheable 209
client-server model 208
code on demand 209
resource management 209
stateless 208
uniform interface 209
REST architectural style
design goals 207
REST attributes
about 209
UriTemplate 212
WebGet 211
WebHttpBehavior 210
WebHttpBinding 210
WebInvoke 212
WebMessageFormat 211
WebOperationContext 210
WebServiceHost 210
REST-based architecture
benefits 204
features 204
resources 207
REST-based service frameworks
Django REST 233
Flickr REST API 233
Google API 233
Restlet 232
Ruby on Rails 232
Yahoo Social REST APIs 234
REST-based Web Services 213, 214
RESTful services 203
RESTful Web API 232
Restlet
about 232
benefits 233
URL 233
REST request
components 208
REST-style architecture
operations 203
row 126
Ruby on Rails
about 232
URL 232

S

Security database
entity data, retrieving from 168, 169
objects, deleting from 198
objects, editing from 198
objects, inserting from 197
objects, reading from 196, 197
Security database, tables
Controls 34
ControlTypes 34
Roles 34
UserAuthenticationTypes 33
UserRoles 34
Users 33
UsersAuthentication 33
UsersLoginHistory 34
SecurityDbEntity
DbContext class 174, 175
Security EDM
EDM layers 72
entity classes 85, 86
Entity Model browser 70, 71
exploring 67, 68
Mapping Details window 68-70
serialization 180
service-oriented architecture (SOA) 214
simple identifiers 125
SiteMapDataSource control 45
spatial data types
URL 27
SQL 118
SqlDataSource control
about 45
reference link 45
state management 193-195
stored procedures
creating 105-107
executing, EDM used 113, 114
mapping, that return custom entity types 114-116
mapping, to functions 108-111
mapping, with no entity set 113
Store Schema Definition Language (SSDL) 15
string canonical functions, E-SQL 129

T

T4 code generation 23
Table per Concrete Type (TPC) 189-191
Table per Hierarchy (TPH) 188-190
Table per Type (TPT) 188-190
transaction 140
transaction management, E-SQL 140
Transact SQL (T-SQL) 117, 118
types, E-SQL
about 126
collection 126, 127
reference 127
row 126

U

update function
mapping, to entities 111
UriTemplate class 212
user authentication database
designing 33

V

variables, E-SQL 126
Visual Studio
Protobuf.NET, integrating with 227

W

WCF Data Services
about 202
creating 223
data, exposing as service 205
features 204
hosting 224
need for 204
versus Web Services 202
working with 217-222
WCF Protobuf-net service
consuming 228
WebGet attribute 211
WebHttpBehavior attribute 210
WebHttpBinding attribute 210
WebInvoke attribute 212
WebMessageFormat attribute 211

WebOperationContext attribute 210
WebServiceHost attribute 210
Web Services
  versus WCF Data Services 202
Windows Communication Foundation (WCF) 225

XLINQ 148
XMLDataSource control 45

Y

Yahoo Social REST APIs
  about 234
  URL 234

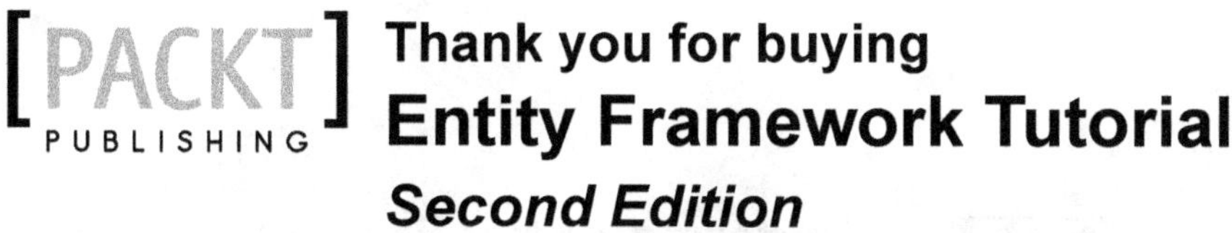

PACKT
PUBLISHING
Thank you for buying
Entity Framework Tutorial
Second Edition

About Packt Publishing

Packt, pronounced 'packed', published its first book, *Mastering phpMyAdmin for Effective MySQL Management*, in April 2004, and subsequently continued to specialize in publishing highly focused books on specific technologies and solutions.

Our books and publications share the experiences of your fellow IT professionals in adapting and customizing today's systems, applications, and frameworks. Our solution-based books give you the knowledge and power to customize the software and technologies you're using to get the job done. Packt books are more specific and less general than the IT books you have seen in the past. Our unique business model allows us to bring you more focused information, giving you more of what you need to know, and less of what you don't.

Packt is a modern yet unique publishing company that focuses on producing quality, cutting-edge books for communities of developers, administrators, and newbies alike. For more information, please visit our website at `www.packtpub.com`.

Writing for Packt

We welcome all inquiries from people who are interested in authoring. Book proposals should be sent to `author@packtpub.com`. If your book idea is still at an early stage and you would like to discuss it first before writing a formal book proposal, then please contact us; one of our commissioning editors will get in touch with you.

We're not just looking for published authors; if you have strong technical skills but no writing experience, our experienced editors can help you develop a writing career, or simply get some additional reward for your expertise.

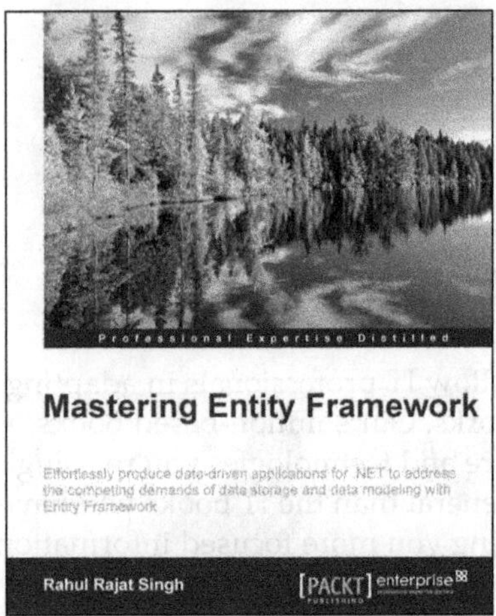

Mastering Entity Framework

ISBN: 978-1-78439-100-3 Paperback: 304 pages

Effortlessly produce data-driven applications for .NET to address the competing demands of data storage and data modeling with Entity Framework

1. Understand everything that requires to effectively start developing and managing data driven applications using Entity Framework.
2. Implement an example-based approach to understand various concepts associated with Entity Framework.

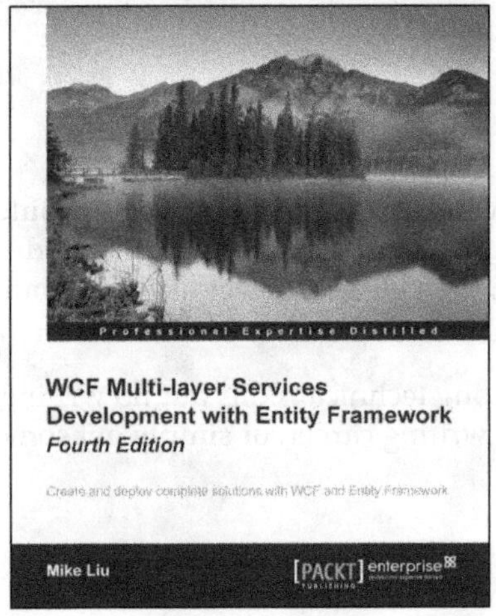

WCF Multi-layer Services Development with Entity Framework

Fourth Edition

ISBN: 978-1-78439-104-1 Paperback: 378 pages

Create and deploy complete solutions with WCF and Entity Framework

1. Build SOA applications on Microsoft platforms.
2. Apply best practices to your WCF services and utilize Entity Framework to access underlying data storage.
3. A step-by-step, practical guide with nifty screenshots to create six WCF and Entity Framework solutions from scratch.

Please check **www.PacktPub.com** for information on our titles

[PACKT]
PUBLISHING

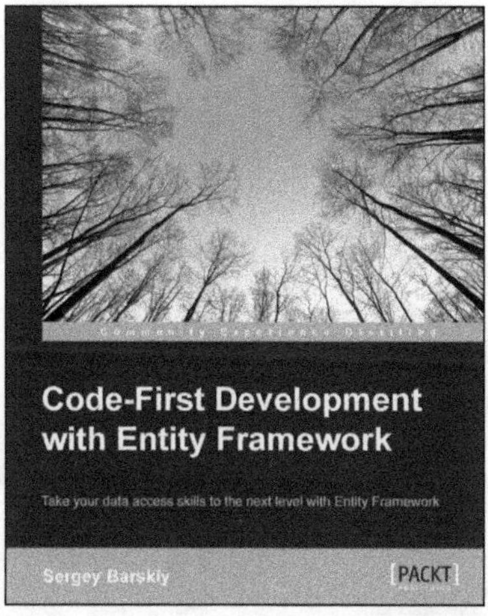

Code-First Development with Entity Framework

ISBN: 978-1-78439-627-5 Paperback: 174 pages

Take your data access skills to the next level with Entity Framework

1. Learn how to create, retrieve, update, and delete the data in a relational database using .NET.

2. Choose from an array of examples in C# and VB.NET that showcase the key concepts of Entity Framework.

3. This is a fast-paced, practical guide based on the code-first approach for the Entity object-relational mapper.

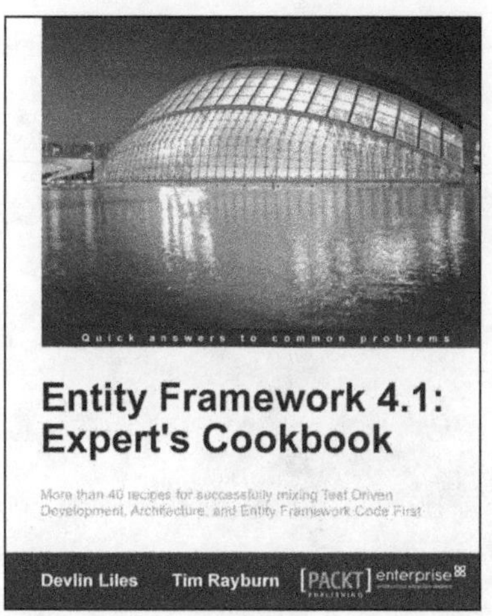

Entity Framework 4.1: Expert's Cookbook

ISBN: 978-1-84968-446-0 Paperback: 352 pages

More than 40 recipes for successfully mixing Test Driven Development, architecture, and Entity Framework Code First

1. Hands-on solutions with reusable code examples.

2. Strategies for enterprise ready usage.

3. Examples based on real world experience.

4. Detailed and advanced examples of query management.

Please check **www.PacktPub.com** for information on our titles

www.ingramcontent.com/pod-product-compliance
Lightning Source LLC
Chambersburg PA
CBHW060530060326
40690CB00017B/3440
* 9 7 8 1 7 8 3 5 5 0 0 1 2 *